D0065617

Successful Mergers, Acquisitions and Strategic Alliances

How to bridge corporate cultures

Charles Gancel, Irene Rodgers, Marc Raynaud

THE McGRAW-HILL COMPANIES

London · Burr Ridge IL · New York · St Louis · San Francisco · Auckland
Bogotá · Caracas · Lisbon · Madrid · Mexico · Milan
Montreal · New Delhi · Panama · Paris · San Juan · São Paulo
Singapore · Sydney · Tokyo · Toronto

Successful Mergers, Acquisitions and Strategic Alliances:
How to bridge corporate cultures

Charles Gancel, Irene Rodgers, Marc Raynaud

0077098757

Published by McGraw-Hill Professional

Shoppenhangers Road
Maidenhead
Berkshire
SL6 2QL
Telephone: 44 (0) 1628 502 500
Fax: 44 (0) 1628 770 224
Website: www.mcgraw-hill.co.uk

British Library Cataloguing in Publication Data
A catalogue record for this book is available from the British Library

Library of Congress Cataloging-in-Publication Data
The Library of Congress data for this book
has been applied for/is available from the Library of Congress

Sponsoring Editor: Elizabeth Robinson
Editorial Assistant: Sarah Butler
Business Marketing Manager: Elizabeth McKeever
Senior Production Manager: Max Elvey
Production Editor: Eleanor Hayes

Produced for McGraw-Hill by Gray Publishing, Tunbridge Wells
Text design by Robert Gray
Printed and bound in the UK by Bell & Bain Ltd, Glasgow
Cover design by Simon Levy Associates

McGraw-Hill books are available at special quantity discounts. Please contact the
Corporate Sales Executive at the above address.

Contents

Acknowledgements   vii
Introduction   ix

Chapter 1   The Alliance Game   1
  Corporate Deals: The Way of the Business World   3
  Marriage Made in Heaven ... or Match Made in Hell?   4
  Culture Defined   6
  How Does Culture Form?   8
  Corporate Culture   10
  How Does Corporate Culture Form?   11
  Points of Pain   13
  Differences? What Differences?   16
  The Case for Action: Why aren't Leaders Rising to the
    Challenge of Culture?   17
  How will this Book Help?   20
  Some Food for Thought ...   21

Chapter 2   Bridging the Cultural Divide   23
  The Two-headed Monster   23
  The Many Degrees of Integration: A Tale of Two Armies   24
  Total Integration: The Irresistible Temptation   26
  Cultural Autonomy: A Culture of Subcultures   27
  An Appropriate Degree of Integration   28
  The Culturally Harmonious Entity: A Holy Grail?   30
  Culture Bridging: A Balanced Response   30
  The Enemy is not Within   32
  A Reality Check: The Market Stops for No One   33
  Some Food for Thought ...   34

Chapter 3   What You Don't Know ... Can Hurt You   35
  You Don't Know What You Don't Know   37
  Like a Fish Out of Water   38
  True Cultural Understanding   39
  Forewarned is Forearmed: The Power of Research   40

Culture Bridging Fundamentals: A Diagnostic Model   42
The Challenges: Three Key Themes for Understanding   43
To Each His Own: Culture-driven Preferences   45
Head, Muscle or Heart? What's Your Style?   47
The Bright and the Dark Sides of Styles   48
Who's Right, Who's Wrong?   49
Some Food for Thought ...   50

Chapter 4 Legitimacy   53
The Legitimacy Challenge: Who Will We Trust and Follow? 56
Legitimacy Preferences   57
The Intellectuals   58
The Entrepreneurs   59
People Like Us   60
Perspectives on Legitimacy: What Happens When
  Preferences Meet?   61
Smoothing the Waters   65
Some Food for Thought ...   66

Chapter 5 Effectiveness   69
The Effectiveness Challenge: How Will We Get Things
  Done Around Here?   72
Effectiveness Preferences   73
Systems and Procedures   74
And ... Action!   76
Network   77
Perspectives on Effectiveness: What Happens When
  Preferences Meet?   79
The Value of Understanding   85
Some Food for Thought ...   86

Chapter 6 Future   89
The Future Challenge: How Will We Communicate and
  Get Buy-in to the New Vision?   92
Future Preferences   94
Organisational Structure   95
Strategic Objectives   98
Heritage   99
Perspectives on the Future: What Happens When
  Preferences Meet?   102

Organisational Structure versus Heritage 102
Heritage versus Strategic Objectives 104
When Two Strategic Objectives Cultures Meet 104
When Two Heritage Cultures Meet 105
Some Food for Thought ... 105

Chapter 7   The Cultural Audit 107
The Cultural Audit: What, Why and Who? 107
The Pay-off 109
Conducting a Cultural Audit: One Approach 112
The Cultural Audit Report in Practice 115
Enhancing the Picture 119
A Question of Timing 120
Some Food for Thought ... 122

**Chapter 8   Merging the Tribes: An Integration Process
                Built on Culture Bridging** 123
The Mother of All Projects 124
The Four Phases of Integration 125
Culture Bridging: No Quick Fix! 130
(1) Understand and Lead: From Shared Values to Share Value 132
(2) Monitor and Solve Problems 142
(3) Communicate and Measure 146
(4) Developing Competencies 155
(5) Celebrate! 158
The Importance of Building a 'Common History' 160
Proceed in Haste, Repent at Leisure 160
Some Food for Thought ... 161

**Chapter 9   Building Your Personal Armoury: Culture
                Bridging Competencies** 163
Culture Bridging Competencies: A Tool Kit 164
Putting it all Together 176
Some Food for Thought ... 178

Chapter 10   Seeing the Light 181
The Culprit Unmasked 181
Putting a Language to the Challenge 182
Back to the Foundations 183
Spreading the Load 184

A Time for Celebration   185
TICs and Task Forces   186
Tooling Up   187
Opening the Channels of Communication   189
Epilogue   191

Chapter 11   The Culture Bridging Code   193
Put the Cultural Dimension on the Agenda   194
Agree on the Real Enemy   195
Embrace and Bend with the Differences   196
Build a Map of the Merging Cultures   197
Plan, Plan, Plan   199
Implement Quickly   200
Communicate Openly and Honestly   201
Make Promises Realistic and Stick to Them!   202
Walk the Talk … and Talk the Walk   203
Conclusion   204

Appendix   Leaders Talk About Their Experience   205
Interview with Gérard de Saint Remy   205
Interview with Ivar Hafsett   209
Interview with Håkan Hallen   211
Interview with Torben Laustsen   214
Interview with Fred Reid   218
Interview with Mr Sheng   219
Interview with Edward Shipka   221

Index   **225**

Acknowledgements

We at ICM have written this book thanks to our clients who have trusted us to accompany them in their postmerger/acquisition and integration processes over the past 18 years. Some have allowed us to include aspects of their experience using a cultural audit and a structured integration process in this book. To them, first of all, we say thank you.

Elizabeth Robinson, our editor at McGraw-Hill, London, gave us her immediate support. This and her enthusiasm helped to push this book from being just an idea to becoming a concrete project.

Thank you to the Chief Executives and senior business leaders from major companies in Europe, the United States and Asia who openly shared what they had found worked and didn't work as they tackled their integration processes. Their stories are sprinkled throughout the book and have brought theory alive.

Two executives who are both clients and friends, Gérard de Saint Remy, who was CEO of Alcan de France, and Austin O'Malley, who was General Manager of PPG Automotive Europe, helped us to meet some of the executives quoted here in addition to sharing their experience with us. Gérard read through the manuscript and gave us precious feedback from the corporate reader's point of view. This was invaluable in helping us to keep an eye on the needs of integration leaders and to avoid only focusing on this subject that we enjoy so much.

Thank you to the consultant team for several years of work in finalising the Culture Bridging Fundamentals model and pulling together valuable data embedded in our client projects. In addition, two of our consultants, Elizabeth Jardine and Sylvie Costa, managed the diverse players on the project, the stringent time pressures and all of the many details of manuscript preparation, ensuring that it got done well and on time.

Claire Forgeot's artwork illustrates a way of representing what we do that lies at the core of ICM culture. This has remained constant for 20 years and is one area where ICM demonstrates a 'heritage' preference. We are happy to be able to share that with you.

Thank you to Stephen Spiesal for providing photography.

Finally and most of all, we'd like to thank Jill Pergant and Mark Tooley of Flying Colours, without whom this book could not have been written at all.

Consultant team: Rachel Amato, Ann Barry, Jürgen Beyer, Elisabeth de Saint Basile, Chilina Hills, Andreas Kaufmann, Lætitia Mazauric, Virginie Peiffer, Alison Perlo, Elisabeth Plum, Monika Thiel, Dick Randell, Beth Shipka, Christopher Stratford, Tran Canh.

Introduction

Globalisation is everywhere. That's a fact.

We may like it or not, but in any case we have to deal with it. Some people see globalisation as a sign of progress, proof of fast economic development and integration; in short, a way for underdeveloped countries to access well-being and modern conveniences. Others see it as a threat to their identity and traditions, a new economic imperialism led mostly by Western countries, and in particular by North American multinational companies.

One of the consequences of globalisation has been the tremendous increase in the number of acquisitions, mergers and alliances across the world. Big is beautiful. As a result, the 1990s have seen numerous companies working with more and more cultures. Differences in corporate and business cultures as well as national cultures have made their activity more complex and challenging. They all recognise that the culture issue is the most difficult one to handle and that it is the first cause for 'merger disappointment'.

We are all having to deal with an unexpected aspect of economic globalisation, in our professional or private lives: the difficult issue of cultural shock. Academics have even talked about this as the source for a 'cultural war'. Is cultural integration possible? Isn't it a trigger we're pulling without knowing who's going to get shot? Are there alternatives to cultural integration? What should we integrate and what should we not? How can we achieve the best and not the worst out of this fundamental confrontation of values and beliefs?

We are sceptical about the notion of cultural integration when it comes to integrating national cultures or religious beliefs. It may work at an individual level, but at a collective level, culture is rooted so deeply and unconsciously that anyway, cultural integration would never happen at the same pace as technical or economic integration. This difference in pace lies at the origin of people's frustrations and, to a certain extent, their potential for violence.

For those of us at ICM who are involved in working with leaders in international companies, helping them to work more effectively across cultures, these differences are something of our stock in trade. Over the years, we have come to hold a few convictions, two of which are driving our approach. First, 'bridging' culture is much more realistic than 'merging' cultures. Secondly, while integration across national cultures seems unrealistic if not undesirable, a clear and open 'corporate culture' offers a basis for convergence because it creates a space within which national differences can be expressed in a constructive, creative and motivating way.

In working with business leaders towards effective culture bridging, we realised that even for founders and owners of companies, corporate culture is simply not 'in the blood' in the same way as national identity is. Corporate culture tells us relatively little about what we consider just, unjust, right, wrong, acceptable, unacceptable, etc., while national cultures do just that. This is important if you are concerned with Culture Bridging, as we are. We have found that by working only on national cultural differences people can sometimes reinforce differences and even stereotypes.

Corporate culture values are more superficial than national culture values because they entail the survival and development of a company, not of an individual or the community. Corporate culture, the set of values that has been agreed upon and turned into management practices, behaviours and systems, is a kind of contract that binds a professional community together. Thus, stressing shared values, attitudes and ways of doing things within a corporate culture, in order to succeed together in a given environment, is a way of bringing people together. This doesn't mean forgetting about national cultural differences. It's a question of timing. It's so much easier to discuss national cultural differences from within the trusting framework of a shared corporate culture. By focusing on corporate culture we have found areas of difference that are far less emotionally charged and therefore more easily resolved.

Therefore, we focus bridging efforts on bridging across corporate cultures. Looking closely at corporate culture tells us a lot about how people work together which, after all, is what people are supposed to do when they belong to the same company. It tells us what criteria people use to determine credible and legitimate managers or executives; it tells us about how individuals and teams go about getting things done, solving problems and making decisions; and it tells us a great deal about how we can motivate people to buy into a shared vision of the company's purpose.

Alliance management and integration processes pose the question of how to reinforce group unity while recognising differences squarely. They raise questions such as: which culture is the 'right' culture for the new entity? The culture of the acquiring company? Or not? Is it better to form a new culture and, if so, how? But, isn't that a bit artificial? Our answer is straightforward and two-fold. The right culture is the one that enables the most effective response to the company's external threats, while taking people's past history and values into consideration.

This leads inevitably to a new set of questions. To what extent should local ways of doing things be accepted? To what extent should common values and norms be promoted within a group? What is the acceptable, tolerable level of difference that allows for sufficient consistency and sufficient respect for diversity? We believe that the debate between universal management cultures and the respect of differences is a central question for managers today. The issue is no longer 'building one shared and global corporate culture', as we were often asked to do in the 1990s. Today the challenge is about building a corporate culture that allows for differences to be expressed without this being considered as a weakness and, above all, to create a new generation of managers whose primary task is to manage diversity in an effective and rewarding way.

This book tells a story about Ingo Janssen, one CEO, and his mishaps as he tries to merge two very different corporate cultures. As the book progresses, however, Ingo reads it along with us; and so he becomes more and more aware of the cultural issues involved in successful integration and begins to apply his new understanding to the integration process of this company with each passing chapter of the book. At the end, in Chapter 10, Ingo, like our readers, has the information, processes and competencies in hand to manage his cultural integration process successfully. He learns the right lessons from others' experience, demonstrates Culture Bridging skills, including calling his own previous approaches into question, invests time and energy into getting it right, and sees the bright light at the end of the tunnel as a result.

With this book, we hope to help all leaders involved in mergers, acquisitions, joint ventures, alliances and other forms of corporate deals to have their own Ingo-like success story. We hope that this book gives corporate leaders the tools to understand the cultural interactions inherent in acquisitions, alliances and mergers, and to identify creative, successful ways of leveraging cultural differences for effective Culture Bridging. We hope that we have contributed ideas for finding a common language for addressing cultural issues with diverse teams and for resolving issues arising out of difference. In other words, we hope to have given leaders insights into how to acquire Culture Bridging skills.

Charles Gancel   *Irene Rodgers*   *Marc Raynaud*

CHAPTER 1

The Alliance Game

What makes the difference, what is more important than who you buy,
is who you are.
Euan Baird, CEO, Schlumberger

Central Europe, November
Ingo Janssen smacked his fist against the steering wheel of his Mercedes. The ice-cool temperament for which he was so renowned showed clear signs of overheating as he squinted through the rain at the brakelights of the car in front of him. Things were simply not going according to his gameplan.

Ingo had always been a man with a mission. While other teenagers dreamed of becoming athletes or movie stars, Ingo imagined himself heading up a great corporation, making decisions that shaped the choices of consumers from London to Lima. One Harvard MBA and a string of fast-track appointments later, he saw his dream realised: at just 34 years of age, he was appointed CEO of advertising and media giant JPMT InterMedia, becoming one of the youngest CEOs the industry had ever known. Yet today, two short years later, he was in the throes of a meteoric fall from grace, at the helm of a merger that should have seen JPMT join the 'big five' of the world's media conglomerates, but that was foundering spectacularly.

JPMT's growth had been a classic tale of a big oak growing from a little acorn. From relatively humble UK beginnings, the company expanded into Europe through the acquisition of smaller, established businesses, steadily building a client list that included some of Europe's most successful technology companies as it did so. In his role as head of European operations, Ingo monitored the integration of each new acquisition into the JPMT family, and was generally pleased with what he saw. True, there were problems – for example, the number of staff leaving the companies acquired was higher than Ingo would have liked – but nothing was significant enough to contain JPMT's continued expansion.

When Emil Devine, JPMT's then CEO, unexpectedly stepped down due to ill health, Ingo was a natural successor. Ever ambitious, he saw his opportunity to make an early mark by addressing JPMT's relative weakness in the North American market. As well as being a natural progression towards JPMT's goal of becoming a major global player, there was a pressing business need to develop a stronger presence in the US as several of the agency's biggest clients were centralising their marketing functions there, so to retain their business, JPMT had to move with them.

InterComm, a large advertising and communications business struggling to 'go global', seemed the ideal partner. Due diligence showed a business with strong financials, an enviable creative record and quality management. It also revealed strong synergies: client lists of similar depth and quality, complementary creative visions and a shared sense that the future lay in technology and the internet. And so it was that, at the dawn of the new millennium, fuelled by a buoyant technology sector, its own success and Ingo's drive, JPMT purchased InterComm in what the press billed 'a media wedding – a marriage of equals'. A new global giant was born. Yet, just one year later, Ingo found himself presiding over a union lacking in either harmony or synergy. Caught in the evening traffic, fresh from another grilling at the hands of a disgruntled shareholder, he asked himself where things had gone wrong.

In retrospect, as early as the first time he and his US counterpart, Jerry Meulen, faced each other across the table, Ingo should have made more of the subtle differences that seemed innocuous, but that spelled future problems. Jerry made such a big thing out of where they were positioned at the table. And the way his team chose to run a meeting was quite amazing! No formal agenda; people leaving the table to get coffee and bagels whenever they felt like it. At the time, Ingo understood these only as small national cultural differences, which could almost be viewed as charming, not as indicators of differences in values and working practices that could spell real difficulty for the success of their partnership.

Ingo saw as far more significant the ease with which he and Jerry had reached agreement on Ingo's assumption of the role of CEO of the merged group. If it had only been that easy as the integration of roles and responsibilities was cascaded down the new organisation. The relocation of several key executives from Europe to support the move of some of JPMT's clients to the US was less than well received by the US staff and a large outflow of talent began. And the talent was not going quietly: many spoke in interviews about being left in the dark on matters of importance related to the merger, as well as about experience being ignored and opinions not being respected. Suddenly, the new organisation was faced with difficulty in meeting deadlines, negative feedback from clients and rumblings from shareholders who were disturbed by the news they were hearing on the grapevine. When a key client was lost, the news was soon public knowledge and the media dogs of war were unleashed on Ingo.

Behind the turmoil lay an all too dynamic business environment. The technology bubble in which so many had placed so much blind faith was well and truly bursting. The burgeoning technology boom had been good to JPMT. Boosted by cash balances generated from venture capital, IPOs and soaring stock valuations, technology companies had been able to afford the luxury of spending heavily on the development of their brands, filling JPMT's coffers at the same time. But the lustre had worn off. Now cashpiles were being burned, dot coms were going bust and profit warnings were becoming a daily occurrence. As their valuations crashed, many of the companies who had been the foundation of JPMT's success went to the wall, and those that didn't were forced to make savage cutbacks in spending. Advertising budgets were slashed and JPMT's revenues plummeted.

Integration problems and market forces combined to take their toll. After years of solid growth, JPMT reported its first ever downturn in turnover and profits, and not a small one at that, declining by 11% globally and by a staggering 20% in the US. Neither market analysts nor the company's shareholders were prepared to accept that the collapse in the technology sector was entirely to blame. They were looking for Ingo's head on a plate.

As the traffic eased a little and Ingo accelerated into the fast lane, the anonymity of a new identity and a beach hut on a small Thai island seemed momentarily appealing. But turning his back on a challenge wasn't Ingo's style. On the contrary, he was sure that with careful reflection, planning and action, he could get these two giants working together in harmony. If it was the last thing he did …

To be continued …

Corporate Deals: The Way of the Business World

A CEO from the corporate class of '72 transplanted to today would barely recognise the business world in which he found himself. Back then, the rules that governed the game were narrower in scope. The focus was on productivity and efficiency, and growth was primarily organic and mainly domestic in focus.

However, the past 20–30 years have seen a world-wide metamorphosis of business. To stay competitive, companies around the globe have had to reinvent themselves in the face of a barrage of technological, economic and market changes. At the same time, they have been expected to stay lean and mean, improving quality and profitability, whilst delivering growth and enhanced shareholder value. Those that have failed to measure up to the challenge have faced extinction in a climate where 'survival of the fittest' is the name of the game.

The sheer *pace* of change has meant that growth can rarely be sustained by organic means alone. If an organisation is even to keep pace in its market, it is unlikely to be able to do so without looking outside its own back yard. As a result, organisations like JPMT in our fictional example have sought new types of partnership, leading to an explosion of mergers, acquisitions, joint ventures and other forms of alliance – deals that the parties involved hope will give them access to new expertise and resources, and that will put them on the fast track to innovation and competitive edge.

The scale of these deals varies enormously. At one end of the spectrum, they can involve two or more organisations coming together to work towards a shared goal, for example airline alliance initiatives such as Star Alliance, One World or SkyTeam. At their most complex, they consist of a full-blown merger or acquisition scenario between two industry giants such as American On-line and Time-Warner. Equally, as in the latter case, they may be between two domestic organisations. However, in this age of globalisation, they increasingly involve cross-border activity: the merger between Daimler-Benz and the Chrysler Corporation and Vivendi's purchase of Seagram to create Vivendi Universal are cases in point.

The permutations are many and varied. However, although corporate deals may be a fact of modern-day business life, few would be bold enough to suggest that they are easily undertaken.

Marriage Made in Heaven … or Match Made in Hell?

'Simple' is not a word you'll find in the dictionary of alliances. The sheer volume of components that need to be integrated can be mind boggling. Sales, marketing, production and human resources are just a few of the functions that may offer synergies on paper, but that present their own unique stumbling blocks over which the unwary corporation can so easily trip and fall.

Then, of course, you have to factor the challenges of operating across borders into the equation. '*Think global, act local*' has become something of a mantra for the modern corporation. It is great advice, but anyone who has had to manage a business towards that goal could probably fill many a night around the campfire with stories of going to hell and back.

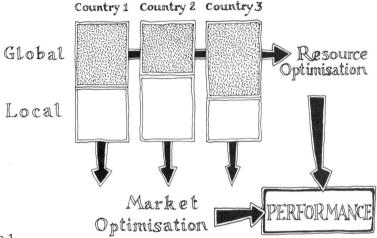

Figure 1

Figure 1 illustrates the particularly delicate balancing act that thinking global and acting local entails. On the one hand, the new organisation will want to work on a **global** level to optimise resources in order to save costs, for example by centralising purchasing. On the other hand, **local** operations will want to ensure that they are doing everything necessary to keep the customer satisfied and to maintain their position in the market. Adapting advertising and marketing campaigns to the local context is a prime example of this.

Both initiatives have the overall goal of performance: delivering results that will please the stakeholders. Yet resource optimisation and market optimisation do not always sit comfortably together. A policy made globally may leave managers in a local operation with their hands tied, unable to add the value that will secure their position and reputation in the local market. For example, when companies move from a regional to a global business-driven structure, they often stop delivering valuable regional management information. Similarly, too many free hands locally may seriously compromise the global ability to optimise resources. An example of this is where local human resource policies are so inconsistent with those in other parts of the group that international mobility becomes impossible.

All of which places the new organisation on the horns of a dilemma, one that it *must* manage and overcome if it is going to live up to stakeholder expectations and frustrate the ambitions of the vultures circling patiently overhead.

In reality, few deals seem to master the balancing act and make it over the tightrope to the other side. An often-quoted fact is that, after five years, 50% of acquisitions are perceived as 'failures'. Mergers such as the one between JPMT and InterComm in our story, launched with talk of synergy and hope, often look quite different a couple of years down the road. The synergy has failed to materialise and the shareholders are getting edgy. The picture is one of conflict, failed objectives and plummeting morale, coupled with the loss of both clients and the organisation's most promising managerial talent. If the end result is a break-up, the financial fallout can be devastating too: when Monsanto and American Home Products broke up in 1998, €10 billion worth of share value went up in smoke.

So what's going on? Why are so many of these 'perfect marriages' failing to live up to expectations? One key factor is a lack of emphasis on planning. Most deals are subject to enormous pressure, conducted as they are under the watchful eye of employees, customers, shareholders, the markets and the press. The stakeholders also expect swift results – the negotiation complete, the deal done, they want to see the synergies that were promised *now*! Placed under such constraints, it's perhaps not surprising that leaders engaged in corporate deals have a tendency to jump to action, forgetting the old adage 'fail to plan and you plan to fail'.

Planning aside, when deals break down terminally, or trundle along in a state of disharmony and inefficiency, observers will be quick to blame the financial or organisational structure, or to focus on some other 'technical' aspect. This may well be true in some cases. Indeed, it is quite possible that these are contributing factors in each and every failed deal. It can be surprising to learn, however, that, more often than not, the *root* cause of the problem is a failure to account adequately for the human factor and the hidden dimension that is ***culture***.

Culture Defined

Cultures are some of the biggest obstacles to change.
Patrick J Rich, Former Chairman, Royal Packaging Van Leer

Culture. You can't see it and you can't touch it. Yet it shapes the thoughts and actions of each and every one of us. In the context that we use it here, culture can be thought of as the values, customs and beliefs that dictate how we view and respond to our environment. Culture is not something that belongs uniquely to you, nor is it universal: it's something that you share with a group and it's part of what distinguishes you from other groups.

Cultures often view the same issue quite differently. Take people's attitude to time. One culture – the German culture would be a typical example – may view time as a scarce and precious resource to be respected and managed carefully. Punctuality is expected and respected. Another culture – the Nigerian culture, for example – may see time as one of the few things in life that are freely available and will use it as others use electricity. Punctuality here is rarely a critical requirement.

Figure 2

Looking at Figure 2, imagine that the German culture is the 'triangle culture' and the Nigerian culture is the 'circle culture'. The two cultures' differing attitude to time falls into the sections of the triangle and circle that do not overlap. In these non-overlapping sections, people often react negatively to the way in which their counterparts go about doing things.

So what falls into the overlapping section? In the case of the Nigerian and German cultures, one answer would be beer-drinking. Here, Nigerians and Germans will find that they drink the same drink, in similar situations, for similar reasons and with similar effects!

Yet cultures are also distributed amongst a population. Not *everyone* will conform to the cultural norms. The majority of Germans may pay homage to punctuality, while the majority of Nigerians assume a more leisurely pace; yet you'll inevitably run into the executive from Stuttgart who's consistently late for meetings with his colleague in Lagos who, in turn, is impatiently tapping his fingers on his desk, because his tight schedule for the day is being thrown out by his thoughtless visitor.

How Does Culture Form?

Culture is both learned and taught. We enter the world a blank canvas on which our cultural identity is gradually painted through our exposure to heritage, language, customs, morals, beliefs, art and technology; in short, everything that is 'socially' transmitted.

Those aspects of culture that we *learn* are taken on in an implicit way. No one tells us how close it's appropriate to stand to a stranger, which facial expressions or gestures are appropriate in a situation, or how long it's polite to maintain eye contact with one another. We just pick these things up along the way by imitating what we see.

Those aspects of culture that are taught are handed down to us by figures of authority. 'Get your elbows off the table!', 'Don't forget to say please and thank you', 'You can't go around hitting people' – just some of the cultural messages that will have been knocked into many of you reading these pages, by parents and teachers!

But how are the elements that define a culture determined in the first place? Figure 3 gives us a picture of how culture forms.

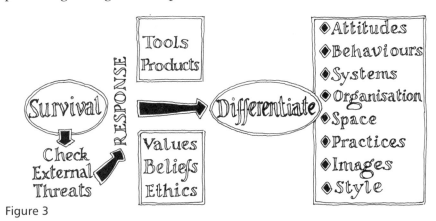

Figure 3

Many of you will be familiar with classic management models that focus on human motivation, such as Abraham Maslow's 'Hierarchy of Needs'. These models identify the most basic human need as that of survival (shown on the left of Figure 3). Whenever a group of people comes together, decisions about 'what to do first' will be driven by this need to survive.

But how will the group ensure that the decisions they make will be good ones? Ones that *will* ensure their survival? The answer lies in understanding the *threats* to their survival. To do this, the group will scan and analyse its environment to identify what those threats might be. Once they have a clear picture, they can begin to develop responses that will overcome them.

Just as circumstances, environment and threats are unique, so are responses. For example, so that they had food during long, cold winters when it was impossible for them to fish, the Inuit developed the ability to preserve fish by salting it, a response that would have been completely inappropriate if they were residents of West Africa! The uniqueness of these responses begins to form the shape of the group's culture; and this uniqueness, and their inextricable link to survival, can help us to understand why they are so often part of people's psyche and therefore difficult to change.

A group's response to its threats takes two forms, one visible, one invisible. The visible responses are the *tools and products* that they create to 'get the job done'. These tools and products are, in effect, the **what** of the group's response to the threats that it faces. For the Inuit, these may be stones or bones, and the harpoons that they fashion from them to spear fish. Tools and products are explicit and relatively easy for outsiders to understand.

The invisible aspect is an altogether more slippery beast. This comprises the *values, beliefs and ethics* that evolve in response to the threats faced by the group. They are, in effect, the **why** of the response. They are implicit and much more closely linked to a sense of identity than are tools and products. As a result, they are less malleable.

Once basic survival is ensured, the driving forces behind the group begin to evolve and the emphasis will shift from *immediate* to *long-term* survival. Invariably, other groups may be competing for the same resources, so the group needs to take on a 'survival of the fittest' mindset and turn its attention to how it can differentiate itself from the others. This quest for differentiation may focus on how the group organises itself (governments and councils), on systems to serve the community (laws): on an array of things that equip the group to survive on both a day-to-day and a generation-to-generation basis, and that further define its *culture*.

This is an abridged version of how culture forms, but one that we hope gives you enough of an understanding to grasp the *strength* of culture. Because, whether learned or taught, once in place, culture becomes ingrained and cannot be easily manipulated. It leaves each of us with our own personal set of 'cultural lenses'. These lenses filter our interpretation of what is right and wrong, appropriate and inappropriate, just and unjust. If we don't like what we see through them, we don't take it lying down.

Corporate Culture

What of culture in a corporate context? The Oxford University Press *Dictionary of Business* defines corporate culture as 'the values, beliefs, norms and traditions within an organisation that influence the behaviour of its members'. Just as our individual cultural programming dictates how we approach and react to day-to-day situations, *corporate* culture presents a framework for acceptable business behaviour. It influences how individuals act, make decisions, resolve conflicts and communicate in their business environment.

Just like culture in general, corporate culture is both learned and taught. During your early days with a company, your mentors, formal or informal, will tell you 'the rules of the game': 'This is a smoke-free environment'; 'You need to get your expenses claim in by the 5th of the month or they won't pay them'. Equally, however, there are things that nobody tells you, often because they don't even think of them, that you pick up simply by observing. What's the company's attitude to meetings? How late is it acceptable to arrive in the morning? What style of dress is appropriate?

Don't expect a company full of clones, though. Again, like culture in general, corporate culture will be distributed through the organisation. Although the majority may conform to the norm, don't be shocked when you run into people who don't.

Wherever groups of individuals have successfully joined together to work towards a common goal, they will have negotiated their own, unique group culture. So, although it may not have existed in name, corporate culture has been with us since time immemorial; but why has it emerged as an area of focus over the past two decades?

First, increased competition meant that organisations were being placed under the microscope to be compared and contrasted. In the early 1980s, writers such as Deal and Kennedy or Peters and Waterman were among the first to identify the significance of 'the way we do things around here' as a differentiator between businesses. Work on national cultures had begun to make cultural values explicit and demonstrated that both behaviour and 'how people do things' are culturally conditioned. When applied to a business environment, the term that seemed to fit the phenomenon was '*corporate* culture'. This phenomenon certainly gave a plausible explanation for the increasing incidence of clashes between companies that was accompanying the trend towards globalisation.

Secondly, internationalisation has meant that people with vastly different backgrounds and education have had to come together around a table to design a common future.

So today, fuelled by management writers and theorists propounding it as a vehicle for improved organisational effectiveness, corporate culture has become a distinctive ethos, shaped and communicated by the organisation's leaders. Many of you reading this will have worked in an organisation that has expended considerable effort in determining its mission, vision and values, and in ensuring that these are truly 'lived' within the organisation. Such initiatives are clear evidence of the drive for a corporate culture that contributes to the development of an organisation equipped to exist comfortably in the world of modern business.

> Corporate culture also has to be taken into account. So Hydro Aluminium goes beyond language and national differences and acknowledges that ways of doing things and managing business are different within companies, even from the same country or in the same business.
>
> *Ivar Hafsett, Strategic Advisor, Hydro Light Metals*

How does Corporate Culture Form?

Not surprisingly, corporate culture evolves in much the same way as any other type of culture. When a company forms, its basic need is for survival: to generate the level of cash flow that will allow it to pay its talent, fund its capital requirements and meet its day-to-day running costs.

To meet the need for survival, it will scan the environment for threats, which may come from competition, changing customer demands or technological and product innovation, and develop responses to them. In overall terms, the response is simply what we know as corporate strategy.

Just like the Inuit, the company will develop products and tools as part of its response. Products will embrace everything that the company offers to the marketplace; tools may range from the production equipment necessary to manufacture product to a logistics solution to get that product to the market. Underlying the explicit elements of products and tools, the values, beliefs and ethics that determine the identity of the organisation will begin to emerge.

Once up and running and sustaining itself in its market, the organisation will turn itself more positively towards what it can do to differentiate itself. At this stage the unique mood and style that makes a company different from its competitors emerges. The company may invest large sums of money in creating strong brand identities, or it may streamline its operating procedures by installing a system such as SAP.

Although these differentiators may change or evolve on a regular basis, as may the tools or products, the values, ethics and beliefs that underpin them tend to be much more 'fixed' once they have formed. The Walt Disney Corporation may one day put Mickey Mouse out to pasture, but it's unlikely that they will ever give up on those good old wholesome values of fun and family.

> There will also be sub-cultures between functions, age groups, talented and non-talented staff, and that also needs to be identified.
> *Cheri Alexander, Vice-President Personnel, General Motors Europe*

Rooted as it is deep in an organisation's history, an established corporate culture is difficult to manipulate and is likely to be staunchly defended by those who are part of it. As the guiding force behind organisational decision making and behaviour, it is clearly visible in the daily actions and behaviour of employees, and newcomers will be immediately encouraged to embrace it. This hints at the potential for conflict when two corporate cultures suddenly face each other in an integration situation.

THE ALLIANCE GAME   **13**

Points of Pain

> Each side is convinced that the way it does things is the only possible way to do them. That's where the conflict and mutual criticism come from.
>
> *Human resources director, petroleum industry*

Anyone researching the subject would not have to look far to see the consequences of deals where cultures have collided. Recent business history is littered with examples that are testament to the failure of the parties involved to account for the cultural dimension.

So what chain of events might you expect to witness in a situation that promises unbounded potential, but in which a cultural divide emerges and is left unmanaged? At the outset, it is likely that one or more of the allying organisations will experience culture shock, a feeling of disorientation caused by being suddenly subjected to an unfamiliar culture or way of life. This can manifest itself in many ways. Let's take communication style as an example:

The chief executive of a US multinational arrives in Paris to meet the managers of the French company it has just bought. His address to the audience of expectant French employees is couched in the language of transatlantic 'direct management'. 'Gentlemen', he begins, 'there are two types of men in this room: those who will stay with us and those who will leave'. In the US organisation, this message would be interpreted as a ritual gauntlet throwing – a direct appeal for commitment to the new challenges ahead. In the French organisation, it was heard as a redundancy announcement...

Clearly, although appropriate for the sender, the approach taken fell dazzlingly short for the receiver.

> It was like the discovery of America by Christopher Columbus. It was kind of a shock. Our people and DT were the old guard and we were facing a new American company like Sprint. They weren't the 'establishment', like AT&T. It was a big contrast for both sides – and a discovery.
>
> There was a good deal of respect and curiosity, but there was also suspicion. They thought we were dinosaurs. We thought they were amateurs – all muscle and no track record.
>
> *Marc Dandelot, President, France Telecom North America,*
> *talking about his experience when partnering with*
> *Deutsche Telekom and Sprint*

This type of mismatch is commonplace throughout the functions of an organisation as integration gets under way. Left unattended, these micro-incidences of culture shock will begin to develop into something far more invidious. If you examine any number of faltering deals, a fairly common thought process begins to take hold at this point:

1. Hmm. We're not achieving our goals. Something's clearly going wrong.
2. Someone must be responsible for this!
3. Of course, its not me!
4. Which means it must be someone else ...
5. And since it couldn't be any of 'us' ... it must be one of them!

Ring any bells? Worryingly, people often feel quite reassured at the end of this thought process. They've got their scapegoat! Each party now knows why things are going wrong and who is to blame. It's those guys from company B. Or it's the French. Or the English. Not only do people feel reassured. It also becomes much easier for them to engage in conflict with a clear conscience, because it's not *their* fault, it's *the others*! This emotional, irrational response may feel satisfying and allow people to absolve themselves of responsibility and guilt, but it also signals the start of a vicious downward spiral that can spell big trouble for the new entity.

For example, having tried and failed to produce results by simply 'putting cultures together', it is likely that one culture, usually that of the acquirer or the larger partner, will begin to dominate and try to stamp itself on the other. One case in point is the merger between Germany's Daimler-Benz and the Chrysler Corporation of the US. Billed as a classic marriage of equals, it promised the harmonious union of two of the world's greatest automotive companies. However, Chrysler executives soon found themselves to be outnumbered and overpowered by the forceful Daimler-Benz culture and, three years on, it is the Germans who have taken control.

How're you going to make a European bank when everyone is trying to make national champions?

Euan Baird, CEO, Schlumberger

Consider also the case of a major publishing organisation, bringing together its three training and development businesses. Ostensibly, all three companies were equal partners in the venture. Yet, a few months in, an executive of one of the companies was heard to say:

> When we joined together, we were amazed at how badly we were treated. From being market leader in our segment we were suddenly the poor relation in the new company. It felt as if company A were in the driver's seat, company B were in the passenger seat, and we were in the trunk!

While the dominance of one culture may leave one partner on familiar ground and feeling more comfortable in the new entity, the remaining partners become disillusioned, frustrated and resentful. If that disillusionment, frustration and resentment is not recognised and tackled by the leadership team, far more wide-reaching commercial implications may result. At best, the deal will progress as if in the grip of an unshakeable head cold, slow to adapt and unable to realise the synergies that were predicted. The more likely scenario is that a serious illness will develop, one that may prevent the new entity from ever reaching its potential; and what you'll see *then* is:

- an increasing amount of negative press, followed by the loss of confidence in all quarters
- key people jumping ship for pastures new and more fulfilling, because they see no light at the end of the tunnel
- the loss of sales and customers, with poor results following close behind
- the loss of shareholder confidence, reflected in a decline in stock price.

However hard it may be, new entities *must* find a way out of the 'us and them' mindset if they are to avoid devastating conflict and years of mistrust, or if they're even to survive at all.

One double-or-nothing, high-risk approach has been taken by Vivendi Universal. Vivendi has taken its own roots and traditional culture and 'parked' them in a separate company, formerly Générale des Eaux, now known as Vivendi Environment. So, for the rest of the company, which is starting from scratch, there is a chance of emerging with something new.

Differences? What Differences?

The world is full of superficial homogenisation. We do all sorts of things in the same way, so one group feels the other is just like it. But that is superficial. Cultural differences are deep.

Cheri Alexander, Vice-President Personnel, General Motors Europe

It only requires the briefest glance at the evidence to deduce that the case for action to address cultural divergence is compelling. Yet our own observations, made during 15 years of experience working with organisations in deal situations, confirm that there is a chronic failure to anticipate and plan for the people and business issues that emerge out of cultural diversity.

Nor are we alone in our observations, which are supported by a number of pieces of empirical research. For example, a 1998 AT Kearney study of 230 recently merged companies cited the lack of appreciation and management of cultural differences as the leading factor for failure of these operations.

On our forays into organisations that are embarking on mergers, acquisitions and other forms of partnership, we have met many cynics who have little or no time for the whole issue of culture. They dismiss it with a wave of their hand and deride it for being a 'soft' issue clouded in 'consultant speak'. 'We're in the same business. All we need to worry about is getting results', they say.

At this point they walk out of the door and march headlong into the 'cultural wall'. When we meet them again in the corridor they say, 'I'm amazed at the level of resistance we're getting. It's the Chinese – they just don't want to play the game. I've never understood them anyway'. For the next hour we engage in conversations about issues that are clearly cultural; yet these managers would still resist labelling them as such if pushed: they would just call them 'management' issues. However, as we hope to show you as we move through this book, a traditional management mindset and traditional management competencies are rarely enough to negotiate the delicate, often hidden nuances thrown up by corporate cultures.

It amazes us just how frequently the smartest people can be gripped by this 'cultural blindness'. On a visit to Maastricht, we talked to a Dane about cultural differences in the EC. 'I've got to tell you – we're not supposed to talk about cultural differences'. 'Why?' we dared to ask. 'It's the basic assumption that there **are** no cultural differences in the Executive Committee, so we're not supposed to talk about them'. That may be the *official* line, but visit the Executive Committee and you'll find that it's the only subject of discussion around the coffee machines!

The Case for Action: Why aren't Leaders Rising to the Challenge of Culture?

> Organisations involved in large, long term projects pay little attention to cultural factors.
>
> *Patrick J Rich, Former Chairman, Royal Packaging Van Leer*

When the consequences of ignoring its impact can be so devastating, why is the tally of leaders who have caught on to the importance of corporate culture so low? Why are so many sharp, strategic thinkers reluctant to give culture the airtime it so richly deserves?

Lack of Awareness
In some cases, blissful ignorance may be the answer: they may simply be unaware that 'the cultural dimension' exists at all. We sincerely hope that this book will go some way towards remedying this particular state of affairs.

Lack of Understanding
Another possible answer is that, although they may be *aware* of it, leaders just don't *understand* culture well enough, and therefore cannot appreciate the impact it could have on day-to-day management practices. Because they lack a language with which they can define and discuss culture, they never uncover the need to bring it to the table.

Lack of Willingness
More worrying rationales for inaction are those where leaders, with misguided judgement, make a conscious decision *not* to address the cultural dimension.

There are four different angles to this. The first is where the management of the cultural dimension simply is not perceived as enough of a priority. Leaders may recognise that cultural issues are important, but rarely as important as the pressure to deliver results. They therefore turn their energies to the more obvious technical and business issues, such as financial analysis or the quest for shareholder buy-in. As a result, there is little time or energy left to give consideration or effort to the management of cultural differences.

The second angle relates to fear of the unknown. Without proper tools and support systems, the issue of culture may take leaders out of their comfort zone and into less predictable waters. Those same leaders who so confidently manage complex technical or financial issues may go weak at the knees at the very thought of having to manage the link between culture, people, emotions and behaviours.

The kind of commitment needed to manage these 'soft' issues is completely different to the kind needed to make tough decisions on the basis of numbers. When it comes to culture, these leaders find it much easier to stay focused on areas that they can more confidently control.

A third reason for a lack of full-scale commitment can come from the fact that cultural integration simply isn't 'sexy' enough. Few CEOs grab the headlines because they have made a great job of bringing corporate cultures together. When the headlines they make *do* refer to integration, be it outstandingly successful or a catastrophic, the article that follows is not likely have much to say about the cultural side of things either. Cultural issues cannot easily be linked to dollars generated, units shipped or increased stock options. Open ten new plants and that's good for your image. The cultural dimension? So what!

The fourth, and perhaps most disturbing rationale for inaction due to a lack of willingness arises when leaders genuinely believe that there is no need to do anything at all. Their unspoken thinking may be, 'Our managers are intelligent. They understand that it's in everyone's best interests to put aside differences and work together'. But it's naïve to think that intelligence alone will drive actions, especially if one reflects on the deeply emotional nature of culture.

Lack of Ability

For some leaders, inaction around the cultural dimension may arise because they just are not equipped to deal with it. They may realise that they need to take action and may even try to do so, but they fail because they lack the 'right stuff', a 'tool kit' of unique competencies that the management of cultural issues demands.

They could hardly be blamed for this, since cultural awareness was unlikely to have been a prerequisite for the senior management positions that they now hold. Part of the tool kit that they lack may be a framework for understanding the key issues that they will need to address. Even if they are clear about these, they may lack the cross-cultural sensitivity or the attitudes, skills and behaviours necessary to deal with culturally diverse stakeholders.

Managers, Educational Systems and the Cultural Dimension

Educational systems have to take some of the blame for the inability of business leaders to confront and manage the cultural dimension. Put simply, we're rarely taught to deal with these emotionally charged issues, so we're ill-prepared when they come along.

For most managers, education – be it at school, undergraduate or graduate levels – will have been number and fact centric, with very little attention being paid to softer issues such as psychology, philosophy or sociology. Yet cultural issues call on them to manage complex people, group and community relationships so that the job gets done and results are produced for the new organisation. Quite a tall order. Yet when it comes to taking the time to add the skills of people and culture management to the literacy or numerical skills of which they may be masters, there are few takers among the management ranks. And few of the companies that they work for encourage them to do so. As a result, they advance through their careers with neither the knowledge nor the skills – the 'tool kit' – that they need to master the cultural dimension.

Our message? If you want to be on the cutting edge, if you want to be a leader in the corporate cultural revolution – be a self-starter. Go out there and take it on yourself to develop the tools that you need to manage culturally diverse situations. Use this book as a starting point. At the end of the day, success is as much about conviction as it is about intelligence.

The message is clear. No matter how 'obvious' the synergies, no matter how 'perfect' the fit, successful deals don't just happen. They critically depend on the ability of the partners to identify and manage any cultural divergence that may exist between them. For whatever combination of the reasons suggested above, as we write, this divergence is being inadequately addressed.

Leadership and management teams at the helm of new entities need to find ways to identify and/or anticipate both cultural similarities and differences. Then, in light of these, they must adapt their integration plan to take advantage of the former and to minimise any negative factors that may be generated by the latter. They must find ways to manage the emotional dimensions of change, minimise internal conflicts and reassure key people more rapidly if they are to keep them inside the company and realise the goals of their deal.

How will this Book Help?

While the past few decades have produced plenty of advice to help us to understand and deal with the cultural differences between nations, similar advice on corporate culture is thinner on the ground. Maybe, having read the evidence presented so far in this chapter, you're wondering if the cultural dimension is something that can be managed at all. We firmly believe that it is.

With this book we aim to demystify the challenges that influence successful cultural integration. We will show you how – with the help of a tool kit that we'll provide, and with the focus that only they can bring to the party – leaders can manage corporate cultural diversity. They can manage it in a way that enables different cultures to work alongside each other in a spirit of understanding that, in turn, enables the effective pursuit of strategic goals.

We will do this by introducing you to a concept that we call Culture Bridging, a concept that has been applied successfully in many organisations to help them to navigate the cultural dimension of deals in which they have found themselves. Specifically, we will look at three tools that are at the foundation of Culture Bridging:

- **Tool 1** is a **diagnostic tool** which provides a structured framework for analysing the 'cultural profile' of your own organisation and that of your partner, to determine areas of cultural similarity and difference. The one that we use – and that we present in this book – is called *Culture Bridging Fundamentals*.
- **Tool 2** is an overall **integration process**, built on the principles of Culture Bridging, that will allow you to manage integration successfully, rather than allowing it to manage you!
- **Tool 3** is a set of **Culture Bridging competencies**: the attitudes, skills and behaviours that enable leaders to work more effectively across cultural borders, and that differentiate great leaders from mediocre ones.

While these tools may only be part of the equation that equals a successful deal, they will place you in a strong position to play your part in what will always be a complex, challenging game. Furthermore, they will enable you to act as a champion for the kind of thinking and action that is so vital to success where Culture Bridging is concerned, but that, in reality, is so often lacking.

> By dealing with cultural differences up-front one can avoid some of the surprises.
>
> *Tryggve Sthen, CEO, Volvo Global Trucks*

Some Food for Thought ...

- Deals between large and small companies are essential for competitive business development in today's global economy.
- Culture can be a major obstacle to change and is often the main culprit in the failure of corporate deals. Managing the cultural component of integration is critical to success.
- Culture, corporate culture included, is for the most part unconscious and implicit. It determines what is considered 'normal' in a given environment. It is ingrained and will be staunchly defended by those whose values, beliefs and ethics it represents.
- The challenges of cultural integration are often neglected as leaders focus their attention on delivering value rapidly. Furthermore, leaders tend to feel more comfortable addressing the 'hard' technical and business issues than they do the 'soft' cultural ones.
- Cultural integration requires understanding, competence and a conscious systematic approach. A cultural integration tool kit therefore includes a diagnostic tool, a set of specific leadership competencies and an explicit process flow that can be implemented and monitored.

CHAPTER 2

Bridging the Cultural Divide

You have to recognise that it's very easy for someone looking from one side to the other to take a totally different view. There's no value in saying 'just do it' – because you'll only antagonise. You have to lead people to the truth.

Nick Scheele, President and COO, Ford

The Two-headed Monster

Fact One. If leaders are to manage integration effectively, they need to think on two fronts: the **operational** and the **cultural**. A no-brainer, right?

Fact Two. Leaders generally create to-do lists as long as their arms around the operational and leave the cultural to look after itself. Chapter 1 hinted at the possible causes of this dichotomy – but how can it be reconciled? In the first place, simply by understanding why it's so important to look at the cultural and the operational as two distinct, yet critically interrelated, areas. Then, by recognising that it's critical to explicitly address the cultural dimension when planning and implementing integration strategies.

At its heart, the operational aspect of integration is about bringing organisational systems, processes and procedures together. It's about pooling resources to improve efficiency or save costs. It may even involve bringing together previously competitive products under a single brand name. *Whatever* it involves, when it comes down to it, it's about the *business* dimension of the deal. It's in the operational that an organisation's visionaries see opportunities to strike gold as they keep a watchful eye out for suitable partners. It's also the place to which stakeholders will apply their magnifying glasses once the deal is done, looking in minute detail for anything that indicates the state of health of the deal. So maybe we shouldn't be surprised that, like the sirens of Greek mythology, the operational dimension captivates hapless business leaders, luring them towards danger with its seductive song.

Mesmerised in this way, how easy it is to forget that it takes *people* to make results happen! Integration is rarely, if ever, achievable operationally if the people who must deal with the details are not enabled by the environment they work in; for example, if they don't trust the people who lead them or with whom they must now work, or if the way that decisions are made is alien to them. That's what the cultural aspect of integration is about, creating an environment where people are both willing and able to work together harmoniously, in a spirit of acceptance and understanding. It's about the *human* dimension of the deal.

Integration, then, is something of a two-headed monster. If, as a leader, you are to stand any chance of delivering the desired level of integration, you must deal with both heads, the *business* and the *human*. You may easily be tricked into focusing exclusively on the business head, because it seems bigger, shouts more loudly or falls naturally into your comfort zone. Take a look at that other head though. It may appear unassuming at first, hiding in the shadow of its more visible counterpart, but on closer inspection, you'll see that it's the source of all the motivation. If you don't respond to its needs or nurture it, it will become disillusioned; and when it does, you'll be able to watch the previously confident business head wither. Before long, you'll find it cowering in the corner at the faintest whiff of a challenge, at which point irrevocable damage will have been done both to the new entity and to its position in the marketplace. This fundamental recognition that you have to balance the human with the business – the cultural with the operational – is the first, maybe most critical, step to achieving successful integration.

The Many Degrees of Integration: A Tale of Two Armies

Leaders also need to take stock of the fact that there's no one level of integration. Rather, there's a spectrum, with total integration at one end and autonomy at the other. Often, the degree to which partners will integrate is defined when the deal is struck. In some cases, they will set out to merge totally with each other, combining products, brands, front and back office functions, etc. (e.g. Lloyds Bank and the TSB, or BP and Amoco). Sometimes they may decide to exist separately, integrating only strategically at the highest level (e.g. United Technologies). Or, in the middle, they may decide to maintain separate faces to the consumer, but merge non-customer-facing functions (e.g. Unilever's purchase of Ben & Jerry's ice cream). The permutations are many and varied.

> When their management asked us what we were proposing we replied, 'We've no intention of controlling your way of doing things. On the contrary, we want to learn from your experience and your practices'.
>
> *Michel Bon, Chairman and CEO, France Telecom, on*
> *France Telecom's approach to Orange*

The degree of integration needed, then, is essentially a strategic choice. Let's think about that choice a little more. Picture this ... you stand atop a hill looking down on two armies. One you know well: you understand its strengths, its weaknesses and its strategies for success; after all, you are its commander. The other you know only as an outsider, from what you have learned through stories and from experience as enemies on the battlefield. But now, thanks to a major political about turn, this former adversary has become your ally in a new conflict, and *you* have been chosen to bring the two armies together.

> I've often noticed in the war of cultures that people have a tendency to take things personally – to feel that they themselves are being questioned. It's very destabilising.
>
> *Véronique Guillot-Pelpel, Senior Corporate Vice-President*
> *Communications, Nexans*

As a leader, you see the potential to achieve something far greater from this new deal than simple suppression of your rival: the potential for a strong, united front against a particularly threatening common enemy. But while you are lost in your vision, imagine what the troops in each of the armies might be feeling. Among your own battalions, so often the conquerors of the second army in the past, you may hear cries of 'Crush 'em' or 'They'll have to do things our way from now on – and heaven help 'em if they don't!' In the ranks of the previously vanquished, things are likely to be rather different: 'I'm going to lose my head' or 'Even if they do spare us, they'll force us to eat that stuff they eat. I wouldn't feed that to my dog!'

As the commander, you face a perplexing challenge. To what extent are you going to allow these two armies to express their individual identities as you ask them to work together to help you to realise your grander vision? Do you simply throw them together and hope that one culture will win out or that a new culture will emerge without too much bloodshed? Or do you allow them to maintain their own unique beliefs and ways of doing things as they work towards the objectives that you set them?

Translate this to an integration situation and the similarities are clear. How far can you realistically integrate two sets of people, who as recently as yesterday may have been bitter competitors in the battle for customers and market share, especially if one is deemed to have taken over the other? Let's look at the potential alternatives.

Total Integration: The Irresistible Temptation

Often when leaders think about their respective organisations coming together, the vision they adopt is one of 'total' integration, and this is certainly an attractive proposition. If it can be achieved, it offers consensus on values and produces consistent actions that lead to unity, predictability and clarity of work experiences. If you were to bet on the chances of delivering results at the operational level, the odds would be much shorter if total integration were on the cards.

But how realistic is it to expect a successful outcome if you throw together two sets of people with differing beliefs, values and ways of doing things, and ask them to 'get on with it'?

Consider our armies. You decide that the two sets of troops are big and bold enough to put aside their differences and find a way of working together. You order total integration, and watch in horror at the mayhem that ensues. Your own army assumes that, as the victors in past battles, it is *their* way that should be adopted. Forced to do things on a daily basis in a way that is completely alien to them, the other army's troops lack commitment and pockets of mutiny abound. So you intervene and order the two sides to come up with something new and different, that both of them can live with. Now *everyone* is on unfamiliar ground, working in the dark with no tried and tested common denominators to fall back on. Gradually, everything falls apart and you find yourself in a state approaching anarchy.

Again, the message in a business context is a simple but critical one: total integration is like expecting bitter enemies to jump into bed together and get a peaceful night's sleep: it's not going to happen. You're on shaky ground from the word go, because most cultures are built on the fundamental belief that their way is the *right* way and is therefore the key to future sustainability. So expecting a new, hybrid culture to emerge any time soon is like wishing on a star. A far more likely scenario is that each side will push for its own approach to be the one that's adopted by the new entity. If the side in question is the acquirer, or has the bigger, stronger culture, it will probably batter its 'partner' into submission, as Daimler did to Chrysler and JPMT did to InterComm. What begins with talk of 'a marriage of equals' rapidly becomes a bloodbath. Frustration, demotivation and the loss of key talent abound.

As for operational results – well, best not hold your breath.

> If you're Daimler-Benz, with its enormously strong culture, you can only impose that culture. The idea of creating a fused culture – no one believed it even if they had to say it.
>
> *Euan Baird, CEO, Schlumberger*

Cultural Autonomy: A Culture of Subcultures

So, if total integration is a non-starter, how about going to the other end of the spectrum and allowing each of the partners to maintain cultural autonomy? Everything would be familiar, and the partners concerned could develop solutions, systems and procedures based on their own corporate culture, beliefs and values. Eureka! This *must* be the answer!

Not quite. Back to our armies. You decide to combine your two sets of troops at an operational level by allowing them to observe their own unique ways of doing things. So they quite contentedly continue to follow their respected leaders and go about making decisions for their community in the way they always have. In the meantime, you educate yourself about the battle strategy of your new ally and learn that it is completely at odds with your own approach. You have to devise a unified strategy quickly, but immediately find that you are stifled by the autonomy you have allowed to develop. In the first instance, simple communication is complicated by the fact that, to allow cultural freedom, you have had to keep the armies physically apart. Because there is no understanding of each other's way of making decisions, you can never make any progress when you *do* get the right people together ... and who are the right people anyway? The game's over before it's begun. If you ever *did* get your two armies onto the battlefield, with their different uniforms, different languages and different ways of giving and receiving orders, they'd be just as likely to savage each other as they would to form a united front against the common enemy.

Once more, the message in a business context rings out loud and clear: autonomy may remove the discomfort involved with bringing cultures together, but it also leads to separatism, as well as a lack of consensus on values, basic assumptions and ways of doing things. Confusion is created as people move between offices and companies or as they participate in mixed teams. Time and energy is wasted, since what is successful in each partner – its best practices – cannot be readily shared or built upon. The bottom line is that there is little or no progress on the operational front.

How long are the stakeholders likely to tolerate a situation like this before they are looking for the leaders' scalps?

An Appropriate Degree of Integration

> Naturally, acquisitions impose systems, people and culture. Ford did not do that. If they had done, the results would be very different. At the time, there was a lot of concern in the UK press – but we didn't send many people to Jaguar. Myself and just four or five other people. Ford nurtured the culture. It was Jaguar people who turned it around.
>
> *Nick Scheele, President and COO, Ford*

So, if total integration is a pipe-dream and cultural autonomy is a surefire way to prevent you from ever delivering operational results, what's the appropriate degree of integration for achieving the goals of a corporate deal?

There is, of course, no prescriptive answer here. The appropriate degree of operational integration will always be a strategic choice. The deal will have been inspired in the first place by a strong business case. For example, one party may have a particular strength in manufacturing, while the other has a particular strength in marketing – strengths that, when combined, will give them a 'step-out' advantage in their industry. It is this business case, along with market, business, product and service – and cultural – considerations that the leadership team should use to frame the decision about how far the new partners will aim to integrate.

If we consider what's happening in practice, all the evidence indicates that companies are getting more 'real' when it comes to integration. Over the past 15 years we've seen a gradual evolution in expectations around how far cultures can, or should, be merged. From the mid-1980s to the mid-1990s, large multinational corporations were definitely shooting for the 'total integration' end of the spectrum, hoping to grow one global culture for the corporation as a whole. Like our general in the first option above, they were seeking a homogeneous set of values, beliefs, rules, systems, practices and behaviours – even dress codes! They would engage consultants to devise integration and communication plans that supported this goal.

In the mid-1990s, however, we saw a shift in perspective. The universal culture myth hit the wall of reality. More companies were learning the lesson outlined above – that total integration was generally unrealistic. Also, for many, total integration wasn't even desirable, particularly in light of business concepts such as 'think global, act local'. Expectations and requirements softened accordingly. Steelcase, and even IBM, for example, came to the realisation that it was acceptable to offer wine or beer to employees at lunch in its European subsidiaries – even though this was unacceptable in the North American operation. New corporate partners now asked consultants to 'help us build a corporate culture that allows diversity – with managers who have the skills necessary to manage this diversity under any circumstances'.

It's clear from this trend that culture is gradually becoming more of a factor in the decision about how far to integrate – a trend that we wholeheartedly support. Comparing and contrasting your respective cultures may help you to determine a realistic level of integration for the partners concerned. For example, a successful deal based on either total integration or autonomy may be possible if you can identify core similarities in your cultures. Conversely, if you identify that your cultures are polar opposites of one another, *any* level of integration may result in failure.

> If there isn't a reasonable cultural fit I wouldn't touch it. We acquired a small company providing telecom services to prisons. We didn't have a thing in common: the wrong business, the wrong people. It didn't have a chance.
>
> *Euan Baird, CEO, Schlumberger*

Although, in reality, corporate culture will rarely be a deal breaker, in such extreme cases the prospective partners may even make a decision not to proceed with the deal at all.

The Culturally Harmonious Entity: A Holy Grail?

It's fair to say that, whatever level of integration the leadership team decides to aim for – be it total integration, autonomy or somewhere in between – there will be work to do at the cultural level.

You could rightly be forgiven at this point for thinking that, as a leader in search of cultural harmony, you're in a no-win situation. You have to demonstrate *quickly* to all interested parties that the deal is delivering (or at the very least is *going* to deliver) value. For that to happen, you've got to get people from different corporate cultures working together effectively. Yet you're told that an attack/defence mentality typically emerges as soon as different cultures come together. So where does that leave your chances of success?

Is corporate cultural harmony *really* a Holy Grail, the quest for which will devour your time and energy, yet leave you with nothing to show for your trouble but cuts, bruises and many a tale of woe? *Do* you have to settle for 'making the best of it', hoping that the truly motivated will find a way to work in the new environment and that you won't lose too many of the star performers along the way? Well, the good news is that you don't.

Our experience tells us that a solution to the challenge of cultural integration can be found by looking at things from a different angle, and not from the angle of 'integration' at all, since the evidence suggests that cultural integration is something of a myth. Instead, we believe that the solution lies in 'linking' one culture with another. It's a solution that demands effort, but that offers significant and timely operational reward, allowing partners to reap the benefits that they first saw on paper. We call this approach Culture Bridging.

Culture Bridging: A Balanced Response

What helped integration at Accor was the space that people were given – by which I mean that people took each other's needs and interests into account.

Evelyne Chabrot, Human Resources Director Hotels, Accor Group

Culture Bridging is both a state of mind and a discipline. It embraces a range of attitudes and behaviours, processes, tools and approaches that together enable the achievement of operational integration at whatever level you may be aiming for, in a way that gets people's buy-in and that delivers sustainable results.

As its name suggests, Culture Bridging builds a 'bridge' between cultures. It helps each side to understand the idiosyncrasies of the other's values, beliefs and practices, and to plan and implement a strategy for working together that takes each of these unique cultures into account. Like a win–win negotiation, successful Culture Bridging leaves each party feeling comfortable, in the knowledge that their needs have been both listened to and taken into account.

When a Culture Bridging initiative is successful, it enables people and organisations of different cultures to build effective, rewarding relationships and high performance across borders, and critically enables leaders to deliver the results that stakeholders are looking for at the operational level.

> In an acquisition, if you arrive like a blockbuster, you won't get anywhere. You need to take small, micro-actions that demonstrate openness and understanding.
> *Cheri Alexander, Vice-President Personnel, General Motors Europe*

Let's not pretend that Culture Bridging is a piece of cake. But be sure that the experience of those who have 'got it right' amply demonstrates that the effort required is repaid many times over by the rewards to be reaped.

> I'm strongly against centralisation. I'm for harmony! If I look at all our 'Maisons', I see that they face the same market, the same consumer, the same distribution network. Therefore we need our managers to co-operate, to share experience and information, in an industry where autonomy is the norm. Even mentioning the word integration in such an environment would generate resistance. At the branch level, it's all about leadership and the capacity to make very different people work together and share a strategy.
> *Christophe Navarre, CEO, Moët-Hennessy*

The Enemy is not Within

> Generally, companies refuse change because it would make an old way of doing things redundant.
>
> *Euan Baird, CEO, Schlumberger*

Culture Bridging has at its heart a fundamental conviction, one that the leadership team must foster throughout the ranks of the new entity if they are to achieve the desired level of integration.

> We were supposed to work with Deutsche Telekom, but each partner was working in its own way and for itself as a company – not in the spirit of a joint venture.
>
> *Marc Dandelot, President, France Telecom North America, on France Telecom's joint venture with Deutsche Telekom*

When two groups face each other, like the two armies in our earlier example, there's an immediate tendency to adopt positions of 'right' and 'wrong'. 'We almost never lost to them in battle, so our way of doing things must be right'. Is it? Does that make the other army's approach wrong?

Let's set the record straight. A new organisation means a new dynamic, one that poses a new set of challenges and that demands a new set of responses. The people who are 'right' aren't those from company A or company B. They aren't those who are drowning in nostalgia for 'the good old days', fixated on how they responded to the past. The people who are 'right' are those who act in a way that will ensure sustainability in the future.

These are the people who recognise that even though they may have been 'enemies' in the past, they aren't any more. They know that the enemy lies outside, in the marketplace, and that, as partners, they must unite against this common enemy if the new organisation is to survive.

> Alliances are never perfect. As you approach them, you have to say to yourself, 'We're making a conscious choice here. It's a choice that means giving things up, but at the same time achieving synergies.'
>
> *Patrick J Rich, Former Chairman, Royal Packaging Van Leer*

A Reality Check: The Market Stops for No One

Soon we'll be beginning an in-depth look at what's involved in successful Culture Bridging. Before we do, it's worth taking a quick side-step for a reality check. By looking at integration in isolation, as we've done so far, we're indulging ourselves. We could easily forget, as managers often do, that integration has to happen simultaneously with regular day-to-day issues.

First, all-consuming as the construction of the new organisation may be, leaders have to remember to keep their eye on the ball with regard to keeping the business running. Take the example of United Airlines' proposed merger with US Airways:

> ... the airline's management has been 'so preoccupied with the merger [that] they are allowing the operation of the airline to be negatively affected'.
>
> 'Since Stephen Wolf came on board [as chairman], he stopped managing the airline', US Airways pilot Nils Mantzoros of Lock Haven, Pa., said before a recent flight. 'I'm afraid if the merger doesn't go through, we won't have an airline to fall back on'.[1]

As if integrating and keeping the business running weren't enough, there are the wider market issues to be addressed – and let's face it, in this day and age, conditions rarely stand still long enough for us to catch our breath. Laws, economics, trends and innovation all shape a shifting environment where today's stability is tomorrow's history. Witness the global economic downturn that's happening as we write. Or the burst of the technology bubble ... Ingo Janssen and JPMT certainly felt the force of that one. Even while they are distracted by reorganisation, companies have to be nimble enough to spot and capitalise on vital opportunities.

At the end of the day, it's of no value to have a harmonious new company if it's no longer competitive in the marketplace. So, we'll occasionally remind you, as we explore the ins and outs of Culture Bridging, that the market stops for no one. Integration efforts have to be juxtaposed with prevailing market conditions and have to bend and sway along with them. On that note of caution, let's get on with the journey.

---

[1] From an article in the *Philadelphia Enquirer*, 24 June 2001.

Some Food for Thought...

- To achieve any level of integration, leaders must address both the business and the human side of the deal. This means thinking on two fronts: the operational and the cultural.
- The appropriate degree of operational integration is a strategic choice. This choice should be made in light of the business case driving the deal, and should factor in market, business, product and service considerations.
- Whatever the degree of integration sought, a Culture Bridging approach is the most effective way to speed up the process, obtain buy-in and achieve results.
- There is no single recipe for Culture Bridging. An individual assessment of the different corporate cultures, with the business case in mind, will allow leaders to determine those areas where bridging is critical and those areas where it is less of a priority.
- A major challenge for the leadership team after an acquisition is to ensure that people do not fall into an attack/defence mindset, where each sees the other as 'the enemy'. They must align people, particularly if they were previously competitors, to face a new, *common* enemy: the competition.
- Leaders must ensure that everyone in their organisation remains focused on the business at the same time as they implement the integration process.

CHAPTER 3

What You Don't Know ... Can Hurt You

A strategy must be undertaken to bridge the cultures. But even before that, one must truly understand the cultures.

Cheri Alexander, Vice-President Personnel, General Motors Europe

'Cream and sugar?'

Ingo chuckled to himself. Americans never seemed to have really understood what coffee-drinking was all about. 'Black. Thank you'.

The 'Fix It' Integration Team, hand-picked from the brightest and best of both JPMT and InterComm's remaining talent, settled into chairs around the long boardroom table at JPMT's European HQ. From his seat at its head, Ingo sensed a glimmer of hope in the darkness that had descended over the JPMT/InterComm merger – the enormous level of goodwill that was now gathered in the room. There was a genuine desire among these people to get it right, no matter how much water had passed under the bridge over the last few months. Both businesses shared a great sense of pride in what they had been able to achieve independently. It hurt deeply to watch the reputation they had worked so hard to build decimated in the media on a daily basis. They wanted to be back on top of the creative pile, and to realise the potential that the merger had originally promised.

Pleasantries over, Ingo threw down the mantle to the group. 'Ladies and gentlemen. When our two businesses came together, we put fear into the hearts of every other global advertising corporation. Yet today I don't think I'd be too far wrong if I said that we're a laughing stock. I know that everyone in this room wants to rectify that situation. Which is exactly what we're going to do. We're going to put our house in order and win back the ground we've lost'.

The group grunted in agreement as Ingo continued his fighting talk. 'If we stand any chance of fixing things, it's my firm belief that we need to begin by working out where we've gone wrong till now. I throw it open to you'. After the customary reflective silence, the ball started rolling. Opinions started to flow. Different approaches to creating design strategy. Different account team structures. Different accounting procedures. The burst of the technology bubble. All were earmarked as culprits and blamed for the merger's lack of success.

A further hand was tentatively raised. It belonged to Jenny Anderson, a British expatriate who'd joined InterComm as Creative Director about a year before the merger. 'You know I really believe we're missing a trick here. Everything we're discussing is about strategy, processes, that kind of stuff. We knew those things were different before we started. And we actually had some pretty good plans in place to bring them together. In fact, we were **so** on the case, we even made space for teething problems. But you know what? We overlooked our people. We neglected the fact that we were merging two different tribes here – both with completely different ways of looking at the world. We just told them how great things were going to be, gave them a goody bag and a handy wallet-sized card with our vision and values on and thought we'd done the job. Well, it's pretty clear to me that we hadn't. It was a whole new experience for them and they felt completely in the dark about it. They didn't **really** know what the future held, there were suddenly all these people around who they didn't know or trust and everyone was doing things differently. We really didn't consider any of that stuff – and we clearly should have'.

Silence. Followed at length by reluctant nods of recognition. It wasn't that it hadn't crossed Ingo's mind: he liked to think of himself as sensitive to the needs of his workforce and fully aware of the need to keep them willing and able to do their jobs. But the extent of his planning here had been to focus on remuneration policies and bringing them into line. He hadn't dwelt on planning for the 'softer' issues, because he simply didn't think that they **were** issues. Both JPMT and InterComm were packed to the brim with bright, motivated people who he felt would rise to the challenge, and enjoy it in the process. Looking at things with the benefit of hindsight, he realised just how much he'd underestimated the importance of corporate culture, and how little he understood about how it worked, not only at InterComm, but also in his own back yard.

The team explored Jenny's comments as they continued their discussions. For many around the table, raising the issue of corporate culture was tantamount to the opening of Pandora's box. On solid ground when discussing strategy or campaigns, this softer issue took them out of their comfort zone to a place where they lacked the language to express themselves. The whole thing was much more comfortably swept under the carpet.

Nonetheless, by the end of the meeting, everyone agreed that JPMT and InterComm's failure to understand each other's culture, and to plan for the issues that integration would bring to the surface, were key to the difficulties they now found themselves in. And that, if they were to move forward, developing that understanding had to be their first port of call.

You Don't Know What You Don't Know

More often than not, senior executives are not in a position to really evaluate another culture and its impact – even though they think they are. What is missing is the perception of what **we** are: not knowing them is an issue, but not knowing oneself may be even more important in the interaction. It's like Socrates said: 'Know yourself'.
President of an international industrial company

If you were suddenly parachuted into the centre of Tokyo, a visitor with no knowledge of the Japanese language, no prior experience of the city and no guide book – you'd have a fairly big challenge on your hands. A million questions would flood into your brain: 'Which direction should I go in to find a hotel?' 'What on earth does that sign say?' 'Why is someone trying to push all those people into a train with a broomstick?'

Every decision, every action would be hampered by a lack of knowledge and understanding. Because of that lack of knowledge and understanding, it will be purely down to Lady Luck whether your decisions produce the outcomes you're looking for. *Did* that sign actually say 'Gentlemen's Toilet'? Well, you may only know once you get inside, at which point you'll either heave a sigh of relief or you'll have a lot of explaining to do. That's if you survive being set upon by twenty outraged Japanese women hitting you with their handbags.

Things can be pretty similar at the outset of a new corporate deal. Unless you're one of the rare companies that goes beyond the 'technical' level that's typical of due diligence to research extensively the 'human' level and support structures that lie below, you'll probably be overwhelmed by a sea of unfamiliarity when you begin to interact with your new partners. Then, like our hapless tourist searching for a Tokyo toilet, your unfamiliarity will soon lead you into trouble.

This was the case for Ingo and his colleagues in the JPMT/InterComm merger. They discovered a little late in the game, to their cost, that **understanding** is the key to Culture Bridging and the place where any bridging initiative should begin.

> If we had understood the nature of their expectations and the need to demonstrate to them that we were a learning organisation, we would have saved 7 wasted years of suspicion, tension and difficulty.
>
> *Senior executive, automotive industry*

By understanding, we mean the development of a shared view of the similarities and differences in the cultural profile of the partners; similarities and differences that will help or hinder the progress and success of the deal.

It sounds simple: deceptively simple, of course! When you embark on a deal, you know the important hard facts about the company you're going to sign with. But what you're less likely to know about is the vast array of elements – the behaviours and customs, systems and processes, recruitment and promotion criteria, communications systems, etc. – that make up your new partner's corporate culture.

Like a Fish Out of Water

> My initial opinion was that their organisation was more decentralised and therefore more egoistic. I didn't feel the team spirit I'm used to feeling in our company.
>
> *Dr Karl-Heinz Schmitz, Board Member, ZF Sachs AG*

For many, corporate culture is surrounded in mystique. It's slippery by nature, with elements that are implicit, elusive and hard to pinpoint *or* decipher. So it's perhaps not surprising that those who are involved in trying to bring two companies together have little understanding of it.

One of the initial challenges when it comes to understanding corporate culture is that it often takes a culture 'clash' to jolt your attention to the fact that you are in any way different from your partners. To the person immersed in a culture, the things that make it up are just part of the fabric of what's 'normal' in everyday life. ('We Japanese are quite used to being helped into trains with broomsticks, thank you very much!') To you, the person who is suddenly confronted with them, these cultural elements may well be completely alien and incomprehensible. Suddenly you become aware that you do things differently and you may act defensively as a result. ('Why do the Japanese tolerate being pushed around like that?! They'd better not do it to me!')

Confronted with a difference in this way, you become like the proverbial fish out of water. This fish only begins to recognise the elements of the water it lives in when it finds itself surrounded by air, where things are discernibly 'different'. At this point, the fish starts to compare and contrast but, by this time, it is already in big trouble: just like our tourist in Tokyo, and just like so many leaders who only become sensitised to the issue of culture once it's begun to cause them significant problems.

But could your new partner help you out by describing his or her culture if asked? Probably not. Come to that, could you describe your *own* culture? Again, the answer is probably not. Even when you *know* there are differences, you can be hard put to define them because, like the folks at JPMT InterComm, you rarely have a common language with which to talk about them.

The long and the short of it is that the issue of culture can be a tough one even to bring to the table. So, where does *that* leave understanding?

True Cultural Understanding

The chairman of a large European multinational company once told us:

> The problem with cultural differences is that they don't lead to disagreements, they lead to misunderstanding. Disagreements are obvious immediately and can be dealt with. But you tend to discover misunderstandings when its too late, when each party has tackled an action plan in its own way.

With this in mind, we'd like to ask you to think about icebergs for a moment, because when it comes to *true* cultural understanding, they teach a salutary lesson!

It may well prove relatively easy to decipher *some* of the aspects of your new partner's culture, because they will be out there for all to see: they are *explicit*. For example, your partner only recruits people from major business schools, or actively pursues ISO certification or makes sure that all of their offices have the corporate mission and objectives displayed for all to see.

But these 'manifestations' of the culture are just the tip of the iceberg, the things that you can see because they are 'above water'. What really counts though is what lies hidden beneath the waterline. It's this part of the cultural iceberg that can lead you into deep difficulties, and maybe even sink you, unless you understand it. This means identifying the values and beliefs that *drive* the culture and that are *implicit* because no one really even thinks about them. It's only when you confront driver with driver, rather than manifestation with manifestation, that you develop true cultural understanding and stand any chance of finding win–win solutions that everyone can work with.

The bottom line is that, as a leader or manager involved in an integration process, you have to understand fully both the *explicit* and, more importantly, the *implicit* aspects of the cultural dimension of your fledgling organisation. If you don't, you'll go through your partnership 'culturally blind', unable to see or do the things that matter to the other parties involved. You may well make critical mistakes that understanding could have avoided; such as closing a site because it's out of date, not realising the symbolism attached to the fact that it was built by the other company's founder.

You may only feel anger, frustration or some other negative emotion when you're confronted with what *they* do. Put yourself in the shoes of our tourist in Japan for a moment: unless you understand that that's the way it is in Tokyo, as well as understanding the reason *why* it's that way, you'll only become outraged the first time you feel one of those broomsticks poking into the small of your back.

> You have to understand the other culture's rules and apply them. If you do so, the readiness to bridge differences is very high. But if you don't – if, for example, you tell your Swedish boss a clear 'no' – the outcome will not be very fruitful.
>
> *Hans Albrecht, Executive Vice-President, Hella*

Forewarned is Forearmed: The Power of Research

> Owners are putting their best foot forward, and you can't always see their socks.
>
> *Ed Shipka, CEO, Pe Ben Oilfield Services*

If understanding is so crucial to your ability to bridge cultures, how do you go about building it? The answer is by being culturally sensitive and doing your research.

By being culturally sensitive we simply mean ensuring that culture is on the agenda and, when it is, watching out for the tell-tale signs that indicate both the explicit and implicit aspects of your own and your partner's cultures.

By doing your research, we mean engaging in activities with the specific objective of building cultural understanding. Ideally, this would involve conducting a Cultural Audit (a tool that we'll look at in some depth in Chapter 7) as soon as possible after the merger has been hatched, as part of the due diligence process.

In many cases, legal considerations may make conducting an audit this early impossible, but that's not an excuse for doing nothing. Apply your cultural sensitivity, keep your eyes open and your ears to the ground and look for cultural clues. They're everywhere: in the way a company's office is designed and laid out; in the way people dress; in the way the company presents itself through advertising and PR; in the way the company's personnel express themselves in interviews or in dealings with you. Talk to them and listen. Talk to other people who know and have worked with them and listen. Ask yourself questions and look for the answers. There's plenty you can do: just do it!

> It's possible to find out a lot about a company's culture just by listening to the market and by using the numerous sources of information at your disposal – business journals, consultants, market analysts, etc. Often this job doesn't get done, which causes big difficulties for management later on.
> *Patrick J Rich, Former Chairman, Royal Packaging Van Leer*

Make sure you do more than scratch the surface. You may be deluding yourself if you believe that everyone is operating in a spirit of openness and honesty in these early stages. During the foreplay prior to the new corporate entity getting down to business, everyone is likely to be on their best behaviour, hiding their dirty laundry from view and trying their hardest to portray an image they think the other party would like to see. So peer through the veneer to the layers beneath, and follow the golden rule: assume difference until proven otherwise!

> Thoroughly research the opportunity. Spend time interviewing key players. Find out what their approach to business is. However, this is very tough, as the company who is trying to sell often does not want you to know what their existing contracts are, what problems they are facing.
> *Ed Shipka, CEO, Pe Ben Oilfield Services*

Acquisitions are time sensitive and are usually focused on the financial and legal issues. Decisions are made on economics and a set of limited criteria, such as a company's reputation. This makes it difficult to know what you're getting into.

Ed Shipka, CEO, Pe Ben Oilfield Services

The important thing is that you make a concerted effort to understand one another. However you do it – through a Cultural Audit or through a less structured approach – cultural observation is made easier if you have a model that you can use to frame your observations and focus them on the areas that are likely to create the most significant challenges when your organisations begin to work together. Our goal in the chapters that follow is to provide you with just such a model: the first of the Culture Bridging tools we promised in Chapter 1.

Be aware that it is very important to allocate enough time in the first phase to investigate the cultural differences and test existing opinions and values. Do this together with your new partners so that you can formulate, together, the values and vision for the new company.

Torben Laustsen, Corporate Head of Group Identity and Communications, Nordea

Culture Bridging Fundamentals: A Diagnostic Model

Diagnostic models for understanding the unique aspects of an organisation's culture come in several shapes and sizes. Over the next four chapters we'll focus on one specific approach, based on our *Culture Bridging Fundamentals* model.

When we've used this diagnostic with our clients, we've found it to be one of the most valuable tools we have to help them to pinpoint and understand the differences in their own and their prospective partners' corporate cultures, and to identify where those differences are likely to lead to problems as they begin to work together.

Like all good models, Culture Bridging Fundamentals provides a common language that helps leadership and management teams to bring their cultural differences to the table and engage in productive discussion on how to bridge them.

The model helps to define an organisation's **style** and **preferences** in response to three **challenges** that are key to successful integration. The resulting *cultural snapshot* of the organisation under the microscope can then be compared and contrasted with the snapshot of a prospective partner to identify the **cultural flashpoints** that will need to be managed if people are to bridge cultures and work together co-operatively. These flashpoints can be *enablers*: points of common values, beliefs or ways of doing things that can be leveraged to help the integration process and increase the likelihood that operational results can be produced quickly. Equally, and perhaps more significantly to our mission in this book, cultural flashpoints can be *detractors*: points where values, beliefs and ways of doing things differ; points that, left unmanaged, create an unproductive workplace and hinder the achievement of operational integration and strategic goals.

> I need to understand and compare, in a detailed way, both 'them' and 'us' and look for areas where we can build together.
> *Cheri Alexander, Vice-President Personnel, General Motors Europe*

The Challenges: Three Key Themes for Understanding

Over the years, we've been privileged to work with a large number of organisations that have found themselves embroiled in the transformation brought on by a major change of shareholder. In doing so, we've noticed a distinct pattern to the questions that inevitably seem to be asked by the managers involved. This pattern suggests three key challenges that exert a significant, often definitive, influence on the chances of success when corporate cultures come together.

- **Legitimacy** concerns the credibility and authority of leaders and managers in the new organisation.
- **Effectiveness** concerns the way decisions are made about how things get done and how problems are solved.
- **Future** concerns the way corporate goals are communicated and buy-in is obtained.

It is in these three areas that leaders must develop understanding, not only of the approach favoured in their *own* corporate culture, but also of that of their future partners.

Legitimacy

The key questions that leaders and managers seem to ask themselves here are:

'How will we choose the right people to lead our organisation?'
'Do I have a chance of being among them?'

When the merging parties suddenly find themselves nose to nose with each other, the first issues to surface often focus on who's likely to be seen as credible and legitimate to lead and manage the new organisation: those to whom people will look for direction and guidance in the days and months ahead. From a purely personal perspective, those involved are likely to be asking whether they themselves have a chance to make it in the new world order!

The challenge here is to make sure that the best people, from both a technical and leadership perspective, stay in the new organisation, establish their authority and leadership, and get people moving forward in their new context.

Effectiveness

The key question that leaders and managers seem to ask themselves here is:

'How will we solve problems and work together to achieve results?'

Whenever companies come together in a merger, joint venture or other form of corporate deal, there is a plethora of 'people-related' operational issues that needs to be addressed rapidly if teams are to work together cohesively and productively. These range from the approach taken to problem solving through the way in which work is organised to the process for resolving conflicts.

The challenge here is to optimise the use of resources, so that integration cycle-time is reduced and value is added.

Future

The key question that leaders and managers seem to ask themselves here is:

'How will we get the buy-in of all our people for our corporate goals?'

Every new entity generates its own unique goals and vision for future success. It's vital that the new partners find a convincing way to communicate these, so that everyone not only understands them, but also feels committed to and motivated by them.

The challenge here is to reduce anxiety and discomfort and ensure that people deliver top-level performance, whilst still giving them 'the company perspective'.

To Each His Own: Culture-driven Preferences

Time and time again as we've worked with our clients and watched the world of mergers and acquisitions in general, we've observed that companies respond differently to these challenges, depending on their corporate cultures. It's not surprising to see two organisations, whose profiles seem similar in so many ways, develop and implement surprisingly contrasting solutions to these same challenges. Let's say that they have different **preferences** for the way that they respond to the challenges.

For example, one organisation may determine who is credible to lead and manage on the basis of **intellectual ability**. Another may make these same decisions based on an individual's track record or **performance**. Yet another may be more focused on people they consider to be part of the '**in-group**', people with shared experience or similar backgrounds to others in the organisation. Together, this set of preferences make up the Legitimacy dimension (Figure 1).

Figure 1

For example:

- A global management consulting organisation will only consider recruiting controllers with an internationally recognised MBA (intellectual ability).
- A computer hardware manufacturer will only promote sales executives into management positions when they have exceeded quota for three consecutive years (performance).
- A large, international, family-owned business will only consider appointing a controller who knows the founder well (in-group).

Turning to 'how things get done', some organisations' preference is to focus on **systems and procedures** to solve problems and work together, believing that the best way to get things done is by formalising their practices. Another organisation may move swiftly to **action**, in the belief that acting quickly is the dominant driver of effectiveness for the new entity. A further preference may be to focus on **networks**, calling on the people they know they can trust to help them. These, then, are the three preferences for the Effectiveness dimension (Figure 2).

Figure 2

For example:

- A venture capital organisation will only launch its new performance management system once all the associated policies and practices are fully and clearly documented (systems and procedures).
- A household goods manufacturer with a new product innovation takes the product straight to national distribution without conducting test marketing (action).
- When looking to expand into a new market, a market research company holds a series of fact-finding meetings with its clients who are already established in the market under consideration (networks).

Looking to the third area of challenge, one corporate culture may communicate and get buy-in to its goals by ensuring that they get the **organisational structure** right. A second may emphasise **strategic objectives**, choosing to communicate clearly where they want the new organisation to go. A third may put its faith in **heritage**, keeping its core values and corporate identity alive. These are the three preferences that make up the Future dimension (Figure 3).

For example:

- A business information company maintains organisation charts in a highly publicised location on its intranet. Updates are made as soon as changes are in the offing and employees are informed by blanket e-mail (organisational structure).

Figure 3

- An international recruitment consultancy employs a highly evolved performance management system that links strongly with the five- and ten-year plans for the business. Employees see the system as a critical part of their day-to-day job (strategic objectives).
- A manufacturer of breakfast cereals ensures that its 100-year-old flag-ship brand name is associated with each and every new product launch. In addition, all of the company's packaging includes the standard statement of the values that the brand stands for (heritage).

Head, Muscle or Heart? What's Your Style?

As you were mulling over the last section, the astute among you may have noticed a common thread between some of these preferences, a thread that gives a sense of the **style** of corporate culture that exists in any given organisation.

Some cultures tend towards a **conceptual** style. You could say that it's the *head* that defines the style here: things in this type of culture are very rational and meticulously thought through. There's a tendency towards certainty and away from risk. The conceptual culture responds to legitimacy questions by focusing on intellectual ability, effectiveness by referring to systems and procedures, and future sustainability by making their organisational structure fit for a purpose.

Other cultures respond in a more **relational** way. Here, the *heart* is the boss. The emotional side of things is much more in play and there's a focus on 'old-fashioned' values such as relationships and tradition. Relational cultures establish legitimacy on the basis of people they consider to be part of the 'in-group', ensure effectiveness by calling on their networks and create buy-in to the future by reinforcing their heritage.

A third style is more **pragmatic**. It's all about *muscle*: acting decisively, in a goal-orientated way. It's also about being prepared to absorb a little risk, rather than delaying action until things have been examined from every angle. Organisations with this type of culture will typically

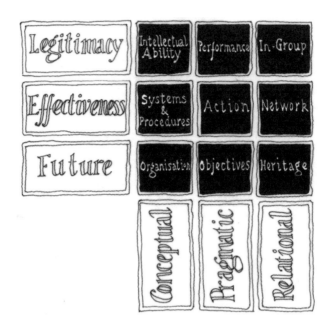

Figure 4

assign legitimacy to those who have achieved concrete and measurable results, ensure effectiveness by moving to action quickly and believe that buy-in to the future will be achieved by clearly communicating strategies and objectives.

We can combine these dimensions and preferences into a single model called the Culture Bridging Fundamentals model (Figure 4). When used as the basis for a Cultural Audit, this diagnostic tool will help to clarify gaps and overlaps in the corporate cultures of new partners (see Chapter 7).

Although a casual observer may be able to make out elements of all three styles in any given organisation, most corporate cultures lean towards one, or at most two, of the styles. In addition, an organisation's style may shift in response to different challenge areas; for example, it may be pragmatic when it comes to Legitimacy and relational when it comes to other preferences.

The Bright and the Dark Sides of Styles

Styles are more or less like personalities, which means that they have both strengths – what we call a *bright* side – and weaknesses – what we call a *dark* side.

The bright side of an organisation's style will lubricate the machinery, helping things to go more smoothly and contributing to more positive outcomes. The dark side will put a spanner in the works, delaying progress and compromising the end result.

At this point we're not going to look at the bright and dark sides of the styles in too much depth: you'll see more of this coming through in the chapters on the Legitimacy, Effectiveness and Future challenges that follow. But let's just think for a moment at a high level about the impact that the bright and dark sides can have on a business.

- On the bright side, a **conceptual** style means that people use their structured, intellectual leanings to ensure a well thought through approach to anything they do. They don't like half-baked efforts and they don't want to make mistakes. But on the dark side, they may succumb to 'analysis paralysis'. Nothing gets done because there are always other options to consider, or because they will not accept any risk whatsoever.
- On the bright side, a **pragmatic** style means that people will always be focused on success and what that means. They're 'better, faster, cheaper' people who want to produce results for their company and themselves. But on the dark side, their focus on action and results may cause them to forget to 'look before they leap'. Their lack of thought before action may lead to costly mistakes and inefficiencies.
- On the bright side, a **relational** style encourages a strong sense of 'we're in this together': people are supported and everyone stands or falls by everyone else's decisions and actions. New people are welcomed and made to feel part of the family. Commitment and loyalty are high. On the dark side, the complete opposite can be true: the 'family' closes ranks and becomes almost sect-like. Outsiders find it almost impossible to crack their code and break into their circle.

Who's Right, Who's Wrong?

Quite justifiably, each culture sees its own solution – be it conceptual, relational or pragmatic – as perfectly reasonable and normal. After all, 'it's the way we do things around here and it works for us'. No problem!

Just as we saw with JPMT and InterComm, however, it *is* a problem if the merging partners have different styles and fail to do what's necessary to understand each other's point of view and to manage the cultural flashpoints that emerge as a result.

A useful example of the difficulties created by an unmanaged clash in cultural styles comes from a senior manager in the chemical industry:

> The French conceptual approach drove the American managers crazy. The few Americans working with the French would come back with war stories about how all the French would do was talk and never take action. And how it was a good thing they 'have us' because we are going to make things happen.
>
> The perception was that nothing ever happened as a result of a meeting in France. You had to be there to represent American interests, but nothing would move forward in those meetings.

If you've come with us this far, you'll be well aware by now of the downward spiral in such circumstances: motivation wanes, people start to leave, customers are lost; and the deal joins the list of those that have become the subject of best-selling business books!

The application of a model such as the Culture Bridging Fundamentals diagnostic early enough in the process of organisations coming together can help to ensure that this point is never reached. The insight and common language that the diagnostic provides allows you to engage in discussions with your partners that focus on win–win solutions.

It's not about subsuming one culture to another. Nor is it about power plays. It *is* about making a concerted effort to draw on the value of each culture to build a win–win outcome across cultural diversity. By encouraging an objective and shared view of the situation, it can help to set partners on the road to success.

> When starting up – both sides were very natural. We saw each other in a fairly black & white way and first impressions clearly demonstrated how 'culture clashes' can prevail in early days of a merger.
> *Commercial vice-president, beverage industry*

Some Food for Thought…

- Cultural phenomena are generally implicit and often unconscious. Most of us can identify our own cultural 'baggage' only when we're confronted with someone else's. Therefore, developing a common language for identifying and discussing cultural differences is an important first step in Culture Bridging.

- Corporate cultural differences have a specific impact on key work processes in an organisation. Although these differences may be easily ignored initially, they will only surface again in the thick of the action; at which point, if there is no common language for analysing and discussing what's happening, mutual stereotyping and accusation can take over.
- No one cultural style – conceptual, pragmatic or relational – is 'better' than another. However, one particular style may be more consistent with corporate strategy than another. A cultural diagnostic allows leaders to identify where the new partners' preferred styles are consistent with the strategy for the new entity and where they are not.
- Companies do not favour one style alone. They usually have a primary stylistic preference, closely followed by a secondary one. The third option is often far less relevant. A cultural diagnostic allows leaders to pinpoint preferences in style that are shared between partners, which can be built on, and those that are not shared, where Culture Bridging may be appropriate.
- A cultural diagnostic provides new partners with a common language for talking about things that are otherwise difficult to talk about. This should allow them to develop greater trust and therefore move from a potential 'attack–defence' spiral into a problem-solving mode.

CHAPTER 4

Legitimacy

Choosing the right man for the right position is absolutely key when going into a merger process. In order to do so, one must look for as much neutrality as possible so that you get buy-in from both sides.

Chairman, telecommunications industry

Authority.

Like some strange form of torture, the word played over and over in Ingo's head.

What was it that Jenny had said when she had dropped her 'cultural bombshell'? 'There were suddenly all these people around who they didn't know or trust'. Yes, that was it.

Staring out of his office window over a cityscape that contained a million people who valued trust and respect as highly as motherhood and apple pie, Ingo asked himself what was really in question here. He reflected on a time in his own career when he'd had to follow the lead of someone who, in his opinion, didn't have the right credentials to be in a position of power. He thought about another situation in which he'd been frustrated by the organisation's lack of willingness to take a chance on someone fresh and new, but unproven – him! – instead focusing their hiring decision on CVs loaded with 'relevant' experience. He thought about how these situations had affected him – recalling, in one key instance, how what was happening had caused him to focus all his energy on finding a new opportunity, a new home for his unappreciated talents. Yet, being completely rational, he also reflected that these approaches to deciding who was credible and entitled to lead were perfectly legitimate for the organisations concerned. They just didn't fit **his** way of doing things.

In a blinding flash, it was suddenly very apparent to Ingo how much JPMT and InterComm clashed in this area.

Take the people who were selected to fill the top jobs in the new US organisation. Ingo had brought in a number of key executives from Europe, believing that the depth of their international experience – coupled with the flexibility that they had developed as they worked across borders in Europe and Asia – made them uniquely suited to piloting the new operation. When they chose them, Ingo and the team believed they'd got it right. They'd assumed that the qualities JPMT valued would be equally valued by InterComm. Yet now he was beginning to realise that JPMT's performance-focused culture was entirely at odds with that of his new American colleagues, who placed their faith in people they saw as 'one of us', particularly when it came to understanding the local market.

He remembered something he'd read somewhere about the leaders in new corporate deals: 'everyone is watching what they do, what they say, how they manage – get this part wrong and you get it all wrong'. Ingo resolved to get out into the business and talk to some of the troops about their experiences. His first port-of-call was one of the few former Inter-Comm Account Directors who remained with the business. Ingo was interested in her perspective on how the JPMT people had managed things during the transition period.

> 'David Daniels, the new VP of Business Development, decided to do account reviews with the teams that ran each of the top five accounts. But he'd only just stepped off the plane from Europe – he just hadn't earned his wings. He'd come in, tell us all about his INSEAD MBA and how he'd worked at this company and that company – as if this qualified him to question all the strategic thinking we'd done before he arrived on the scene. I don't doubt how smart his degrees make him, and I'm sure he knew his clients back to front. But he'd never worked in our market – and he didn't seem to place too much value on the fact that we had. A lot of the guys were really upset. To be frank – we didn't trust him and we didn't think he was the right person to be calling the shots.'
>
> When you think about credibility and leadership, you put your faith in qualifications and experience. For us it's more about family – about people who understand us, what we're about. Sure we want to be surrounded by people who can do the job. But, make no mistake, if it stops feeling like family – well, that's when people start to run for the doors. And it's no good thinking that a fat salary and the promise of stock options will cure things. They can get those elsewhere. For InterComm people, it was important to feel good about where they worked. When they didn't, they jumped ship.

As Ingo continued on his journey around the business, he talked to a lot of the junior account handlers and copywriters who worked in the engine room of the business. Many of them spoke about what they saw as a lack of support from their new European colleagues. InterComm's culture was one built on feedback and coaching. Employees who found themselves reporting to former JPMT Account Directors were suddenly deprived of this. Their new bosses seemed to work in silos with their heads down, and the team only really heard from them when targets weren't met or results weren't delivered. InterComm people quickly began to feel that they were being kept in the dark. The natural consequence was that they found it very difficult to trust their new bosses and respect for their leadership dwindled by the day.

Ingo thought about the effect the trust and credibility issues might have on other functions within the new organisation. He talked with the VP of Human Resources, whose story gave him fresh evidence of the cultural divide between JPMT and InterComm.

> Out of the blue, we got this call from HR at headquarters, telling us to put a temporary freeze on recruitment until they'd been able to review 'the approach we took to hiring'. We just couldn't believe their nerve! These people had never set foot inside our business, yet they were trying to tell us what raw material we should be looking at.
>
> Even then they didn't bother to come to see us personally. Everything was done by videoconference and it quickly became clear that we saw things very differently around the type of people we hire. We've always looked out for bright, creative minds – be they for copywriters, design directors or account handlers. That's just our way and it's worked for us. To us experience doesn't necessarily equate with quality. Some of the best people we have had never worked in the industry before they joined us. JPMT were different though – industry experience was everything to them. Maybe that's just because of the way they grew, I don't know.
>
> I guess the good thing is that now we know what we're dealing with – so we've at least been able to start work on finding a middle ground. We're trying to thrash out a picture of the culture we want for the business, as well as the behaviours that would drive it and hiring accordingly. But it's caused a lot of friction.

Walkabout over, Ingo tried to summarise what he'd learned. Although he'd always known it, these meetings had hammered home the fact that a successful organisation needs a workplace built on trust – and leaders who are credible. Yet somehow, in the mêlée, he'd overlooked the fact that different groups of people define trust and credibility in different ways and that this needs to be factored into those oh-so-critical selection and deployment decisions. It was clear that JPMT was an organisation that saw qualifications and experience as measures of who should legitimately hold power and be trusted. For InterComm the picture was quite different – they placed trust and respect in people who were 'part of the family'.

For his own part, Ingo realised that he'd been relying on his gut when he made decisions about key posts. He'd simply looked at who he thought would be the best person for the job, based on his trusty old yardstick, 'related experience'. He hadn't thought about who would command the respect of the teams and who would embody the 'cultural blueprint' that would equal success for the merged business. He'd got away with it in the past, but this time the feeling ran deeper and, because of the scale of the operation, the stakes were higher.

The price that had been paid for failing to recognise and bridge the divide was high. Although some turnover was to be expected, JPMT had lost both chaff and grain. The number of key people leaving had turned from a trickle into a torrent and when they left, they took with them not only proprietary knowledge of creative strategy and customers, but also the spirit of InterComm. The American business was left a shadow of its former self with people in positions who were neither respected nor even effective in the way Ingo had imagined they would be. The company's competitors couldn't believe their luck.

Ingo reflected on a saying he'd heard recently, one that he now latched on to as he thought about the road ahead. 'Mistakes are the portal of discovery'. Ingo was sure that the differences in approach weren't insurmountable. Challenging as it may be, he was confident that, with the base of understanding he was starting to develop, he and his various teams held the key to bridging between two very different perspectives on 'legitimacy'.

The Legitimacy Challenge: Who Will We Trust and Follow?

The moment news hits the grapevine that a merger is on the cards, gossip and speculation become everyone's favourite sport. Who will the new bosses be? Who and what will they be responsible for? What will it take to 'make it' in the new organisation?

These are questions that the powers that be must wrestle with quickly in order to build confidence. But as they do so, they should remember that it's not just about putting names in boxes on the organisational chart. Allocating roles and responsibilities will count for nothing unless the **credibility** and **authority** of the people *behind* the names are established. If this doesn't happen, people are unlikely to buy in to the new entity and the rot will set in. It's this issue of who will be trusted and followed that we call the **Legitimacy** challenge.

Legitimacy Preferences

Problems arise in responding to this challenge because teams and organisations have different perspectives on what constitutes 'credibility' and 'authority'; in other words, they have different *preferences* around the issue of Legitimacy. What inspires trust and a willingness to follow someone in one partner may be completely alien to another.

There are three distinct preferences when it comes to responding to the Legitimacy challenge:

- a preference for people with conceptual skills, degrees and titles, who have clear **intellectual ability**
- a preference for measurable **performance**, for people who have a proven track record and have demonstrated significant, measurable results and achievements
- a preference for people who are part of an '**in-group**', who share some kind of common bond based on experience, background, social grouping, etc.

These preferences lie at the three angles of the Legitimacy triangle (Figure 1).

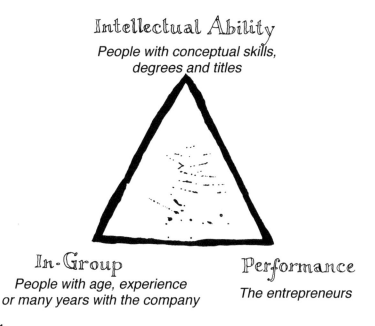

Figure 1

The Intellectuals

We look for people who demonstrate intellectual capabilities in the way they manage their ideas and construct their arguments. How you present yourself and your ideas is important in getting ahead in this company.

Senior executive, consulting company

I was absolutely amazed when I saw the CEO of our new French partner present during a European management meeting. He stood on stage, and gave a well-structured, forty-five-minute, five-point speech, in perfect English. His message was eloquent and persuasive, and delivered without any notes or stumbling. It really was quite a performance. Then, as I watched the rest of his team make their presentations, I realised that they were **all** like this!

The cynical amongst you might question the effectiveness of such a slick approach. But one thing's for sure: in order to climb up the ladder in this French organisation, you'd have to demonstrate outstanding **intellectual ability**: no mumbling, no hesitation, no checking written notes, no visual aids.

In organisations that see intellectual ability as the key prerequisite for credibility and authority, the people who get hired and get ahead will be highly educated, with prestigious degrees and titles. Take a look at the company's leaders. Are they publicly recognised as experts in their fields? Then the chances are that you're looking at an organisation that associates Legitimacy with intellectual ability. These leaders are highly articulate with highly developed analytical skills. Their strategic thinking skills are strong and they expect fast 'thinking on your feet' from their colleagues, rewarding those who demonstrate it.

When it comes to Legitimacy, you can expect a high intellectual ability score to come from engineering firms, medical companies and major consulting firms, where academic prowess and official qualifications are the order of the day.

The same is true of many state-owned companies. The monopoly status and protection from competition that they often enjoy means that the focus is more on politics than economic results. However, there is often pressure for technical achievement in these organisations and, to address it, the powers that be will try to lure and develop the brightest and best experts. It will be difficult for anyone to establish Legitimacy in these organisations without the right degrees and qualifications, in the right fields of competency from the right schools. In the past this type of culture has flourished in Europe, where the state-owned sector has always been significant. Today, the ongoing trend towards deregulation is forcing their evolution into more results-orientated organisations.

It's worth noting that in many cultures with a preference for intellectual ability, the overwhelming focus on intelligence and brain power can dominate the focus on results, in some cases making an 'intelligent failure' more acceptable than a 'simplistic success'.

The Entrepreneurs

> Here, who gets promoted is purely based on results and who you know. But they're innovation driven – it's **how** you achieve that matters. The results and numbers are less important.
>
> *General manager, beverage industry*

Things would be quite different in a culture with a preference for **performance**. Here the 'simplistic success' would have everyone cracking open the champagne.

The people who are trusted and followed in this type of culture are 'entrepreneurs': people who take risks, but deliver results. They may or may not have strong academic track records. They may or may not be part of the 'in-group'. But they most certainly make things happen.

Picture a scene. The German VP of HR for a large chemical company is considering applications for a senior project management position, and comes to the CV of an American project manager in the US subsidiary. She notices, with amazement, that a few years before joining the group, the candidate set up a company which had ultimately gone bankrupt.

'This is unbelievable. No German professional would ever mention this sort of information', she thinks to herself. 'On the contrary, he'd do everything possible to hide it'. Hedda calls her American counterpart to ask about the candidate. 'Well, it proves that he's entrepreneurial, doesn't it?', he replied. 'I expect that's why he put that in'. Hedda returns to her desk, intrigued. She's just come face to face with a performance culture.

The performance culture is all about results and individual or team performance. Internal competition is often used as a way of stimulating effort and reaching peak performance. Employees must get used to the fact that everyone is accountable, no matter where they sit in the hierarchy. So performance evaluation, formal and informal, is part of everyday life. Promotion opportunities, career and succession plans will all be determined by it. If you deliver results, you're likely to get ahead. If you don't measure up, you're likely to be shown the door.

When it comes to Legitimacy, you can expect to see a strong performance culture in multiproduct fast-moving consumer goods companies in highly competitive markets. It's something you may also see in emerging markets, where opportunities for growth often lead to a 'can-do' attitude. One illustration of this was given to us by Euan Baird, CEO of Schlumberger:

> We opened a research centre in Tsinghua – the premier university in China. They have provided facilities for research within the university itself. I met the President of this university and of Beijing University – they aren't even 40 years old and speak perfect English. I asked whether it had been difficult to get this to come about. They said 'we thought it was a good idea'. It seems to be that's all it takes.

People Like Us

The people we accept as leaders are 'people like us'. They share – and respect – our values, our history and our traditions. Our leaders and managers all come from similar backgrounds and the relationships they develop with their people go well beyond the professional arena. This makes it difficult for newcomers to find their own place in the company.

CEO, entertainment industry

The scene is an orientation programme for a group of European managers in the chemical industry, about to take up appointments in Africa. The African General Manager, trained in Europe, is addressing the group:

> I know that most of you here today have a commitment to developing local managers. But there's something you have to understand about the way we recruit and promote people in my country. 'Local' doesn't simply mean 'national'. Ethnic group is often far more important than simple citizenship. I've always made sure that there's

an appropriate balance of managers from the major ethnic groups in the country, and you'll need to do the same if you want things to work smoothly. You'll never get people's loyalty and commitment if you don't.

What we have here is a case of a company trying to avoid the pitfalls of the **in-group** culture. When the preference is for the in-group, people relate to and respect one another like clans, tied together by a common bond. The bond itself can vary widely in nature. It may be based around some regional affinity, where you're 'one of us' because of where you come from. Or it may involve 'old-boy' school networks, where you're one of us because of where you attended school or college. In the most deep-seated cases, it can be based on religion, race or, as in our example, ethnic origin.

> If you speak German, you are accepted. They are so German leaning – if you don't have anything to do with Germany or accept the German way, then you're dead.
>
> *General manager, beverage industry*

Yet, although the 'group' varies from situation to situation, groups all have one thing in common: you're in or you're out, depending on whether or not you belong. If you're not part of the group, it can be difficult to gain acceptance or get ahead. If you *are* part of the group, you're linked by more than just a contract.

When it comes to Legitimacy, you can expect to see strong in-group cultures in family-owned companies and start-ups.

Perspectives on Legitimacy: What Happens When Preferences Meet?

> If you talk to an American applicant during recruitment, s/he will stress his or her capabilities and point out what he or she has achieved. As a German, I find this embarrassing, but it's the way people learned to behave. Here we tend to be a little more modest.
>
> *Hans Albrecht, Executive Vice-President, Hella*

We have presented three very different perspectives on who to trust and follow. Each one is completely valid for any organisation that adopts it and each is perfectly fine as long as the organisation is working in isolation. But what happens when this organisation needs to form a partnership of some kind and the new partners have different preferences where Legitimacy is concerned?

All too often, the answer is 'trouble'. The difficulties experienced by JPMT, with preferences for performance and intellectual ability, and InterComm, with its strong 'family' atmosphere and in-group preference, are only one illustration of this. David Daniels, JPMT's VP of Business Development, almost certainly thought that it was a good idea to stress his intellectual pedigree to his new account management team. However, he would have had more success in earning their trust and respect by taking the time to learn about how *they* operated and what *they* held in esteem. This is one example of what we'll call a 'disconnect', an area of subtle or overt discord that can create potentially destructive rifts in the relationship between partners.

But it's not all bad news. Although cultural *clashes* may make themselves more immediately obvious, it's worth remembering that there can also be *positive* outcomes, or 'connects' as we'll call them, when different preferences come together, sometimes because the preferences are complementary in some way, sometimes because fresh input stimulates fresh thinking and fresh approaches.

In a perfect world, there would be only 'connects'! The reality, however, is that it's *disconnects* that grab the headlines in most mergers and other forms of corporate deals. And it's disconnects that slow down integration and that create the need for Culture Bridging. The moral of the story? Identify and understand them as early as possible.

It's not our intent to cover all of the possible connects and disconnects between the different preferences in these chapters on the three challenge areas. Nonetheless, in the hope that it will heighten your awareness of the potential issues to watch out for in your own situation, we will provide you with a little food for thought in each of the challenge areas.

For example, what might happen if two cultures with similar preferences around Legitimacy come together? Let's take two **performance**-driven, pragmatically orientated cultures as an example. Potentially, this is an incredibly powerful combination, as everyone is focused on getting results and there's an all-round willingness to take risks to achieve them. The downside might come if perspectives on what constitutes 'good' and 'bad' performance differ greatly from one group to another. Similarly, two **in-group** cultures may blend well, but only if the 'group' in question is similar in each case. It's worth remembering that many terms and concepts, no matter how familiar, may need to be redefined in a multicultural context. Otherwise, there could be fireworks!

Turning to combinations of different preferences: if yours is an organisation that leans more towards *intellectual ability* when it comes to assigning legitimacy to leaders and other key people, what can you expect to encounter in a partner with a more *performance*-orientated culture, where results and entrepreneurial spirit are particularly valued?

One possibility is that your own people, who value and esteem intellectual credentials, would be reluctant to take a risk on performers who aren't backed up by degrees. This was certainly the case in one situation we know of, where a German manufacturing company, with a clear preference for intellectual ability in its managers, acquired its smaller American supplier. The supplier's culture was strongly orientated towards the achievement of results and very little attention was paid to people's academic background or skills. When the German company president visited the new subsidiary and met the plant managers, he found them to be relatively inarticulate and lacking in both written and presentation skills. His predisposition to equate credibility with intellectual ability blinded him to the fact that these people had consistently produced excellent results for the company. His somewhat inflammatory reaction was to ask the local General Manager, 'Are these really the people we should have in these jobs?' A disconnect took place and a rift was born. José-Maria Aulotte, Director of Integration at the Lafarge Group, expanded on this idea of 'cultural blind-spots' when he shared the following example with us:

> In Lafarge we sometimes tend to react negatively to people who don't demonstrate their intellectual ability – for example in a presentation. I can think of a couple of instances recently where, after hearing the acquired management team's initial presentation, the Lafarge team was questioning their ability to work to our standards. Of course, this was an instinctive reaction, and we felt differently once we'd given them more time. But it's indicative of our culture, which favours intellectual 'brio'. We have to be careful not to make these hasty judgements.

If you look at our earlier scenario through the eyes of the American supplier, you'd probably see a different angle on the disconnect. With credibility in their culture being strongly attached to the achievement of impressive business results, the German acquirer's apparent lack of focus on this type of performance would quickly lead to irritation and frustration. This is a shame, because the marriage of one side's 'smarts' with the other's drive could inject much needed energy and focus into the new venture.

One Senior Vice-President of Human Resources gave us another example of what can happen when a culture that favours performance meets to do business with a culture that favours intellectual ability:

> One of my first projects in global compensation was to create a global bonus program applying to a certain level of management in the three companies. This meant that the people in France were suddenly accessible to bonuses. I had a meeting with them and said 'we will measure your performance based on your objectives and you will get paid according to how well you meet them'. People were outraged. 'How dare you think I would work harder for more money. I'm here for science. I'm here for my contribution to humanity. How dare you think that for money I would do more'?

How might an in-group culture react to cultures with other preferences? Imagine company A, with a strong **in-group** culture, merging with company B, with a preference for **performance**. When it comes to appointing the managers who will wield authority and power in the new organisation, company A's representatives suggest mature (read middle-aged!) candidates who have been around the company for a long time, who come from similar backgrounds to their own and who have steady, but unremarkable track records. Company B's representatives see things quite differently. The candidates they put forward are hungry, young, high-flyers. Sparks fly and a culture clash ensues.

A senior executive in the automobile industry gave an illustration of this when he spoke to us of the difficulties that he and his European organisation had experienced in working with a little-understood Japanese partner and the differences in how each party assigned credibility:

> We had two totally different engineering systems and we might as well have come from different planets.
>
> For example, the Japanese engineers were dedicated experts. They had an engineer who worked exclusively on tailgates. During his 30 years' experience he would have designed more tailgates than our engineers would have had hot dinners, but our engineers were filled with arrogance about the difference in approach. They sneered at the idea of working in just one specific area, where they

would expect to be involved in a variety of jobs. They couldn't appreciate the value of being so specialised.

But when a question came up in meetings, the senior people in the front row of the Japanese team would defer to the tailgate expert on the back row. They recognised and respected the value his experience could bring. This type of speciality expertise was totally alien to and unappreciated by our senior management.

We also know of the merger of two publishing companies owned by the same parent. One company was highly creative and people focused, with a strong **in-group** preference. The other favoured performance, being disciplined and results driven. The charismatic leader of the creative company – one of its two founders when the company was born 35 years earlier – was made CEO of the new organisation. The managers of the other company, whose culture prized results above all else, found it difficult to respect their new leader, considering his approachable, down-to-earth style and emphasis on people and values as 'soft'.

Smoothing the Waters

These are not isolated examples of the problems that can be caused by different perspectives on **Legitimacy**. Every day, around the world, similar cultural clashes manifest themselves in meeting rooms, on factory floors and in front of customers. They stand as testament to a general lack of sensitivity to the cultural dimension.

Yet, by using a tool such as the Culture Bridging Fundamentals diagnostic, problems like these *can* be anticipated and, as a result, action can be taken to avoid them. Take the example of a German–US joint venture in industrial hygiene. Looking back over ten years of successful operation, the Human Resources Director for the combined operation told us:

> Look at the origins of the two companies – one had strong German and French roots and had developed a culture focused on its products. **Legitimacy** for them was focused on the **intellectual ability** to develop these products and the relationships between technicians and engineers in the teams.
>
> In contrast, the US partner developed more as a service company. Here **Legitimacy** was more a question of individual and team performance, coupled with relationships between people. The

company had a strong and charismatic CEO, who tended to mobilise this in-group feeling within the company. So, although they had differences, they also had a common relational link through the in-group.

What made the venture successful was the fact that both sides were aware of – and managed – their differences as well as the areas where they complemented each other. They were in different geographic markets. Their sales approaches were different. But they were able to achieve synergies, something quite rare in the history of mergers and alliances.

Remember that, as a general rule of thumb, if you're trying to establish early credibility and authority with new employees, colleagues or shareholders, don't use what builds credibility in your eyes as your yardstick. What matters is what builds credibility in *their* cultural environment.

This is a lesson that the people at JPMT would do well to learn. If they had applied the Culture Bridging Fundamentals diagnostic as they planned the merger with InterComm, they might just have learned it. They would have developed an early understanding of their different perspectives on Legitimacy, an understanding that may well have helped them to avoid a great deal of the pitfalls and pain they are experiencing. Instead, they find themselves deep in a hole, feeling the full effect of their disconnects.

> When you nominate managers for the new company, it's important to choose people who are respected in both companies. Each manager must be seen as the obvious choice. It's tempting to choose only managers that you already know, but be aware of the signals this sends.
>
> *Kjeld Johannesen, CEO, Danish Crown*

Some Food for Thought ...

- **Legitimacy** – credibility and authority – means different things to different cultures.
- Some cultures attach **Legitimacy** to **intellectual ability** – conceptual skills, degrees, etc. Others attach it to **performance** – the achieve-

ment of results. Still others see it in the **in-group** – 'people like us' or those who have served with the company for many years.

- When cultures with different preferences come together, there can be both *connects* – areas of synergy that contribute to forward momentum – and *disconnects* – areas of discord that can cause rifts that slow down progress.
- To increase the chances of successful integration, both connects and disconnects need to be identified and understood as early as possible in the relationship. This is where a cultural model can help to build understanding.
- Once differences have been identified, managers have to learn how to accept and manage them. For this to happen credibly, leaders must demonstrate their **Legitimacy** in a way that is acceptable in the cultures in which they operate.

CHAPTER 5

Effectiveness

The way things roll out it's always the same. They say to you, 'What an interesting way of doing it. We'll have to see what we can keep. *We* do it differently though, and that's how we're going to do it'.

Véronique Guillot-Pelpel, Senior Corporate Vice-President Communications, Nexans

♪ You say tom-ah-to, and I say tom-ay-to ♪

The needle was definitely stuck in the groove. The line from the old classic played over and over again in Ingo's head. He was making a concerted effort not to allow himself to get to the refrain ...

♪ Let's call the whole thing off ♪

Hmm. Tempting!

The song had come to mind in the first place after a discussion with Holly Arthur, a financial controller who had moved to New York after the merger to help integrate JPMT and InterComm's financial systems. The conversation, and the passion with which Holly delivered her message, had alerted him to a common thread in much of the feedback he'd been getting from people during his walkabout. There was often talk about the way the two companies went about things, problem solving or decision making for instance, and how their respective approaches were often at odds with one another.

He thought specifically about what Holly had said.

Our problems weren't so much about bringing the financial systems together. Certainly that had its challenges, but we're used to that sort of thing – it's our bread and butter. Where we really got into deep water was around understanding how each other worked.

Take the way decisions were made. I was used to having to follow a pretty regimented process. My bosses expected me to document everything and to make my case clearly and completely. It's not that I had to run every decision higher up the organisation – on the contrary, I had a lot of authority in that regard – but I had to be able to justify everything I'd decided to the nth degree.

When I started to work with my colleagues in New York, I soon realised that their way was the polar opposite of ours. They looked at the alternatives, tossed them around a little, chose one and then said 'let's do it'. And that was more or less it!

To be honest, I could see the appeal – and the logic – of their approach. They were bright people. They'd been hired to make just these kinds of decision and they'd be held accountable if things went down the toilet. Who needed lengthy reports and analyses? But I couldn't just throw out the European operation's way of doing things. They were expecting their reports and my head could have been on the block if I hadn't supplied them. So I had to force these free thinkers to sit with me and follow 'the process'. They were **not** happy! They were like a bunch of caged animals.

I suppose the bottom line is that they have a culture of risk taking and we have one of thoughtful, process-orientated decision making. What we see as professionalism, they see as restrictive red tape. Maybe we make fewer mistakes but, more often than not, they get results more quickly. I don't think that either way's right or wrong – but if you don't acknowledge the differences, it causes major headaches. And that can have quite an impact on the quality of solution you come up with.

The good thing about the pain we went through, though, is that it helped us to recognise our differences – probably because we were so directly confronted by them. I'm not sure that people in other parts of the business have been so lucky. Their differences haven't been so immediately apparent, so they haven't been able to carve a way of working that suits everyone – which, amazingly enough, we have.

Like so much in life, once you were aware of it, you wondered how you could ever have missed it. But miss it Ingo had. Holly's words now made him think of a hundred and one instances – some small, others far more significant – that highlighted different ways of doing things between JPMT and InterComm. Even yesterday when the Integration Team met to start the mop up, he realised that they'd been working in 'the JPMT way', with everyone seated around a classic boardroom table. If they'd followed Inter-Comm's style, they would have found a more informal setting, with plump, feather-filled sofas and fruit juice on tap.

He thought about the many months of meticulous planning that had gone into merging JPMT and InterComm's systems and procedures, from payroll through billing to the whole domain of IT infrastructure. Yet scarcely a thought had been given to the **human** systems and processes that actually made it all happen. Everyone was so focused on mechanics that they just didn't see the 'people' problems coming. And when they **did** come, no one seemed to be confident enough in each other's company to voice their concerns. Instead, there were whispers by coffee machines and secret trysts in neighbourhood bars after the work day was done.

One situation, which had almost turned into a serious conflict, suddenly came into Ingo's mind. It was all about purchasing rules. Ah! Purchasing! Over the years, JPMT had developed a well-oiled purchasing policy, establishing quality standards such as cost, reputation and style, against which all potential materials providers were assessed. Some suppliers had been listed as 'preferred' and Art Directors were expected to review this list first before selecting any other external resource. It wasn't that choosing from the list was compulsory, but if any manager chose an alternative supplier, he or she had better have a good reason for it – a reason that they had to communicate to the purchasing department at that.

Presenting this process to the InterComm Art Directors had been an unforgettable experience, to say the least, for speakers and audience alike. InterComm's nervous laughter quickly evolved into polite incredulity. 'You cannot be serious' summed up their thoughts fairly succinctly! This was just not 'the InterComm way'. Their suppliers, photographers and copy writers were a network of friends, so close to the company that they were considered to be 'part of the family'. JPMT had doggedly tried to implement their process anyway. Before long, the sight of a normally mild-mannered InterComm Art Director issuing threats to a defiant purchasing assistant became a common one.

Returning to reflections on his walkabout, a second key discussion came to Ingo's mind, this one with Jaime Esposito, an Art Director from InterComm.

> Suddenly we seemed to be having endless meetings about accounts. The Europeans would arrive armed with thick folders and painstakingly detailed agendas. Right there at the outset, they'd be asking 'so who's going to be responsible for the minutes?' We didn't know whether to laugh or cry. We come to meetings with a completely different mindset. We like to let it roll, with everyone sparking off everyone else. Yet they wanted it all recorded in minute detail – afraid they'd miss the slightest nuance.
>
> For us, their approach just stifled the creative process. Whenever we got on a roll, the minute taker would call a time out to review some point that we'd long since left behind. And in most cases, the thing they were fussing about wasn't even relevant any more.
>
> Generally, they just seemed obsessed with a process for this and a system for that. It was as if they felt everything would fall apart if they didn't play it precisely by the 'rules'. We just wanted to get down to it – let those juices flow.

Ingo imagined how the transition period must have felt for his American colleagues. With their unfamiliar approach to almost everything, coupled with the fact that they had yet to win any kind of credibility in the eyes of their new brothers and sisters, JPMT people must truly have felt like interlopers to them. It wasn't surprising that the environment had quickly become one of stony silences, frosty glances and furtively raised eyebrows.

Ingo took encouragement from Holly's comments about having reached 'a way of working that suits everyone'. Armed with a desire to succeed and a strong common goal, the financial people had been able to work around their differences. There was no reason why they couldn't replicate this success in other parts of the business. But that meant getting people to assume value in their colleagues' ways of doing things, no matter how alien they may seem, and viewing them as opportunities to learn and grow.

The thoughts of his colleagues prompted Ingo to carry out a little self-reflection. Early in the integration of JPMT and InterComm, he and Jerry Meulen, InterComm's CEO, had been faced with one particularly significant problem to solve. My word, how differently they'd approached it! Ingo, a business school alumnus to the end, tended to put his trust in the empirical approaches he'd learned through his academic career. So, naturally, he had a beautiful lock-step approach to problem solving that he loved to bring into play at such moments.

Jerry looked at the world rather differently. He'd always found that the best way to arrive at a solution was to get others involved: it may have been less scientific, but putting a number of minds to work and seeing things from fresh angles had always resulted in something bigger and better than he'd ever felt he could achieve on his own. Besides, as the head of the business, he felt that it was critical to be seen as a team player.

The Effectiveness Challenge: How Will We Get Things Done Around Here?

Ask a few men at random how they go about tying a bow tie and you'll probably get several quite different responses. 'I like to do it the old-fashioned way and tie it by hand. It can be a bit complex, but if you do it step-by-step it always gets the best results'. Someone else might say, 'Tie it? I don't have time for that. I just use a clip-on tie. Gets the job done much more quickly', and a third person might say, 'It's far too difficult to do on your own! I get a friend to help me'.

Three different approaches to the same task. Who's right? Who's wrong? The answer, of course, is that nobody is. In each case, the end result is perfectly acceptable. However, if you pushed these people, they'd probably have all the 'right reasons' for telling you that their way of doing it is best and they wouldn't thank you for having to do it any other way.

There is a parallel here with the way that organisations do things. Each tends to have its own approach to 'getting things done' – to decision making, problem solving, conflict resolution, meeting organisation, conflict management, evaluation and delegation. The list goes on. Their particular method may not necessarily deliver results that are any better than any other organisation's approach, but their perception may well be that it does; and perception is reality.

So, when an organisation is suddenly faced with a new collaborator who has an approach different to its own ... well, you can see the potential for problems! But the alliance game is all about survival of the fittest. The companies that flourish are those that adjust quickly and effectively to their new reality. So when, as the Americans say, 'the rubber hits the road' and the new organisation's people get down to the business of working together to manage integration, they *have* to find an approach to 'getting things done' that works for everyone and that allows them to focus on staying competitive in the marketplace, rather than focusing on each other.

We call this issue of determining 'how things get done' in the new organisation the **Effectiveness** challenge.

> We underestimated the way people come to conclusions. The problems we face are the same. The hard thing is that people can come to the same conclusions through different logical structures. If you argue over these, you lose.
>
> *Fred Reid, President and COO, Delta Airlines*

Effectiveness Preferences

Just as they do around Legitimacy, organisations have different *preferences* when it comes to getting things done:

- a preference for referring to **systems and procedures**: the company's formalised practices
- a preference for 'getting on with it' and moving to **action** quickly
- a preference for working through **networks** of people whom they count on and trust.

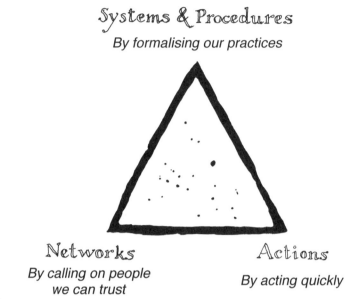

Figure 1

These preferences lie at the three angles of the Effectiveness triangle (Figure 1).

> We spent more time discussing **how** to do business together than in **doing** business together. In the end, it didn't work. Each partner was still working in its own way and for its own company and not in the spirit of a joint venture.
>
> *Marc Dandelot, President, France Telecom North America*

Systems and Procedures

Cultures with a preference for getting things done by referring to **systems and procedures** are *conceptual* in style. Whatever they do, they follow specifications. They believe that it's important to do it right, even if it takes a little longer or costs a little more. When it comes to bow ties, these are the people who 'like to do it the old-fashioned way and tie it by hand. It can be a bit complex, but if you do it step-by-step it always gets the best results'.

This type of culture will use systems and procedures to avoid errors and provide a process for accessing resources efficiently. Investments are made in total quality initiatives and the pursuit of industry-accepted quality standards. Job descriptions are clear and hiring and performance evaluation follow explicit formulae. There is a specific hierarchy for decision making. As we've seen it through Ingo Janssen's eyes, it would seem that systems and procedures are the preferred style of JPMT when it comes to getting things done.

A focus on systems and procedures is commonplace in companies that are particularly large or complex in terms of product ranges and geographical spread. Here, as remote, multifunctional project teams are put in place to deliver strategic results, process formalisation becomes a critical success factor. It ensures a common language that helps to speed up decision making and enables 'right first time' results.

We can also expect to see a strong preference for systems and procedures in industries whose products or processes represent a high level of risk to people or the environment. Chemical companies, pharmaceutical firms, nuclear power plants and aircraft manufacturers have no margin for error. Systems and procedures help them to ensure that knowledge and best practice is readily available, that errors are effectively debriefed and that learning points are logged.

Getting Things Done at Lafarge
At Lafarge we try to apply a 'project/action' perspective to integration. We use systems and procedures, as well as networks, as the means to integrate – but we make sure that the actual integration process is adapted to each unique case.

Through the project approach we involve people from both companies – the acquirer and the acquired – and set out the Integration Plan. This sets out the business objectives which we then communicate to our local partners.

'Becoming Lafarge' means setting ambitious objectives, making use of our proven systems & procedures and involving our people. We emphasise a 'common language'. That doesn't mean French or English, but having a common vocabulary about accounting methods, the organisation of an efficient plant and so on. For example, in the HR function we have standardised job descriptions which help promote exchange and internal mobility.

José-Maria Aulotte, Director of Integration, Lafarge Group

And ... Action!

When the preference is for **action**, the focus is on results rather than the means to achieve them. In this 'just do it!' culture, flexibility and agility are applauded. Red tape is derided and people feel stifled by weighty procedures and guidelines. When it comes to bow ties, these people don't have time to mess around with the lengthy process of tying them, they want the effect now! They're the ones who 'just use a clip-on tie'.

> When I have my European team here, we don't always need a meeting for every decision. Someone tells me in the hallway 'I have an idea'. Providing it is good, I say 'do it'.
>
> We get together informally – we have many informal meetings here – we kick around issues on our minds and make decisions fast and they are kicked into an action plan or a 'let's do it' approach.
>
> *Ken Bell, President, Invensys Appliance & Climate*
> *Control Systems Europe*

Action cultures are *pragmatic* in style. They use what they have at their disposal and try to get more, here and now. Up-front planning isn't a big part of their modus operandi and they may require some cajoling to fall into line with structured project management tools or other processes. But they're good at *self*-management and change and will get organised and deliver results rapidly. What motivates them and drives them to produce these results is the opportunity to sink their teeth into a problem, pulling together the most appropriate people to work on it, and getting down to it.

Another thing you'll see in action cultures is decisions being taken by the people closest to the action, the belief being that it's the best way to ensure that a problem is solved swiftly and efficiently. In line with this, people are encouraged to take initiative and risks at all levels of the organisation.

Action cultures are most easily sustainable in organisations that are relatively 'simple' in structure, scope and spread. As these organisations grow in complexity, for example through diversifying product ranges or widening geographical spread, the action culture may need to be complemented by a focus on systems and procedures.

Ours is a very down to earth team that is 150% committed to getting the job done. We often work on several projects at a time and that means keeping a lot of balls in the air. But we always get the job done. Team members know and accept that they will be expected to chip in and sort out a problem no matter how high up they are in the hierarchy.

Development director, software producer

Network

American managers are much more involved in and connected through social life. People use their relationships to influence decisions far more than we do here.

Hans Albrecht, Executive Vice-President, Hella

The **network** culture is *relational* in style. It uses its contacts and connections to get things done. People in these cultures tend not to act alone; they put their faith in individuals and teams who have the right knowledge, skills or experience to help them to do the job better, faster or cheaper. When it comes to bow ties, these people know that they'll end up with a better result if they 'get a friend to help them'.

Because of the energy that they spend building a web of resources, people in network cultures often know who to call to get the job done. We were given an excellent practical example of how this can work in a recent focus group:

We were facing a critical situation – the territory where the development project was to run included 200 different owners, each requiring separate negotiations. Given our tight time scale, this was a disaster waiting to happen. We spent the whole night pulling together a plan that would allow us to speed up the process by lobbying and putting pressure on the key people. In the morning, one of our partners told us 'Just a minute – I know who we should be talking to'. He went to his office and called someone. Two days later the problem was resolved. Where we would have spent weeks working through the system, he knew who to call to get the ball rolling.

So it is that problems are solved, by calling on experts, specialists or just those who are willing and able to help get the job done, from inside or outside the company.

We have found three loose groupings of organisations where the network culture flourishes:

- *family-owned companies*
- *start-ups* where there's a strong 'founding father' figure
- *Asian companies*, where the national culture has led to 'loyalty contracts': in return for loyalty to the company, the company supports and even defends the employee and his or her immediate family.

Different as they may be, there is plenty of overlap in the way that these three groups of companies operate. In each case, the corporate culture is tied to the relationship between individuals. The better you know someone and the more you share with that person, the greater the co-operation, service and support he or she is likely to give you.

In each case, there's an underlying feeling that the way to survive is to close ranks and pull together. Oddly enough, when they *do* close ranks, they can draw in people from outside the company, if those people are trusted friends and mentors who can be counted upon to 'deliver the goods' when necessary. In a start-up, closing ranks may mean calling on people for funding, knowledge, entrées to business opportunities, bank references, introductions to venture capital firms and a host of other things necessary for speeding up business development.

A family-owned company will close ranks because family shareholders want to protect their patrimony. They may trust family members more than anyone else, and so may structure the business in a way that obliges family members, and only family members, to work together. The family, or extended family, becomes the core network for decision making and access to resources. This scenario is particularly common in Asian companies, where family ties combine with values of cultural solidarity.

To outsiders, organisations with a network culture can seem like 'an enigma wrapped in a riddle', because it can be tough to figure out what's really going on. When it comes to management information, for example, the 'clan' at the head of the network may be very reticent to share information with the public at large or with newcomers. They've been used to making decisions and allocating resources and they'll continue to do so; so information is their business! The frustrations for newcomers can be immense. They can peruse the organisational chart all they like, but what they really need to understand is the network that may be well concealed behind it.

Perspectives on Effectiveness: What Happens When Preferences Meet?

> People in the company which acquired us have a very strong connection to their local communities. Because their company is owned by a community foundation, shareholder value so far was not that relevant for them. So sometimes I'm missing that driving force.
> *Dr Karl-Heinz Schmitz, Board Member, ZF Sachs AG*

In the last chapter we considered the potential fallout when very different preferences around Legitimacy find themselves working side by side. At this point, let's make a similar assessment for the Effectiveness challenge.

Because they relate to 'doing things', different preferences around Effectiveness are often easier to spot, in terms of both timing and scale, than the rather more subtle differences that arise around Legitimacy. Many of the leaders we interviewed as we wrote this book had stories to tell us about 'visible' differences in this area. Here's what some of them had to say:

> Their focus is partly different. Whilst efficiency and speed seem to be important for us, they are driven by other values like social responsibility and continuity of development. This causes some uncertainties in both parties.
> *Dr Karl-Heinz Schmitz, Board Member, ZF Sachs AG*

> Distillers was in a time warp in the 19th century. Business was done in a gentlemanly fashion. Some of them had no notion of creating value for shareholders. We on the other hand had high expectations for performance and were really driven into reducing cost and so on.
> *Senior manager, strategy consulting firm*

> The closer the culture is to the customers the faster it goes. State-owned companies have a different sense of urgency, for example, they allow more time for meetings. Differences in decision-making styles, which create frustration in multicultural meetings.
> *Håkan Hallen, Executive Vice-President Human Resources,*
> *Volvo Global Trucks*

The differences aren't *always* obvious. It's a positive thing when they are: painful though they may be, at least they're out on the table and can be addressed. Far more dangerous are the less obvious misunderstandings that occur. These often go undetected until well into the attempted integration, when what can feel like irreversible damage has been done to the relationship. Under these conditions it's easy for mistrust and suspicion to settle in and block the emergence of a new and efficient corporate culture.

But let's look at specifics. What can you expect to see when different preferences for Effectiveness meet? Let's select just one or two of the possible permutations and look at them more closely.

Systems and Procedures versus Network

Imagine company A, where a strong, relational, network culture is mixed with an action-orientated pragmatic way of doing business. Sales people are used to providing tailored solutions to their customers, each handled by an account manager who works closely with product development and implementation specialists to deliver precisely what the customer needs. The team can react rapidly to client requests, exercising its own judgement when it comes to pricing projects and producing comprehensive proposals to win business.

Then company A is acquired by company B, a large industrial conglomerate with a multilayered hierarchy and a focus on financial and resource management for decision making. Clashes begin when the sales team members in company A try to work as they always have, quickly and independently, and find themselves blocked by the new system. With the new rules of the game lacking in appeal both internally and externally, the fallout begins. Customers grow impatient and begin to doubt the account managers' earlier assurances that, in spite of the take-over, it would be business as usual. The account teams lose motivation and enthusiasm as they wait for decisions on pricing and custom product to make their way through the system.

They weren't used to operating in an environment that encouraged independent thinking and problem solving. Employees came from a parochial style of management where roles and responsibilities were clearly defined and boundaries were not to be crossed. Employees were not motivated and looked to others to make decisions.

(continued)

> Our values are based on building and enhancing organisation suc-
> cess through our employees. Their value system did not encourage
> independent thinking and did not provide employees with a sense of
> the bigger picture.
>
> *Edward Shipka, CEO, Pe Ben Oilfield Services Ltd (Canada)*
> *on the different approach of an acquired company*

It's true that the 'natural' opportunities for these two types of culture
to connect are few and far between. The things that make network cultures tick are often invisible to the naked eye: personal knowledge, relationships and insights. With a systems and procedures culture, things
are much more visible: policy documents, procedures manuals and so
on are testament to what they stand for.

The inability to understand or decipher 'what the problem is' with
the other party leads to mutual irritation and alienation. When a systems and procedures culture meets a pragmatic culture, the two sides
have their work cut out. In our example, they would *have* to surface and
discuss the issues around responding to customers and preserving
important relationships. Only then will they be able to make adjustments
to the way they do things that will be acceptable to both of them and
that, more importantly, will keep the customer satisfied.

It's frequently the case that a network preference develops within a
systems and procedures culture where the latter has become bureau-
cratic and ineffective. In this type of environment, activating your personal network, by calling on who you know to get things done, can often
be the only way to make things happen. Where might you see this? Take
a look at administrations and state-owned monopolies – it's their
traditional cultural profile.

Systems and Procedures versus Action

As an illustration of what can happen when a systems and procedures
culture meets an action culture, let's look at two airline companies
involved in an alliance.

One of the partners focuses on quality through systems and procedures: their modus operandi is to take as much time as is needed to
'think things through and get it right'. The team faithfully checks and
double-checks all of the details, aiming for a zero defect solution. Doing
anything less would be considered unprofessional.

The second partner has an action culture: they want to move quickly and they'll take risks to do so. Their irritation and frustration at the seemingly endless discussions that surround every little decision is palpable. They can be heard to say: 'Let's just get on with it! You can never plan for every possible eventuality. You have to be willing to take risks and fix glitches as you go along. That's what continuous improvement is all about'.

You could be forgiven for thinking that these two will *never* make good playmates. Yet, there are mutual advantages to this kind of cultural mix, provided the parties are willing to learn from each other. The energy of an action culture can shake up the bureaucracy that's so often characteristic of a systems and procedures culture, injecting new life into the old dog as it does so. Action cultures, can often draw on the experience of a systems and procedures-orientated culture to bring rigour and discipline to their creativity and 'go get 'em' attitude, particularly in situations where they suddenly find themselves part of a much larger organisation where it's harder to achieve quick results.

However, they'll have to manage the mutual frustration caused by the differences in operational tempo to get to these synergies. One route to this is the joint development of an integration plan that clearly and publicly establishes ambitious milestones, thus reassuring the action side and stimulating the systems and procedures side.

Effectiveness and Mixed Task Forces

The merging of two companies into one poses an enormous 'problem-solving' challenge. A large number of core systems, processes, policies, organisational rules and guidelines have to be reviewed within the new context of the merger. Each must be evaluated, one against the other, in light of the relative contribution they might make to the new organisation's effectiveness in the marketplace. The resultant redesign may be minimal or it may involve a complete over-haul. Whatever the level, the changes need to be communicated, understood, accepted, implemented, evaluated and – take a deep breath – continuously improved – phew! Quite a task – one usually implemented through mixed task forces that bring together managers from both sides to work out solutions.

Now let's not be naïve – the mindsets and agendas of task force participants are going to be very different – even contradictory. Those

(continued)

who lean towards **systems and procedures** will come along to 'analyse the situation' and report back through their hierarchy. Those with a preference for **action** may come with the objective of finding solutions that can be implemented straight away. And those who favour **networks** might sit at the table, planning to use the task force as an opportunity to promote their own people and get them into critical jobs in the new organisation.

Suddenly, the task force – supposedly a solution provider – turns into a counterproductive exercise in wheel-spinning, leaving everyone frustrated and disappointed. In Chapter 8, we'll look more closely at how you can manage task forces so that they don't succumb to these cultural pitfalls.

To conclude this section on what happens when different preferences come together to get a job done, let's go back to the words of some of the many people we've worked with and talked to who have been in the thick of integration-related change. They've told us many stories and anecdotes that illustrate the particular challenges of trying to 'get things done' with people who sometimes seem to have come from another business planet!

One international project manager talked about trying to get a mixed project team off the ground and working effectively:

> In our division, we get along very well. When we work on a project, even though we'll put all our energy into the job, the atmosphere is very relaxed. We're all on a first name basis, our doors are always open for an informal chat and we frequently bounce ideas off one another. They're just the opposite. Everything seems very formal and controlled. There's a strict process to follow and a hierarchy to respect. People feel that you're attacking them if you step into what they consider to be their territory. And every decision has to be approved by the boss. I find it hard to be effective in that type of atmosphere – I can't work like that.

Another manager reported big differences in approaches to performance evaluation:

> In our company, performance evaluations are guided by a specific, detailed structure and process – the same one for everyone. I don't really understand how their people are evaluated. Their approach

is vague at best – lots of open questions and content that varies from one branch to the next – how can they ever work out who's doing what ... ?

A third talked about differences in documentation processes:

> Their emphasis was on the importance of process. Everything centred on accepted standards, written procedures and non-negotiables. We were expected to follow the same formal process for every situation and every client. We found that very irritating and frustrating – to open a door, all you need to do is turn the handle and push – you don't need to dissect the whole process and then document it to get people to do it.

Yet another found it difficult to get decisions made in the face of differences:

> When the project teams had a meeting, it was difficult because in our organisation, when someone tells you something, he or she will commit for the company. This wasn't the case with them. You needed to have the boss in front of you. It was a big source of misunderstanding. In a meeting, we would come to an agreement and then afterwards, we'd hear from one of their senior managers, 'oh no, I don't agree to that'.
>
> When we started talking about empowerment in the company we had just acquired, it seemed as though we were speaking in a foreign language. People always agreed but then nothing ever happened. They always went back to the boss to solve the problem. There was never any attempt to take a risk or show some initiative.

Effectiveness and National Cultural Differences

Although we are all Nordic, significant differences exist between us. Both the Danish and the Swedish decision cultures are very consensus-driven. You are expected to involve all stakeholders who will be affected by a decision in how that decision will be implemented so they can feel part of the decision process. Swedes continue to discuss the matter until they have found a solution that everybody feels good about and can support while Danes might reach a decision

(continued)

faster and respect that a decision has been taken and then implement it, which may sometimes lead to changes later in the process.

Torben Laustsen, Corporate Head of Group Identity and
Communications, Nordea

I experienced the difference between the Finnish and the Danish way of making decisions in my own organisation when I found out that my Finnish middle managers were already implementing a decision we had **talked** about, but in my mind not yet taken. 'But you said that you preferred this decision and you are the boss', said my Finnish counterpart. 'Yes, but it is your responsibility to provide me with the necessary information regarding local conditions so we can avoid making the wrong decision. I don't intend to overrule your professional expertise', I answered him.

Torben Laustsen, Corporate Head of Group Identity and
Communications, Nordea

Our first task was to integrate the Belgians into the team. They are very different from us. For example, family life and being involved in the community are very important to them. We had to consciously discipline ourselves and recognise that our way of working before – when we were all in the same location – was no longer possible. Meetings had to alternate between Brussels and Paris. We had to be more organised, explain our ways of working, have an agenda and stick to it.

Christine Gastinel, Head of Cultures, Languages and
Social Evolution Department, TotalFinaElf

The Value of Understanding

Each of these examples highlights the significance of developing a shared understanding of issues that can influence the way that things will be done in a new organisation. The Effectiveness challenge touches so many aspects of a business that it simply must bring to the surface those issues that will affect its ability to be efficient, and therefore competitive, in the marketplace.

JPMT failed to do so and now find themselves with a lot of back-tracking to do. With an earlier understanding of the differences between JPMT and InterComm, Ingo's team would have been able to spend their time finding common ground for agreement on working principles. They would have been better placed to set collective objectives and define action plans that people from both cultures could buy-in to and be committed to carrying out.

To this end, a cultural diagnostic would have made it possible for them to develop this understanding, to anticipate and avoid the pitfalls, and to move themselves sharply up the learning curve.

By way of example, this is what happened to a Japanese/European acquisition in the automobile manufacturing industry. As one executive put it very neatly:

> We didn't get there (to partnership) through a deliberate strategy. We got there because we now better understood their way of working. We had learned, for example, that the role of engineer could be very fulfilling. Whereas we had been taking our best engineers and making them into managers, we learned to take pride in experience and put in place a reward system to recognise specialist engineers.
>
> Why the almost overnight change in our working relationship with the Japanese? 'Because', they said, 'we saw you were willing to be a learning organisation. Before, you were not willing and so we saw no reason to help'.
>
> If we had understood the nature of their expectations – for us to demonstrate that we were a learning organisation – we could have saved ourselves seven years of wasted effort.
>
> Seven years characterised by arguments and disagreements, difficulties, debates and suspicion. With better cultural understanding, the way they spoke and nit-picked would not have been a source of irritation. We would have understood that it was just their way. We eventually learned to let them be who they are and not try to fight/change that.

Some Food for Thought ...

- *Effectiveness* – 'getting things done' efficiently – means different things to different cultures. Some cultures relate Effectiveness to *systems and procedures* – sticking to formalised practices. Others relate it to *action* – getting on with things quickly. Still others relate it to *networks* – calling on people whom they can count on and trust to help them get things done.
- As cultural integration gets underway following a merger or an acquisition, the Integration Team's number one priority is to develop

a common process for decision making, and agree it with as many different teams as possible throughout the organisation.

- Empowerment is a highly cultural thing. A manager at the same level may be able to commit for the company in one organisation, but may require more senior approval in another. If new partners understand this difference, they can agree on a decision-making process that meets both their needs. If they don't understand this, people are likely to lose confidence in one another. One side will feel that decisions are slowed down or rejected, and the other will feel unduly pressured.
- When an acquired company has a strong *network* culture, the acquirer must distinguish between effective and dysfunctional networks – a difference that may not immediately be clear. The acquirer should avoid a 'knee-jerk' network-breaking reaction and take care not to destroy or weaken those networks that add value.
- Companies need to increase their emphasis on systems and procedures as they grow or become more complex. It is important for leaders to be able to communicate this need in a convincing way during periods of cultural integration.
- Demonstrating *why* a new way of doing things is good for the group is a strong lever for getting people to *accept* that new way of doing things.

CHAPTER 6

Future

When you go into an alliance, acquisition, etc., you have to be very clear about the whole picture and the vision of where you are going. What made our partnership wrong from the beginning; the vision wasn't clear and there were three different interpretations of it.

Marc Dandelot, President, France Telecom North America

A handy, wallet-sized card. They'd viewed it as a simple, practical way of outlining JPMT InterComm's new vision and values to their people.

Ingo winced as he reflected on the fact that a small plastic card had become central to the merged organisation's internal communication strategy. And how, more tellingly, it had become a poisoned chalice, a symbol of the leadership team's abject failure to help people to understand and feel secure about the future direction of the business. To cap it all, he had to acknowledge that he and his fellow JPMT executives were the guilty party in this particular fiasco.

The more he investigated 'what had gone wrong' with the merger, the more Ingo became aware of the many instances where JPMT, as the larger party, had steamrollered InterComm, circumventing their heritage and imposing – albeit with impeccable manners! – their own way of doing things. With a string of apparently successful acquisitions behind them, JPMT felt that they knew best. As a result, they listened far less closely than they should have to any wisdom offered by InterComm, digging themselves into a hole in the process.

This was particularly true when it came to the issue of communicating and getting buy-in to the future. With hindsight, it was clear to Ingo that InterComm knew exactly what was needed to ensure that their own people felt reassured about where things were heading and the role that each of them would play in the new world order. They wanted to ensure that, in addition to clear overall strategic objectives, each and every individual had their own measurable objectives to perform to. If they could simultaneously build on the 'family' values that had seen them through good and bad times, they felt that they had a strong recipe for future success.

If JPMT had just been able to listen and understand, they could have accommodated InterComm's approach to good effect, even if it seemed a little alien to them. But history told them that, in a merger situation, people needed a well thought through organisational structure, supported by precise job descriptions to drive the business forward. InterComm's protestations fell on deaf ears.

As was so often the case in those early weeks, JPMT's opinion won the day. In what they intended as a gesture towards InterComm's approach, the Integration Team set about crafting the visions and values that eventually appeared on the famous plastic card. However, more than a little deflated by the heavy-handed approach of their new 'partners', Inter-Comm's representatives lost the will to fight for their heritage to be reflected in the values. The result was a set of statements destined to haunt the leadership time and time again in the months that followed.

Anna Black was one of the InterComm managers who'd been involved in the Integration Team's discussions about defining and communicating the future. Ingo asked her how she'd felt at the time:

> I felt really strongly that the JPMT people didn't understand what it would take to keep everyone on board. People here are used to trans-parent information and clear direction. We see ourselves as a fam-ily and we keep everyone in the picture. It doesn't matter whether you're the CEO or the night cleaner.
>
> Things were obviously very different at JPMT. Their management kept things close to their chests, and they seemed determined to adopt the same style for the new organisation. We gave it all we'd got, but we just couldn't convince them otherwise. What little we ended up doing really didn't help anyone picture the future. You don't calm the nerves of an apprehensive workforce with values cards and a pep talk from the CEO.

If members of the Integration Team felt this strongly, how deep was the feeling on the ground? Ingo began to ask people around the busi-ness how they'd felt about the future in those early days. In response, he'd been on the receiving end of a lot of straight-talking, none more direct than that of Jim Morrison, a long-serving member of the InterComm Art Department:

> I've always known where I stood in this company. I knew what was expected of me and I had a pretty good idea what was around the corner. The merger was a surprise, but I wasn't too worried because I knew that we'd be told clearly what it all meant and what was expected of us.
>
> I couldn't believe it when the weeks went by and we didn't hear a thing. People from Europe started arriving to take up new jobs and

we'd only hear about it a few days in advance through blanket e-mails. Naturally we started to get edgy. Who were these people? Why were they coming to New York? What was going to happen to the old InterComm family? I can tell you, it had a pretty strong effect on morale.

If the comments of senior and middle managers, like Jim, gave cause for concern, the feeling away from these levels was even more worrying. For example, Jenny Powell, a junior in the InterComm Accounts Department:

We hear the news of the merger and then there's deafening silence. Followed by more silence. We were desperate to know what this meant for our jobs. Would we even **have** a job in a years time?

We were kept totally in the dark. Except for those ridiculous values cards that came through internal mail. Everyone was up in arms. I mean, I'm sorry, but that's not communicating!! It's a joke.

Ah! Those values cards! Dispatched in such a positive spirit yet received with such hostility. Ingo turned a copy over in his fingers and perused the words again. He was struck by how bland they now seemed. He could also see how they might cause such cynicism in people who were used to so much more direction.

As he read the values out loud to himself, one set of words in particular stuck in his throat:

We undertake to keep our people informed of anything that will affect their willingness or ability to perform their role within the JPMT family.

Oh boy. JPMT's understanding of what affected people's willingness or ability to perform their role had clearly missed the mark where InterComm employees were concerned. Ingo recalled something else that Jim Morrison told him:

In the workforce's eyes, management simply didn't walk the talk. We left people living with uncertainty – how could we expect them to crew the ship well?

Ingo's mind turned from plastic cards to the second prong of what he'd laughingly thought of as a 'communication strategy': his flying visit to New York to address the troops. He'd intended his presentation to excite his audience as much as he himself felt excited about what lay ahead. The reaction? Ingo bravely listened in on an internal focus group:

Well, at least he took the time to pay us a visit. But I just found it scarily slick. The big suit dropping in, sweet-talking us and then flying out to do who knows what. Replace us all with Europeans maybe? Mr Janssen may ooze degrees and experience but, to me, he also oozed insincerity. It takes a little more than a well-scripted speech to make me feel confident about the future.

Food for thought indeed.

So what did all this tell him? Understanding, as he now did, the consistency, clarity and transparency with which InterComm communicated the whats and whys of change to its people, Ingo realised that JPMT really weren't big communicators at all. Their primary response to anticipated future challenges was to keep the organisational structure fluid, tweaking it whenever a new challenge presented itself. As long as everyone understood that structure, as well as the specifics of their job within it, they felt that people would be on board and that future sustainability would be assured.

The approach worked for former JPMT personnel in the new set-up, as they were used to it. They'd even helped to create it. But for the InterComm people, who made up the bulk of the US workforce, the approach was an anathema. Ingo began to understand the discomfort that InterComm people felt, faced with what must have seemed like a dictatorial, business-focused approach that took little account of their individual needs and left them without clear personal objectives.

JPMT's past acquisitions had involved smaller businesses. The problems created by their unwitting bully-boy style could easily be absorbed by the mighty resources at their disposal. The merger with InterComm was a completely different ball game. Played out on a much bigger stage, for much higher stakes, the cracks were less easily concealed.

Ingo pressed a button on the intercom on his desk. It was time to go back to the future.

The Future Challenge: How Will We Communicate and Get Buy-in to the New Vision?

The chances are that, like most of us, you give a lot of thought to your future. When you do, what do you find yourself thinking about? Do you focus on all the things that you need to do to make sure that you're organised when the day comes: your pension plans, legal arrangements, etc.? Or do you set yourself personal or business targets to achieve: to see the ancient Inca settlements of Peru or to reach the board before you turn 50? Or are you someone who believes that the future will look after itself, if you just keep doing things the way you always have and draw on the network of family and friends you've built up over the years?

Although you probably engage in a little of all of them from time to time, the chances are that one of these three approaches fills you with the greatest sense of security about the future and provides part of your motivation to go forward into it.

Things are remarkably similar when it comes to corporate deals, whatever their nature. Their success is fuelled in large part by the enthusiasm and commitment of the people involved, and much of that enthusiasm and commitment will relate to the way those people view the future.

But in the early stages of coming together, the future often looks a little hazy, to say the least. As soon as announcements are made about the new partnership, anxiety levels begin to rise as people grapple with the uncertainty of their individual and collective future. The leadership team may have a vision, but the workforce has questions and concerns. Going back to our friend Abraham Maslow, these questions and concerns usually cut to their own need for survival:

- How does this affect me?
- What will it mean for my future?
- Will I have a job?
- Can I be successful in this environment?
- Can I operate in the way that will be expected of me?

Often, as was the case at InterComm, these questions are accompanied by the expectation that everything will be made clear: that the leadership team, who must surely have taken this decision with wisdom and foresight, will clarify precisely how the business will operate and how they, the people, will be affected.

In reality, this clarification often does not come. With the technical aspects of the deal still sapping all their time and energy, leaders fail to communicate key information to their anxious employees. What little information is communicated often raises more questions than it provides answers. The rumour mill steps in to fill the communication void, people begin to paint their personal nightmare scenarios and motivation plummets.

> People get very concerned and worked up about whether they'll have a job and what that job will be. The sooner people know, the less turmoil you have.
> *Lord Colin Marshall of Knightsbridge, Chairman, British Airways*

The long and the short of it is that people *have* to find answers to their questions and resolve their personal concerns before they'll ever be able to buy into the new vision and make the journey to the future. For the leadership team, this means anticipating those questions and communicating responses in a way that reduces anxiety and allows people to focus on performance and on moving the organisation forwards.

This means that it's not enough just to communicate. Confidence, commitment and buy-in are secured by different things in different cultures, so leaders must also determine *what* they need to communicate and *how*.

It's this issue of communicating their common vision in a way that gains commitment and buy-in that we call the **Future** challenge.

Future Preferences

Just as we've seen with the Legitimacy and Effectiveness challenges, different cultures have different *preferences* when it comes to gaining their people's commitment and buy-in to the future.

- Some prefer to focus on **organisational structure**: they believe that if the organisation is engineered in the right way and if everyone understands their role within it, it will be well placed to respond to the market forces that it will be subject to.
- Some prefer to focus on the communication of **strategic objectives**: it's their conviction that people feel most secure when they have a clear understanding of where the organisation is going – its strategy and goals – and of what's expected of them specifically.
- Some prefer to emphasise and build on the organisation's **heritage**: it's their belief that people's buy-in comes from an ability both to identify with strong corporate values and traditions and to project them into the future.

There's an interesting angle around the Future challenge that relates to time. The power of a culture that focuses on organisational structure is the power of reassurance, *here and now*. The power of heritage culture is the strength of a successful *past*. The power of a culture that focuses on strategic objectives is their call to arms for the *future*.

These preferences lie at the three angles of the Future triangle (Figure 1).

Organisational Structure
By getting the organisation right

Heritage
By keeping our core values
and corporate identity alive

Strategic Objectives
By clearly communicating
where we want to go

Figure 1

Organisational Structure

> Organisational structure determines behaviour. Setting up a pan-European organisation has allowed us to get things done more quickly – turf protection is gone. Key people are thinking European. Certain people who don't want to be managed like that have gone but most have stayed. For example, implementing a pan European accounting system has led to job scope development for some.
>
> *Ken Bell, President, Invensys Appliance & Climate Control Systems*

Cultures with a preference for getting buy-in to the future by empha-sising **organisational structure** are *conceptual* in style. The prevailing opinion here is that the business and the people who are part of it will be best positioned to manage the challenges that lie ahead if the organ-isation is engineered specifically to meet those challenges. If you're the type of person who focuses on pensions and legal arrangements when you think about the future, you'll probably feel quite at home in an organisational structure culture.

The belief is that if infrastructure and systems and procedures are clear, if people know precisely where and how to obtain resources, if there is a defined method to handle customer service and a clear troubleshooting process, etc., then people will feel confident about the future and their place in it.

Cultures with this preference put significant effort into keeping organisational charts up to date. They also make a point of publicising them, and take pains to point out both *who* people are and *where* they are. There is a clear job description for every job, in part to motivate people by demonstrating the clear career development opportunities and possibilities that exist.

Applying a Preference for Organisational Structure

Organisational structure was the strong preference of one of the units of a high-technology industrial firm, which moved from a geographical to a business unit based structure in the late 1990s. The company's sector management team placed great strategic emphasis on the change in structure, linking individual career plans to the successful implementation of the matrix. Although there were strong performance goals, the primary emphasis was on making the new structure successful.

To maintain continuity and build business performance, the company took a step-by-step approach to the changeover. Power and decision making were migrated from the geographical to the business unit structure gradually, by implementing a transition period during which managers were asked to fulfil the roles of both Country Manager and Business Unit VP.

Time and energy went into ensuring that the structure delivered on its promise. Task Forces were put together to look at systems, mobility, global account management and new roles for country-based people, the goal being to ensure that these would support the new vertical structure.

Senior managers even asked their clients to insist on the importance of the company 'thinking global and acting local'. They then used these expressions of customer need to help to get their people on board with the change.

To support the process of change itself, change management initiatives were implemented to ensure that people understood the new organisation and their role in it. Internal surveys were then used to measure how successful these initiatives had actually been.

(continued)

In this situation, the preference for *organisational structure* was a dynamic contributor to change. The *primary* strategic driver for the future success of the business was to get the global matrix up and running successfully.

For some companies, a fixed approach to organisational structure is a long-term asset for ensuring sustainability. McDonald's and Starbucks are prime examples of companies that, wherever they go, implement a similar organisational structure, a tried and tested 'winning formula', and count on that structure to drive success.

How else might you spot a company that has a preference for organisational structure when it comes to the Future challenge? You're probably familiar with the company that seems to be perpetually announcing reorganisations, the company that changes its structure in the same way that we might change our socks. This is the company with a preference for organisational structure, continually reinventing itself to respond better to market forces.

Although all companies have traditions that they want to maintain and results they need to achieve, the company that has a cultural preference for organisational structure will insist that its *competitive advantage* lies first and foremost in its organisational structure, whatever it may be. They'll say, 'Look at our clients, look at our competitors. And now look at us. We're structured in the best possible way to meet our clients' needs and to compete effectively with our competitors'.

As an illustration of this cultural preference, consider the example of the European CEO of a large express mail conglomerate, communicating the company's strategy for becoming a truly 'European' company, able to compete with the global giant of the sector. As he addresses the top 150 executives in the company, the first slide he shows is entitled 'Our Vision of the Future'. What does it include? A complex organisational chart, with lots of boxes, lines, functions, names, countries and TBAs. No goals, no strategy, not measurable; but a very well thought through structure, designed specifically to meet the market and client challenges.

When leaders are building the communications piece of their integration strategy, they'll need to emphasise the way that the new organisation will be put together if they're going to win the minds of this culture.

Strategic Objectives

My experience is that, on day one, you should start making clear to your new colleagues what, for you, constitutes 'success' and how it's going to be measured. Is it growth, profit, innovation, etc. ... ? This conversation, held early in the process, will avoid many future misunderstandings.

CEO, global telecommunications organisation

The culture that stresses **strategic objectives** as the key to future sustainability is *pragmatic* in style. People in this type of culture know where the company is going and what they'll be expected to do to help it get there. They often think, 'I don't know exactly what structure or processes we might have in place to rely on, but I **do** know where we're going. Our management has clearly outlined their vision and described it well enough for me to understand how I can contribute. With my manager, I've also been able to translate the company's objectives into my own personal objectives. I know where I'm heading'. If you're the type of person who has goals and milestones set for their business and private lives, you'll probably feel quite at home in a strategic objective focused culture.

The conviction here is that objectives are the trigger for motivation and therefore performance. The objectives in question are usually ambitious and always measurable. In general, they are expressed in terms of numbers such as market share percentage or ROCE. Some companies, such as 3M, express them in terms of the number of innovative products that they have brought to market. For a small, but growing number of companies, such as Air Products or Monsanto, strategic objectives can also be qualitative, with goals set around issues such as diversity. Whether quantitative or qualitative, progress and accomplishment must be visible to all.

When leaders are building the communications piece of their integration strategy, they'll need to emphasise where the organisation is going and what will be expected of people if they're going to get this culture to apply its muscle.

Perspectives on Strategic Objectives

Although they may both see strategic objectives as the driver of future success, different groups don't necessarily share the same

(continued)

understanding of what's actually meant by the term! One American manager told us the following story:

> When I first arrived in Italy, I was appointed CEO of our recently acquired local unit. I had a good management team – local people with good international experience and professional expertise. At the end of the first year we met to analyse our results, which, by the way, were significantly lower than expected.
>
> To me, it made no sense to enter into any bonus discussions since we weren't even on plan. Imagine my surprise when the team made it clear to me that, since they had all worked hard, we should still consider applying the bonus policy. In other words, we should reward not on the basis of results – which were poor because of the economic climate – but on the basis of effort and commitment.
>
> I was flabbergasted! Why did they believe that they had been set objectives if they were just going to be set aside at the end of the game? Their response was that the objectives were useful as guidelines for action but were not, for them, an indication of anticipated results – since 'no-one but God is in a position to control the future'.
>
> It was clear to me that for this team, setting objectives had a very different meaning than it had for me, with my North American background. Our sources of pride and motivation were poles apart. I realised that 'Management by Objectives' is a very North American result-oriented management philosophy that cannot necessarily be easily or automatically applied elsewhere. Indeed, in some cultures, it would be considered unacceptable arrogance to believe that any individual is responsible for his or her own destiny, or that he or she will 'make it' by acting according to set objectives, dreams or desires.

Heritage

Ask me how our organisation can survive 25 years from now and I'll tell you how we've handled the last 25 years. What else do you need to know?

Board member, beverage company

The **heritage** culture is *relational* in style. It builds confidence and buy-in to the future by emphasising the organisation's core values and common history. There is a focus on traditions, shared experience and the value of people when projecting future sustainability. In effect, a heritage culture uses the successes of the past as a basis for assuring its future potential. If you're the type of person who thinks the future will take care of itself if you stick to your principles and do things the way you always have, you'll probably feel quite at home in a heritage culture.

Cultures that favour heritage can be found both in industries that have been around for centuries and in businesses that have worked long and hard to create lasting brands, for example vintners or luxury goods manufacturers such as LVMH. You'll also find them in businesses that place an emphasis on tradition and craftsmanship, such as Rolls Royce. In each of these categories, companies will feel that their survival has been, and will continue to be linked to the 'authenticity' of their product and a genuine respect for values and ways of doing things that have been handed down from past to present.

> Our treasure, our capacity to create value and our future lie in our 'Esprit Maison'. At their very heart lies a unique savoir-faire, which is expressed in the brand and understood by our consumers. This is our heritage. A unique savoir-faire that has been transmitted from person to person and that allows the company to achieve the highest level of quality in a sustainable way. Think that, for example, in a high range Cognac today, we use spirits issued from grapes which were cropped two centuries ago.
>
> *Christophe Navarre, CEO, Moët-Hennessy*

People within a heritage culture also place tremendous importance on values, convinced as they are that their success has been built upon them. Managers in Heineken, a family-owned success story, for example, are immensely proud of Heineken corporate values. They consider these values to be the primary driver of their success and use them to make consistent, appropriate strategic choices in all aspects of their business, everywhere. This, also makes them very proud of their past. The Heineken museum in Amsterdam is one magnificent example of this.

> Where you can have many cultural differences is when you take over a family-run business.
>
> *Senior manager, strategy consulting firm*

A preference for heritage carries similar hallmarks to the other relational preferences: those for looking to the **in-group** when it comes to Legitimacy and for calling on **networks** when it comes to Efficiency. This means that you'll often find a preference for heritage in young, start-up businesses or organisations where there's a strong family presence. The sense of 'family' that these types of organisation share contributes to the feeling that people are doing more than just a job. Although strategic objectives and organisational structure are still important, they must maintain a clear connection with the organisation's values.

These organisations are often built around a charismatic leader, a strong founder or a patriarch. While that person remains in the business, he or she is often seen as a role model who embodies the strengths of corporate success. Employees tend to respect this person and derive a sense of security from him or her. When the person dies or leaves the company, they are often replaced by someone in their image – an heir – who maintains the values, code of conduct, principles and attitudes embodied by the founder. Beware the dark side though! Charismatic leaders can turn into authoritarian despots when threatened. Check the history books.

When leaders are building the communications piece of their integration strategy, they'll need to emphasise how values and history will be harnessed to shape the future if they're going to win the hearts of this culture.

> All the people in Jaguar, from the guy sweeping the floor to the engineers share a passion for the product. Love for the look and performance of the car. It's transcending. Everyone know what a Jaguar is and what makes a Jaguar. It's a visceral thing.
>
> *Nick Scheele, President and COO, Ford*

Heritage versus Objectives and Financial Results
Incredible as it may sound, despite globalisation, *heritage* can still be a more important driver for some companies than *strategic objectives* and *financial results*.

As one Swedish Managing Director in a service industry told us:

> Corporate identity and core values are very important for the Swedish company: Since people spend a lot of time at work, they
> *(continued)*

need to be proud of being part of one company and, more precisely, of one team. The company communicates openly and transversally on its heritage and what it has achieved to nourish the sense of contributing to more than 'just a job'. Financial objectives cannot be the only way to project the team and the company in the future.

Accor: The Challenge of Going Global for Heritage Cultures
The challenge for heritage cultures when going global is to maintain their prized, but often local, value system, while at the same time organising the global optimisation of their resources.

The Accor hotel group is known as an example of a heritage culture with strong links to its founders and to the way its very first hotel was managed: by a manager and a small, yet cohesive team devoted to customer service.

It was this 'paradigm' which spread all over the world and led to the creation of one of the leaders of the industry. So, when the group faced the need to optimise shared resources such as purchasing, reservations systems and common regional maintenance teams, top management met with significant resistance as the 'unit' structure, the cohesiveness of the small teams – the whole sense of **heritage** – was called into question.

Perspectives on the Future: What Happens When Preferences Meet?

Why was it so easy to merge the two companies? In both co-operatives, the decision makers and owners were trained in strategic thinking. They were used to dealing with future perspectives and visions about how to strengthen their company's position as an important player in the European food business.

Jens Bigum, CEO, Arla Foods

Organisational Structure versus Heritage

An Italian manager – let's call him Marco Conti – had worked his way through a prestigious European hotel school and graduated with honours. He was snapped up by one of Europe's leading five-star chains and placed in their six-year management development programme. The programme ultimately promised a senior management position but, to get there, Marco had to work his way through each of the chain's hotels, in a variety of capacities, to understand fully the company's operational style and the distinct nature of the client offering.

He spent time in Rooms Division, Housekeeping, Sales, Food and Beverage, Engineering and Conferencing. This is where we find him, five years on, as the group is acquired by another European hotel chain looking to expand across the continent.

The style of the acquiring company is quite different from the one that Marco has been used to. Whereas his company's managers are very much 'old school', traditional hoteliers, steeped in tradition and hierarchy, the management team from the new group is made up of young, go-getting creative talent. They quickly restructure the senior positions in all of the newly acquired hotels, often replacing old managers with new ones from their own ranks.

Marco and his colleagues in the management development programme learn, via e-mail, that the programme is to be discontinued and that the positions they currently hold will become permanent. Marco is aghast. While his friend Anthony, who at that point in his tour of duty is working as the assistant to the General Manager, is left with a position he could have expected had he completed the full programme, Marco, after five years of hotel school and five years of 'doing the rounds', is frozen in the role of a conference service salesperson.

> I was totally demoralised. After investing all my energy into a future with the company, these people walked in and wiped out any chance I had of promotion. With the organisational structure they put in place, it became immediately clear to me that I would have to wait years to get anywhere decent. It was also obvious that they had no intention of continuing with the traditions that made our group both distinct and distinguished. I, and others, soon started to look elsewhere. I eventually moved abroad to work for a North American start-up.

This example illustrates what can happen when different preferences around Future meet. It shows that the **conceptual** focus of getting buy-in to the future through **organisational structure** can easily be at odds with a **relational** focus on **heritage**.

Heritage versus Strategic Objectives

In another example, the scene is the management convention of a powerful, American multinational with a cultural preference for *strategic objectives*. This is the first convention since they acquired a small, traditional, French state-owned niche market company, strongly bound to its *heritage* culture. All of the newly acquired company's managers, many of whom speak no English, are concerned about moving from the security of ensured employment to a company that is notorious for restructuring.

The American managers are on the podium. All around are banners bearing the corporate slogan in English: 'Go For One'. Before they know it, the 'Go For One' T-shirts are broken out and, along with the others, the French managers are invited to put them on. Under the pressure of the situation, most do so, but all of them feel uncomfortable and some of them are downright hostile.

To the acquiring company, this was all part of laying out its *strategic objective* and rallying the troops to meet it. It was intended to lay down the gauntlet for its hungry, *pragmatic* team and to generate excitement over the challenge of being first. To the French managers, deprived of their *heritage*, out of their secure *relational* environment and feeling more than a little nervous about their future, the challenge felt threatening and the T-shirts ridiculous.

Cultural integration with a *strategic objective* orientated culture can be risky because, far more than the other two types, they tend to feel that they have the 'right answer' on how to motivate people. After all, isn't this the model that seems dominant in today's global economy? Leaders of these companies will expend considerable energy communicating strategic objectives, making sure that *everyone* hears. Objectives appear on office walls and everyone is expected to know what they are. This works well for the culture that believes in it, but can be irritating to those who don't share the same preference. In heritage cultures particularly, strategic objectives pushed to an extreme can lead to demotivation and low levels of commitment, precisely the opposite of the intended effect.

When Two Strategic Objectives Cultures Meet

What about when two companies who both have a preference for strategic objectives come together? Here, it is essential that the Executive

Committee agrees on what constitutes an 'ambitious objective', since different national cultures may have different perspectives on what this concept means. The SMART (Specific, Measurable, Achievable, Realistic, Time-based) formula works in North America and many parts of Europe, but not in Asia. In North America, unrealistic objectives would demoralise, as goals need to be perceived as achievable. Yet in Japan, 'achievable' is not motivating, and an objective needs to 'stretch' more than that to inspire real motivation. Similarly, in Beijing 'time-based' will refer to a very different time-frame than the 'quarterly focused' Wall Street mindset in New York.

When Two Heritage Cultures Meet

As we've seen when looking at the other cultural preferences that are relational in orientation, a company with a cultural preference for heritage can be by far the toughest type to merge with another. Although many companies may have an element of heritage blended into their culture, there is a step-change in the degree of pride and belonging that people in a company focused predominantly on heritage feel as opposed to one focused on organisational structure.

It's worth noting, by way of conclusion, that some companies *are* consciously trying to integrate different cultural preferences into their approach to sustainable high performance:

> I feel that today's Lafarge is focusing on setting the 'objectives and vision' first, and then on using 'organisational structure' and 'tradition' (core values) as the *means* to ensure a sustainable future. Quick wins – such as increasing profits through reducing or squeezing the workforce – are important but are not the sustainable approach. Sustainable performance can be ensured through the application of our culture, values and systems.
>
> *José-Maria Aulotte, Director of Integration, Lafarge Group*

Some Food for Thought...

- Some cultures gain commitment to the Future by focusing on *organisational structure*, believing that the organisation will be best positioned to manage the challenges that lie ahead if it is engineered specifically to meet those challenges. Others gain commitment by focusing on *strategic objectives*, making sure that employees know where the company is going and what they'll be expected to do to help it to get there. Still others gain commitment by focusing on *heritage*, emphasising the organisation's core values and common history as a basis for future sustainability.

- In a period of intense change, employees will need to be reassured about the Future of their new entity. Whatever the cultural preference, top management has a stronger communications challenge than ever. It must share the new picture of the Future in a way that attracts the different preferences of each partner. The benefits for the whole organisation must be explained, and cascaded down to allow each unit and individual to work out what it means for them.
- The Future dimension is not only about how leaders articulate the basis for development and growth. Just as importantly, it's about the ways in which they will communicate this to their people.
- Communications are the primary lever for responding to the Future challenge. Cultural differences being what they are, it makes sense to involve local managers to help to formulate key messages that make most sense in their local culture.
- Merging with an organisation with a strong heritage culture is difficult. Merging two organisations who both have strong heritage cultures is *very* difficult. The identity issue at the root of a heritage culture is deeply emotional and much harder to shift than pragmatic or conceptual positions.

CHAPTER 7

The Cultural Audit

It's easy to underestimate the challenge. Even if cultures seem
alike, they may be very different. It helps to get an analysis up-front
about the differences between us and the company we're planning to
acquire. Then you can deal with it up-front – not as a problem – but as
a fact of life.

Tryggve Sthen, CEO, Volvo Global Trucks

Over the past four chapters, we've placed a magnifying glass over the
first of the three Culture Bridging tools that we'll cover in this book:
a diagnostic model that will allow you to build a better understanding
of those aspects of your own and your partners' corporate cultures
that will directly impact on the effectiveness of the integration process.

At this point, the pragmatic among you are probably thinking, 'Nice
theory. But how do we work with it *practically*?' Perhaps the most valuable way to harness the power of the model is to use it as the foundation
to what we call a **Cultural Audit**.

The Cultural Audit: What, Why and Who?

You need to see the points of congruence between the two companies – the shared values.

Patrick J Rich, Retired Chairman, Royal Packaging Van Leer

Whenever an organisation aspires to the development of a new culture,
it needs a benchmark, a clear picture of where it stands today that can
be compared with its vision of tomorrow.

The Cultural Audit is a vehicle for defining just such a benchmark.
In simple terms, it examines and compares the values and behaviours
that make up the corporate cultures of prospective partners. The raw

data that this process provides – in the form of a *cultural profile* of each partner – helps to identify the nature and extent of any cultural divide that may exist, and what that divide could mean in terms of working together.

A full-blown Cultural Audit involves a number of steps – a questionnaire, one-on-one interviews and focus groups – each of which we'll look at in detail a little later on. But for now, let's just think about *why* you should engage in a formal audit at all and why, if you do, you should enlist outside help. Why not just use the Culture Bridging Fundamentals diagnostic, or any other diagnostic that you may favour, as a framework for discussion and planning within the Executive Committee? This kind of culturally focused thinking is definitely something to be encouraged. However, when it comes to bridging cultures, there are risks and missed opportunities associated with using this type of approach in isolation. We've already discussed the challenges of articulating a culture when you're within it, and of discussing it dispassionately even if you *can* articulate it. Your ability truly to make sense of the cultural dimension is severely hampered under these constraints. You're trying to develop some fairly in-depth understanding here, about how a corporate culture works, what microcultures exist within that, what pockets of resistance you may come up against and what risks you run by changing the organisation. To do this, you'll need to explore mutual representations, or stereotypes and views of the merger. This is impossible to do by questionnaire alone.

Any conclusions you may draw might well be inaccurate and inactionable, lengthening the odds that you'll be able to bridge your cultures and therefore build a fruitful way of working together. A full, externally run audit can overcome these limitations. The neutrality, lack of 'agenda' and trained expertise of an external resource mean that they can more easily spot things such as gaps and overlaps that people *inside* the organisation may not be able, or even willing, to highlight. The result is honest, accurate and actionable data; data that may just make the difference between success and failure for your new partnership.

> You need to look at the painting of the other company and of your own company and see if they could be from the same period, if they're of the same style – or if they were painted by different artists.
> *Cheri Alexander, Vice-President Personnel, General Motors Europe*

The Pay-off

So what are the benefits for the new entity that commissions a Cultural Audit?

Ask anyone who's worked extensively in the arena of cultural integration and they'll tell you that an objective 'cultural map' provides the mutual understanding that enables the new entity to make the right decisions to accelerate a successful integration process. Looking at specifics, a Cultural Audit helps you to do the following.

Put the Cultural Dimension on the Table

When it comes to culture, whether national or corporate, you're dealing with implicit, often unconscious and even historical factors. Technically, these can be difficult to put a 'language' to. Emotionally, they may be uncomfortable to acknowledge. Yet, if you're to understand your respective cultural differences and then figure out how to bridge them, you *have* to bring these unconscious features into the light of day.

A Cultural Audit makes it easier for this to happen. By providing a shared language for talking about cultural factors, the Audit opens up a 'space' that makes it acceptable and legitimate to talk about these things.

Incorporate the Cultural Dimension into the Decision to Buy or Not to Buy

No acquisition will ever be made purely on the basis of cultural issues. However, a Cultural Audit conducted during due diligence or immediately following the announcement of a merger or acquisition allows the prospective partners to anticipate any issues related to cultural compatibility that might slow down or even jeopardise the integration process.

For example, in one case we know of, a Cultural Audit – by giving people the opportunity to talk about emotional drivers – allowed a Western European firm looking at an acquisition in Poland to spot a number of critical issues that a technical human resources audit would have missed. Among these was the realisation that the Polish senior managers had such high expectations, in terms of the personal career opportunities that an acquisition would bring, that the potential acquirer would never be able to avoid disappointing them. This factor reinforced an ultimate decision not to acquire, which was based on a business case.

Even when the Cultural Audit does not form part of the go/no-go decision, it can provide invaluable guidance on the degree of integration that is realistic to aim for between the merging partners, occasionally leading to a greater or lesser degree of integration than originally planned.

Develop a Shared View of Future Values and Management Style

Any new set of partners needs to define 'the kind of company we would like to be', to make the common values and management style of the future explicit.

With the common understanding of each other's cultures as a base, the Audit helps new partners to negotiate a shared view on what the values and management style should be, particularly in the areas where differences exist that could affect the achievement of top management's objectives.

In cases where the Executive Committee have already *made* decisions on future values and management style, the Cultural Audit allows each partner to position itself against the proposed model and to compare itself with the other partners involved.

Develop an Integration Plan

Earlier in this book, we highlighted the lack of planning for the cultural dimension as a contributory factor to the failure of mergers, acquisitions, joint ventures and various forms of alliance. No surprise then that one of our major recommendations is to develop a clearly defined plan for integration, just as you would for any major strategic project – an area that we'll look at in some depth in Chapter 8.

A Cultural Audit allows you to build an integration plan that takes cultural issues into account from the outset. There's no question that this can save time and pain down the line.

Take the example of a large European multinational that used a Cultural Audit as part of the process of acquiring a small Canadian start-up operation. The audit highlighted, in no uncertain terms, the importance of team spirit among the Canadian managers, a group that had been with the company from the word go. The acquirer was able to factor this information into its planning and revisit its initial intentions for expatriate staffing levels, reducing them accordingly.

Accelerate the Integration Process

Even if you do everything by the book, integration is going to take time. However, although there are some issues that just can't be short-circuited, there are others that can be. A Cultural Audit can make significant contributions here.

- It provides Integration Team members with a tool for interpreting any difficulties and misunderstandings they may come across. With this base of understanding, they're more likely to be able to make decisions that get it right first time, saving time, energy and resources along the way.
- It balances top–down leadership with bottom–up input on how the new partners view their challenges, options and future together. An integration process is effectively a negotiation between the leadership and the troops. In a negotiation, the better you understand the other party's interests and needs, the better you are able to meet them. The better you're able to meet them, the more quickly you meet your objectives.

A Cultural Audit provides this insight into interests and needs. Skilled integration leaders are then equipped to factor this information into their integration plan.

- It allows the Integration Team to adapt internal communications to reflect cultural preferences, and so to reinforce confidence and commitment on all sides and avoid misunderstandings. Effective communication is all about matching the *intent* of the communicator with the *impact* on the receiver. The more both sides understand one another, the less risk there is of crossed wires.
- The actions that flow from a Cultural Audit help to minimise internal disruption, allowing people's energy to remain focused on the customer.

So often in both integration and change situations – for example, a shift from a regional structure to a global, product-driven one – people have a tendency to mistake the enemy. They fight with a new subsidiary. Or with the global product manager who's arrived from another country and who speaks a different language. They forget that the real enemy is not within. It's outside, in the marketplace, and goes by the name of 'the competition'.

By helping leaders to meet the needs of newly integrated teams, a Cultural Audit channels energy from internal struggles to the real battlefield: the marketplace.

Adapt Human Resource Systems

Human resource systems have an enormous part to play in ensuring that an organisation recruits, motivates and keeps the best people. That puts remuneration policies, promotion criteria and performance management systems among the most 'sensitive' systems to be found in an organisation. At the very least, a merger or an acquisition will mean that these systems require some tweaking, and in many cases they require a complete overhaul. Once that's happened, the new systems need to be 'sold' to those for whom they are new and unfamiliar and to those who would prefer to preserve the status quo.

A Cultural Audit allows human resource teams to anticipate potential resistance in these areas and to develop a plan for minimising it.

Add all the benefits up and the bottom line is that a Cultural Audit allows the *right* decisions to be made and actions to be planned to facilitate and speed up cultural integration.

A very significant 'soft' benefit also comes from conducting a Cultural Audit. Most people who are affected by a change of shareholder will be silently (and in some cases vocally) concerned about the implications for the culture that they know. They'll be seeking reassurance that the cultural dimension is being taken seriously by those at the helm of the new entity. The decision to run a Cultural Audit sends a clear message that this is indeed the case. As a result, tension is eased and everyone can feel more confident that their own culture will be taken into account as the future takes shape.

Conducting a Cultural Audit: One Approach

We mentioned earlier that a full-blown Cultural Audit involves a number of steps. Let's turn our attention to these now and take a look at a roadmap of what's involved (Figure 1).

Building on the idea that an integration process should be managed in exactly the same way as *any* important strategic project, the Cultural

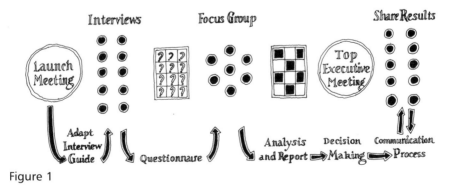

Figure 1

Audit should kick off with a **launch meeting** involving the Integration Team.

This meeting is all about spelling out the different steps of the Cultural Audit and agreeing the action plan for its implementation. Along the way, it should identify the specific data that need to be collected through the questionnaires, interviews and focus groups that make up the components of the Audit.

The direction clearly set, the Audit begins with a series of **interviews** with top management and individuals who will be interacting with counterparts or colleagues from the other partner(s). The target interviewees are those individuals who are likely to have the greatest influence on the success or failure of the merger, or on its capacity to deliver visible results in the shortest time-frame possible. The interviews, which typically last between one-and-a-half and two hours, can be run face to face or by telephone, and explore issues such as:

- perception of the merger
- the key characteristics of the company: 'how do you do things around here?'
- information about the past: the critical events that have shaped the company
- perception of the other partners.

The second key component of the Audit is a **questionnaire** on culture. This can be sent either exclusively to management or to the company as a whole. Whichever option is chosen, we recommend that the questionnaires are sent out and completed at the same time as the interviews are being run.

The questionnaire can be administered electronically (e-mail or web-based) or by hard copy (paper or fax). However it's done, it's critical to guarantee that all responses will be treated as confidential.

At its heart, the questionnaire contains a series of statements. For each of these statements, recipients indicate:

- the degree to which it is descriptive of their organisation
- the extent to which they would *like* it to be descriptive of their organisation.

The data are processed and an initial analysis is produced. Typically there are some obvious findings that confirm perceptions from the management interviews conducted. Occasionally, there will be additional, more unusual findings that require further clarification.

As soon as the initial analysis is available, we recommend running **focus groups**. These involve homogeneous groups of ten to fifteen employees, in sessions that generally last for two to three hours depending on the situation.

The primary goal of the groups is to act as a sounding board for the findings that have emerged from the interviews and questionnaires. They serve as a forum for gaining deeper insight into some of the issues raised.

The available quantitative results are informally shared with the groups, who are asked to comment on any area that requires clarification. After all, culture is not a 'precise science'. Some interview or questionnaire responses may require 'home-grown' analysis to provide the sharpest insights.

At this point, we'll stress again our recommendation that the focus groups, and indeed the entire Audit, should be run by an external resource that is not seen as biased towards any specific part of the organisation. The emphasis during the focus groups is on finding examples and stories that can be used to determine the *true* driving forces that characterise the culture of the company. An independent external resource is more likely to be able to maintain this focus. People are likely to be more open with their perceptions of the merger or acquisition, integration process and partners involved, and propose recommendations for next steps.

It's worth mentioning that, in addition to the invaluable qualitative data they provide, there's an important side-benefit to focus groups. By their very nature, they allow a greater number of people to be involved in the Audit and therefore in the integration process. Furthermore, focus groups send out a clear message that the Executive Committee leadership is concerned with cultural issues and open to listening to employees in that area. Focus groups therefore make a major contribution to getting the buy-in that's so necessary for success.

The combined findings of interviews, questionnaires and focus groups are then synthesised into a **written report**. A fully fledged Cultural Audit of the type we're describing here makes it possible to include both an analysis and a series of recommendations for next steps that are based on both quantitative *and* qualitative data in this area of corporate cultures. The result is therefore far richer than the audits that generally make up a standard due diligence exercise.

The completed report is presented initially to the Integration Team and then to the **Executive Committee** during a **working meeting**.

Ultimately, these data can be used to communicate more broadly, as the integration process is implemented.

Inevitably, the Audit will raise a host of issues that typically fall into three distinct areas: **business issues**, **human resource issues** and **communications issues**. These three areas and the issues that they encompass form the 'cultural core' around which an integration process should be built. We'll look more closely at precisely how it might go about building that process in Chapter 8.

Building a clear, objective process around the Cultural Audit ensures that it acts as a springboard for the thinking and actions that need to go on to ensure successful cultural integration. It doesn't guarantee success – that still depends on leaders *using* the data that a Cultural Audit throws up to take action. Yet even the act of conducting it begins the move away from the dangerous position of simply making a token nod in the direction of culture.

The Cultural Audit Report in Practice

Now we've looked at the Cultural Audit in theory, let's get a little more practical for a moment. If you commissioned an Audit, what could you expect to see in the report that emerged from it? What kind of information would it tell you that might help you to face the cold reality of cultural integration?

Although Cultural Audit reports can take a myriad of forms, they generally always include a combination of both *quantitative* and *qualitative* data. Like all other studies they will include demographic information on the sample used to gather data, as well as information on the methodology that was used. By way of an example of the actual data that may be generated, let's take a look at some elements of a typical report resulting from a Culture Bridging Fundamentals-based audit.

Questionnaire Results

For each of the dimensions – Legitimacy, Effectiveness and Future – the report presents the responses to the relevant questionnaire statements in a way that allows the management team to compare the preferences of one partner with those of another. Responses are colour coded, with green indicating positive responses, red indicating negative responses and grey indicating that no response was given.[1]

---

[1] Different patterns substitute for colours here, but the Audit reports are in colour.

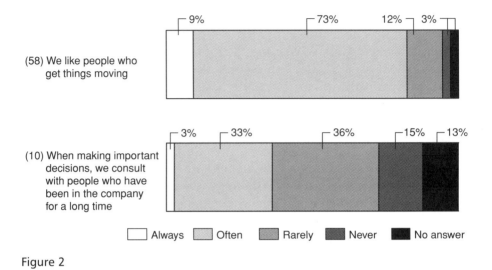

Figure 2

Although the results can be similar, they can just as often be different, as shown in Figures 2 and 3. This example, drawn from a real survey, relates to the *Legitimacy* dimension. It tells managers about the kinds of people who will be recruited and who are likely to succeed in each partner.

The responses to the first statement ('We like people who get things moving') indicate that recognition and legitimacy are orientated far more towards *performance* in company 2 than in company 1. Getting things moving, reaching objectives and producing results comprise one of the most important behaviours within company 2.

The responses to the second statement ('When making important decisions, we consult with people who have been in the company for a long time') indicate that, for both companies, the blessing of the elders is not seen as necessary when taking or validating decisions. In other words, 'length of service', or being part of the *in-group*, is not synonymous with credibility or legitimacy in the organisations concerned.

Responses to all questionnaire statements are presented in this way, sorted from 'most green (positive)' to 'most red (negative)' to aid comparison.

For each of the three dimensions, the audit report presents summary diagrams that allow managers to see the overall preference of each partner for the dimension concerned. The example shown in Figures 4 and 5 relates to the *Effectiveness* dimension. It tells managers about the

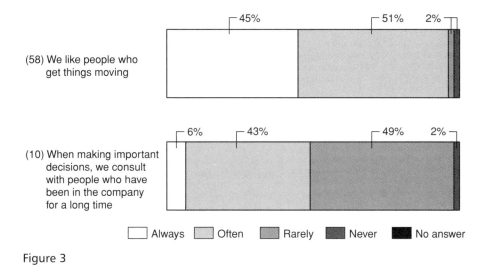

Figure 3

way in which each partner goes about making decisions and getting things done.

These diagrams show that company 2 places greater emphasis on ensuring its effectiveness by establishing *systems and procedures* and jumping into *action* from the word go. Although, as in company 1, personal *networks* are important, they are likely to be used primarily to fulfil objectives rapidly. This may lead to important differences at the start of a common project: for company 1, with its emphasis on *networks*, it will be very important to take the time to work out who is in the project team before springing into action; for company 2, this may be seen as 'time lost' and they are likely to want to get down to work immediately, using existing procedures to co-ordinate the project.

Comparative Positioning on the Dimensions

After the questionnaire responses for a dimension have been presented, the report goes on to use triangles to illustrate the comparative position of each company for that dimension. The example shown in Figure 6, again from a real survey, relates to the Future dimension.

While both companies share values around *organisational structure*, they don't put the same weight on *heritage* or *strategic objectives*. To build the future and guarantee success, company 1 will underline the importance of heritage and of what has been achieved so far. Company 2 will focus more on strategic objectives and a clear vision, to show the way to go. As we saw in Chapter 6 on Future, these differences will have

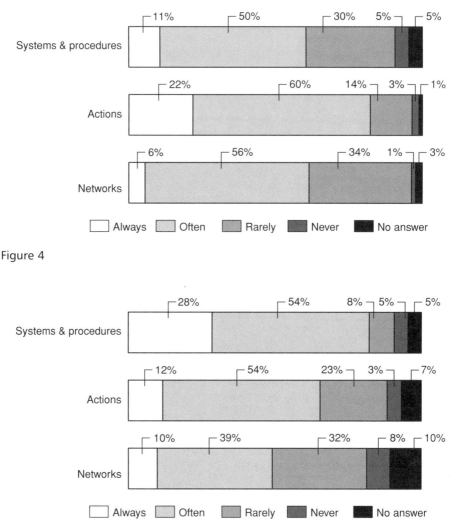

Figure 4

Figure 5

an impact on issues such as buy-in and motivation, communications styles and messages.

Overall Analysis

By way of conclusion, the report provides a summary analysis that draws both on the results of the Audit and on broader experience and comparisons whenever relevant. This analysis is made triangle by triangle and then for the companies overall, including recommendations for next steps.

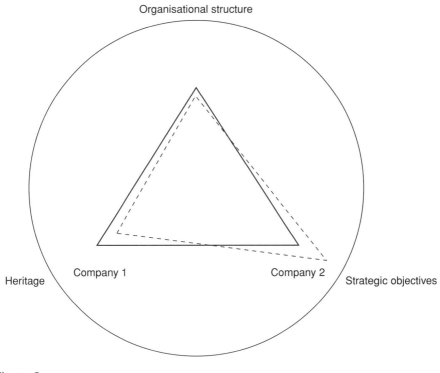

Figure 6

Enhancing the Picture

At this point, we'd like to draw your attention to two additional forms of survey that can be used to generate cultural profiles and that are complementary to the Cultural Audit components that we've just described.

The first is a *semiological* study. Semiology is the study of 'signs' and the meaning behind them. A semiologist will be able to draw conclusions about a company's culture by looking at the way in which it presents itself through its website or advertising campaigns, its corporate publications or logos. The analysis can be enriched by looking at aspects of corporate life, such as dress codes or office layouts.

Semiologists are also able to tell a lot through what's called a *discourse analysis*. This examines the deeper meaning behind what key executives of a company say in speeches, interviews, letters and so on. The analysis highlights words and phrases that appear consistently in communication and that generally give clues to the company's basic values – often embedded unconsciously in the corporate culture, but that are nonetheless important in 'how things are done around here'.

All of this can be included in a semiological study, which in turn can be integrated into the overall Cultural Audit report, giving a richer picture of the company under the microscope.

The second approach rests on a detailed analysis of the *history* of a company. The specialists who carry out these kinds of survey focus on the landmark battles that have created the value system of the company under scrutiny.

Moet Hennessy provides an interesting example of this approach. A fundamental value in Hennessy had always been respect for diversity, something that made itself clear in all aspects of the company's business. For example, the company had long made a specific target of the black American market. However, no one understood why: black Americans were no stronger a customer base for cognac than any other American community. An explanation was ultimately found by looking back into the company's history. This revealed that Hennessy's Irish founder had been wounded in battle in France and forced to stay there to recuperate. The end of the eighteenth century wasn't an easy time for the Irish in France and our hero was very much the alien. But, despite being a foreigner from the enemy ranks, people accepted him, took care of him and nursed him back to health. Not only did he survive, but he began the business that we know today. As that business flourished, he vowed that this fundamental value of acceptance, a value that had enabled both his personal survival and commercial success, would forever form the backbone of the company.

You may be asking yourself how this knowledge can add value in the integration process. Establishing any kind of new relationship with another organisation is a rebirth. It requires the partners to question the fundamentals that underpin their business, something they can only do if they understand where those fundamentals came from in the first place. Throwing light on corporate history is one more way for leaders and employees to acquire just this type of understanding.

A Question of Timing

Forewarned is forearmed: a phrase that many of us know and love, but whose advice we all too rarely heed. Projects of *any* kind stand little chance of success without a solid foundation of information on which to plan confidently. This is never more true than when the project concerned is a new form of partnership or relationship, where the potential for misunderstandings, confusion and defensiveness is enormous.

It makes sense then for the Executive Committee to commission a Cultural Audit as early as possible in the integration process. In an ideal world, this would mean conducting the Audit as part of the due diligence process, or immediately following the announcement of a merger or an acquisition. In reality, legal considerations may make this impossible, meaning that the Audit can only be conducted once the deal has been signed and the partners have begun to work together.

When an Audit is conducted *early*, leaders can reap the full range of benefits that it can bring, particularly those that relate to anticipating and avoiding problems related to culture clash. Conducted *later* in the process, a Cultural Audit still brings value, although the focus may be slightly different. By virtue of the fact that they have begun to work together without a full appreciation of each other's culture, the partners may already have run into problems. The Cultural Audit therefore becomes a tool for building understanding of what's gone wrong and for helping to *fix* problems, as would be the case if our friends at JPMT were to commission one.

Whenever it takes place, a Cultural Audit and the activities that flow from it can place the leadership team at a distinct advantage over those who opt to stick their heads in the sand, in the hope that the cultural dimension will look after itself. It opens up a space for acknowledging and mourning the past. Further, by encouraging an objective and shared view of the way things are, it allows new partners to define the way that things will be, and to lay out the map that will set them on the road to success.

All of this takes place in the knowledge that they're different and, quite possibly, all the better for it!

> It gave us a language – a set of descriptions of what the company stands for, how we express ourselves and how decisions are made. It was an eye-opener for us – a basis for discussion and how we wanted to have it. Now, rather than being irritated or annoyed, we say 'Let's see how we can tackle it'. Rather than spending time on the surprise, we accept that this is how it is, so we can go to the next stage.
>
> *Tryggve Sthen, CEO, Volvo Global Trucks*

Some Food for Thought...

- A Cultural Audit helps partners to identify the nature and extent of any cultural divide that might exist between them, and what that divide could mean in terms of working together.
- A Cultural Audit helps to bring the issue of culture to the table by providing a language and framework for discussing the issues in a non-threatening way.
- The profile generated by a Cultural Audit contributes to the mutual understanding that enables the new entity to make the *appropriate* decisions more *quickly*, and thereby to accelerate a successful integration process.
- A Cultural Audit should ideally be run by an external resource. The neutrality, lack of 'agenda' and trained expertise that they bring encourage more honest and open feedback, and perhaps more accurate and actionable data.
- We recommend that the Executive Committee commission a Cultural Audit as early as possible in the integration process in order to anticipate and avoid problems related to culture clash, and to demonstrate that people are being listened to.

CHAPTER 8

Merging the Tribes: An Integration Process Built on Culture Bridging

> When you decide to identify the similarities and differences between corporate cultures, you must have a clear concept of what you want to do with them to move things forward.
>
> *Håkan Hallen, Executive Vice-President Human Resources,*
> *Volvo Global Trucks*

At the beginning of this book, we promised you three tools that, taken together, would help you to navigate a course to successful integration at whatever level you might be seeking it; three tools that would help you to manage the cultural dimension of the integration process that you found yourself in by applying the concept of Culture Bridging.

Over the past few chapters, we've been focusing on the first of these tools, a diagnostic model to help you to build the kind of understanding of your respective cultures that is so fundamental to successful Culture Bridging. We also looked at the practical application of that diagnostic through a Cultural Audit.

But knowledge is only of value if you do something with it. So, in this chapter, we're going to focus on the second tool, a process for managing integration that's built on Culture Bridging, and that will help you to make effective use of the information that the diagnostic can generate.

Delve into text books, visit seminars around the globe, talk to experts and you'll uncover a range of models for managing integration. There are lots of them out there. Although they can be extremely valuable in the advice and guidance they provide, there's one piece that is consistently missing: the cultural component.

However, having come with us this far, you'll be well aware that we believe culture to be at the heart of the matter, and that, if it's not taken into account, integration simply will not happen.

Although we've said it before, it's important enough that we'll say it again: culture has to be on the agenda from the word go. Culture Bridging is as much a state of mind as it is anything else, and if you want to avoid the kind of turmoil that besets so many mergers or acquisitions, it's a state of mind that needs to be present from the moment the new entity is born.

This may seem like a small addition to the basic principles of integration. But, in reality, it represents a qualitatively different approach, one that is fundamental, that has huge implications and that seems to represent a quantum leap for many CEOs.

Let's begin by acknowledging that, sadly, Culture Bridging is far from a precise science with nice clean formulae for success. Quite the opposite, it's something of an art. Each fusion of business units – be it through merger, acquisition, commercial partnership or any other scenario – brings with it a unique set of variables. These unique variables demand unique solutions.

Yet, from our observations and experience, it *is* possible to define an integration **process** built on Culture Bridging that improves the partners' ability to manage differences in cultural profile highlighted by the Culture Bridging Fundamentals model. So, in looking at the recipe for Culture Bridging, the specific ingredients may vary from situation to situation, but the method of preparation is remarkably similar.

The relevance of the approach that we're going to look at over the following pages will differ depending on the degree of integration that is being sought by the two partners. For the merger or acquisition that's going for total integration (even if it's not the best route forward), everything we cover should be of use. For the 40% of mergers or acquisitions that don't involve integration at all, the chapter will be of more limited use. The advice that it gives on Culture Bridging, however, is of use whatever the degree of integration, to help the partners to deliver results as quickly as possible, to maintain solid relationships with suppliers and clients, and to ensure that the best people are motivated and retained.

The Mother of All Projects

One of our key convictions around the integration process is that it should be viewed as a strategic project and should be managed accordingly. It may be the single most critical project you undertake during your career, and if you don't manage it well, it may be your last.

All of which means taking it seriously. Back it with the level of senior management sponsorship and allocation of resources that would be given to any strategic project considered vital to the survival of the business. Give it a budget. Make it easy for the right people to be available.

Why are we such staunch advocates of the project management approach? Simply because it's so well suited to the type of globally diverse, multievent and multiactor initiative that a merger, acquisition or joint venture represents. Integration isn't down to a department or a function. It's down to remote multifunctional, multicultural teams getting together to sort out business issues. A project management approach to it will help you to ensure that you involve the right people, in the right way, in the right place, at the right time.

Another reason for applying a project management approach is that, when you're trying to get people to explore another way of doing things, especially when it involves their values and beliefs, the best way is to involve them in defining the solution. A project management approach to integration encourages this.

The Four Phases of Integration

As a foundation for understanding the integration process that we'll be considering, it's useful to look at the different phases that this type of process can expect to go through, from the time when the powers that be give the deal the green light, to the point where the new organisation is functioning as a single, fully integrated entity, and at what you can expect to happen in the absence of a project-based integration process built on Culture Bridging. We can represent the four major phases of this process in the following way (Figure 1).

Figure 1

Preparation

Few leaders will have reached their positions of power without having the old adage 'fail to plan and you plan to fail' indelibly stamped on their brain. As a result, most *do* engage in integration planning. It's what and how much they prepare that differs.

Preparing for integration is similar to preparing for an important negotiation. The goal in both cases is a win–win solution for the parties involved. In both cases the quality of forward planning distinguishes an outstanding performance from a mediocre one.

It's during the Preparation phase that the issue of culture should be put squarely on the map. From the very first meetings, as representatives from the merging organisations begin to interact, the DNA of the new entity is being formed. If cultural sensitivity doesn't appear on the agenda now, the new entity may already have placed itself on a slippery slope to failure.

This, ideally, is where the Cultural Audit comes in. However, as we stressed earlier in the book, if a Cultural Audit isn't possible, don't think that you have a licence to forget about culture! Put your cultural specs on and do your research. Establish an 'informal cultural profile': analyse the communications of the company, look at their exhibition stands, examine their history and talk to their clients; there's plenty that you can do without actually going into the company. Then factor whatever you learn into your integration plan. What's important is that the parties involved should enter into this early stage of their relationship in a way that reflects the cultural profile of both sides.

The Due Diligence Team

Traditionally, the preparation phase of integration involves the set of audits called due diligence. Typically, a due diligence team will assess the company up for acquisition, focusing on balance sheet, inventory, contracts in the pipeline, headcount, compensation and benefits, etc.; in other words, measurable numerical elements. Companies are finding that if they add a Cultural Audit to the human resources part of the due diligence process they save a good deal of time later on.

There's something else to think about when it comes to due diligence. Many companies miss a trick with the due diligence *team*. All too often they are established, go in and do their work, and are then disbanded when the decision is made to acquire. Yet these are the people who have been immersed in the new partner organisation, on site, meeting people, making relationships, building trust and *feeling* the culture.

(continued)

From a cultural understanding perspective, it makes sense to ensure that at least some of the due diligence team are included in the leadership team that will be at the helm of the new organisation. The cultural insight that they will be able to offer can prove invaluable.

In an ideal world, an integration process would be launched right after a 'go' decision is made, even before the final deal is signed. However, this is rarely possible. There is a considerable lack of clarity during the Preparation phase of any integration process regarding what new managers can and cannot do. Most people, senior managers included, don't know what the legal restrictions really are and have little idea about how to optimise their position before everything is signed, sealed and made public.

For example, in an M&A situation in the UK, the partners should talk to the Stock Exchange before talking to the unions. In France it's the other way around. Afraid to risk going outside the law, managers from the acquiring company often do nothing. There are exceptions, of course. We know of one French manager who chose to ignore an edict not to talk to people before talking to the unions. The pay-off was high, but so were the risks.

However, this is not about short-circuiting the law: it's about working out how you can humanise things when an 'information blackout' is imposed on you. Because, quite simply, this is the time of maximum uncertainty for anyone touched by the integration process who's not in the driving seat. 'How will this affect me? How does it affect my future? Will I be happy? Will I be able to cope?' Such burning questions are likely to be passing through the minds of a good percentage of the workforce. The answers to these questions may not always be the ones that they hoped for, but knowing them enables people to make intelligent choices, both for themselves and in support of the new company. One of the leadership's key challenges in this phase is to find ways to give them the answers.

This may be particularly true in the most dramatic scenario, when the deal has been signed just to add one partner's existing physical assets to the other partner's portfolio. In this case, integration may well be a 'one-way street' and the sooner that's clear, the better able people are to make decisions about whether they'll stay with the new entity or not.

How do the different cultural styles typically act during the preparation phase? *Conceptual* types tend to focus immediately on systems, procedures and organisational structure. *Relational* types won't do anything until they've made their mind up about the people with whom they may have to share their future. *Pragmatic* types will go straight to results and performance. Given three completely different entry points, it's not hard to see why it's so crucial to understand your future partner's orientation if your early interface and interactions are to go smoothly.

Preparation – The Importance of Cultural Respect
A large European building systems company, the subsidiary of a Canadian-based multinational, was looking to acquire a small entrepreneurial unit in its field of business.

The acquirer was conceptual/pragmatic in style, with a preference for systems and procedures and results. The small, family-owned company, in contrast, had a strong preference for the 'in-group' and results. Preferences for systems and procedures, organisational structure and intellectual ability didn't feature prominently amongst their managers. Despite the common ground around results, the deal was made more difficult because of the acquirer's preoccupation with auditing the systems and checking the results. Not only did they pay little or no attention to building relationships, but they also attempted to push one of their people into the tight-knit management team of their new acquisition without any consultation whatsoever.

This was the smaller company's first exposure to its potential acquirer, whose owner and leader finally turned the deal down because as he said, 'he did not feel considered or respected in the preliminary meetings'.

In an ideal world, preparation – as we've discussed – will address both the technical and the 'human', or emotional, dimension. The reality is that, more often than not, the planning that gets done focuses on the technical components only. The human, and specifically the cultural elements are left in the lap of the gods. Meanwhile, all the evidence tells us that failing to prepare for the cultural dimension is sowing the seeds of future disruption.

Transition

During this phase, the partners begin to work together and to orientate themselves to the new venture. The main organisation charts will be in place and preliminary plans are put into action. Integration teams are formed to develop more detailed plans for the amalgamation of business processes, resources and responsibilities.

If the leadership has not given careful prior thought to the way in which they'll bridge their corporate cultures, now is the time when trouble begins. As people work together to solve problems, or at least try to, their differences appear in full light. The cultural dimension comes into play in the most painful way as the initial euphoria is replaced by culture shock: a collision of values and beliefs that baffles and frustrates the individuals concerned. Conflicting perspectives on 'how things get done' emerge to hamper the decision-making capability of integration teams. Different angles on who's credible and who should hold positions of power undermine efforts to put people in jobs. Different ways of envisioning and communicating the future clash and have a negative impact on quality of information.

During the transition phase, everyone will have a tendency to look at the challenging new environment with their own cultural background as a frame of reference. *Pragmatic*, results-orientated companies will be frustrated by what they consider the slow tempo and inability to act of a *conceptual* counterpart. The *conceptual* company may consider its *pragmatic* counterpart somewhat reckless, since it apparently makes risky decisions without conducting a thorough analysis. Similarly, *pragmatic* people will feel shut out by the secrecy of *relational*, in-group orientated colleagues, whose tendency will be to install and protect a network within the new corporate environment that 'works the system' of their *conceptual* counterparts for their own advantage.

Alliances, mergers, acquisitions and joint ventures that fail to underpin their integration process with a Culture Bridging mindset may find themselves in a *perpetual* state of transition, unable to get past the idiosyncrasies of the individual partners to the land of milk and honey beyond.

Integration

If the transition to a new organisation is well planned, or has a favourable wind behind it, it will proceed to the integration phase. During this phase, detailed strategies and plans are implemented. People will start working together more comfortably, processes will be combined, and the first synergies should start to become apparent.

It's worth noting that, even with the best laid plans, operational and cultural integration may well be out of step with one another during this phase. While technical aspects may move along to a predictable schedule, people's natural suspicion and reluctance to change means that it may take more time to build true commitment to new ways of doing things and for people to let go of the past.

However, if the cultural dimension has been factored in, positive signals will begin to emerge. The 'old' cultural profiles and preferences of the partners begin to play a less critical role, as people begin to build a common history and agree on the basic values that will drive the 'new' corporate culture that they'll share. Fresh blood will have joined, while dead wood will have left. The balance between the 'movers and shakers' and the 'blockers' will tip in the direction of the former.

At this stage in the integration process, it's important to use the strength of each cultural style. Allow the *conceptual* types to formalise the lessons learned from the integration, in order to prepare better and manage the next one. Ask the *pragmatic* types to focus on improving efficiency. Let the *relational* types nurture the vital emotional and symbolic link between people and the company's identity.

But what if the cultural dimension hasn't been accounted for? If that's the case, the fledgling entity may well be experiencing fallout by this stage. The rumour mill will have ground into action, morale and productivity may take a nose dive and disillusioned talent could be bolting for the door. All of this will combine to produce a negative effect on revenues, profits, customer retention and shareholder confidence.

Consolidation

An organisation that has bridged corporate cultures whilst integrating the appropriate technical aspects of the operations involved will eventually reach consolidation, typically around three years after coming together.

During this phase strength and stability come to the new organisation. Stakeholders begin to see clear evidence of the synergies that encouraged them to back the deal in the first place. Common ground will have been found and a new corporate culture will be emerging, built on the bridges made between the individual corporate cultures of the partners.

Of course, if an integration process does not include a Culture Bridging component, this 'cultural nirvana' may forever remain a dream.

Culture Bridging: No Quick Fix!

Integration then is something of a minefield. If the leadership, both at the most senior level and at the implementation level, are not prepared for the cultural dimension, or don't *truly* understand the nature of the beast, they may never make it through. The really unlucky deals will fall apart, whilst others become paralysed where they stand, trapped on every side by mines of their own planting.

Yet it doesn't have to be this way. We firmly believe that there's a key to unlocking success where integration is concerned, and that's a well thought through integration process built on a foundation of Culture Bridging.

We want to stress that Culture Bridging isn't a one-point-in-time thing. Leaders must be prepared for Culture Bridging to form part of their integration process throughout its life cycle, from the Preparation through to the Consolidation phase.

At this point, it's worth mentioning that not everyone will greet a structured integration process with enthusiasm! Some cynics, those who in terms of the *Culture Bridging Fundamentals* diagnostic model are *pragmatic* by nature, may well question its value, preferring instead to 'just do it'. Those who are more *conceptual* may implore you to 'give it to a guru'. We'd certainly agree that the *way* in which the process is implemented should reflect the preferences found in your own situation, but we also hope that we've presented sufficient evidence to show how dangerous it can be to proceed with no process at all.

With that caution, let's get down to the nitty gritty. What does an integration process driven by a Culture Bridging mindset involve? If we express it visually, it looks like the diagram in Figure 2.

At the head of the integration process is a piece that focuses on ensuring mutual understanding on behalf of the partners and establishing the leadership that will drive the rest of the process (*Understand and Lead*). Three strands typically flow from this initial phase:

- a core business-related subprocess that focuses on resolving the business issues that the new organisation faces, a major factor in ensuring that it delivers operationally (*Monitor and Solve Problems*)
- a subprocess that focuses on what's communicated and how, a major factor in addressing the issues of uncertainty in the workforce (*Communicate and Measure*)
- a subprocess that focuses on developing the leadership's ability to manage the issues, including cultural diversity, that will be thrown up as the partners integrate, a major factor in ensuring that people feel they've 'got what it takes' to succeed (*Develop Competencies*)

The glue that holds the process together is the use of transparent tools to monitor progress, and the occasional use of *Celebration*.

In the sections that follow, we'll look at each element of this process a little more closely.

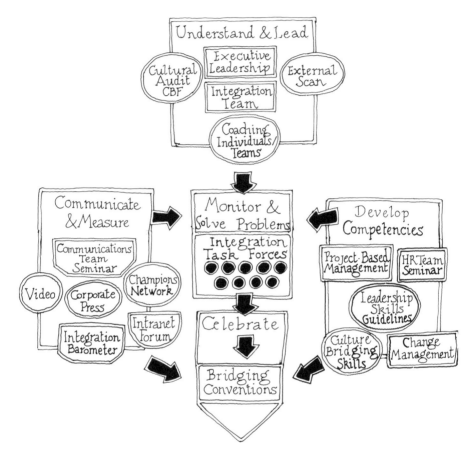

Figure 2

(1) Understand and Lead: From Shared Values to Share Value (Figure 3)

Be aware that it is very important to allocate enough time in the first phase to investigate the cultural differences and test existing opinions and values. Do this together with your new partners so that you can formulate, together, the values and vision for the new company.

Torben Laustsen, Corporate Head of Group Identity and Communications, Nordea

Figure 3

The deal has been signed. The reality of integration begins.

An effective integration process starts with the leadership team, or Executive Committee as we'll now call it. For the *Committee* to be effective, its members must share a clear and common understanding of the importance of the cultural dimension to the diverse groups that they're leading. Unless they have this understanding as a base, they'll never be able to provide the kind of leadership that will be necessary to help their people to navigate the new, culturally different waters that the new organisation is sailing in to.

One of their initial tasks then should be to commission a **Cultural Audit**. We looked at the whys and hows of Cultural Audits in Chapter 7, so we'll focus here on output. Inevitably, the Audit will raise a host of issues. These typically fall into three areas.

- **Business issues**: these can be wide-ranging and may touch each and every function within the partner organisations. For example, decisions may need to be made around how a new, combined sales team needs to work. How will the team be structured? Who goes after which client? With which product? How will sales people be remunerated? There may be issues around a new management information system and how it should be deployed. The financial officers may need to devise and implement new reporting procedures. The list may go on.

- **Human resource issues**: as we mentioned earlier, the systems that come under the human resources umbrella are among the most sensitive in an organisation. They're also quite unique to each organisation, so it's no surprise that a Cultural Audit throws up issues in this area. These will typically include how to develop mobility plans, how to reconcile different remuneration and pension plans, how to establish a set of common performance management guidelines, or how to define a shared matrix for job analysis and classification.
- **Communications issues**: in times of change, people's thirst for information increases dramatically, particularly at the outset, a period characterised by maximum uncertainty. Again, it's no surprise that different communication needs emerge from a Cultural Audit. Will any locations be shut down? Will our jobs be combined? There will be many questions, all demanding responses.

These three sets of issues – business, human resources and communication – form the 'cultural core' of the integration process, driving the three subprocesses involved.

Determining the Degree of Integration and Culture Bridging

When a Cultural Audit is conducted early enough in the preparation phase, the Executive Committee should use the data it generates to inform their decision on how far they will attempt to integrate the partner organisations, keeping the original business case in mind at all times.

An understanding of how similar or different the partners' cultures are can provide insight into the level of integration that will be realistic, allowing the Executive Committee to build more effective plans and to avoid costly mistakes. As we explored earlier, although this issue of culture will rarely be a deal breaker, it can lead initial thoughts on the way that ownership will be managed to change.

Just as it helps to make decisions about the degree of integration, the Cultural Audit can, and should, inform decisions about the degree of Culture Bridging that will be appropriate, again keeping the original business case in mind at all times. Here's how ...

Once the Executive Committee understands the similarities and differences between cultures, it can determine what's critical to preserve or extend from one culture to another, in order to achieve the required business outcome; for example, alignment on an *action* mode of effectiveness in marketing and on a *systems and procedures* mode in manufacturing.

This will help to specify precisely where Culture Bridging will be necessary to achieve the targeted business result, and will provide a clearer, 'hardwired' case for action for the Bridging initiative. Conversely, it will clarify areas where Culture Bridging is *not* essential to the business case and, hence, may not be a priority for the Committee.

> We were cutting the Jaguar workforce by over 50% in 18 months. At the same time, we decided to close an engine plant and build a new line of engines in a Ford plant. Ford top management insisted that within the Ford plant there should be a mini Jaguar plant. Visibly Jaguar. With a separate entrance so they could maintain cultural independence.
>
> *Nick Scheele, President and COO, Ford*

The External Scan: Balancing the Internal Viewpoint

A Cultural Audit provides the Executive Committee with a strong *internal* base of understanding from which to develop integration leadership. But what about *external* understanding?

Two key themes that we've explored through this book are those of 'finding a common enemy', to help to pull people out of an attack/defence mindset *vis-à-vis* their new 'partners', and 'keeping your eye on the market', to avoid losing out to the competition as a result of an overly internal focus on integration.

Initial responsibility for responding to both of these issues lies with the Executive Committee. In both cases, the response requires the focus to be *external*, balancing the viewpoint given by the Cultural Audit.

That's where the **External Scan** comes in. Although each partner will have carved out an approach that ensured its own survival in the marketplace, that approach was appropriate for a certain time, in a certain context. Just by definition of being a new entity, that context has changed and those individual approaches are no longer adequate for survival. As a client said to us: 'Both of us have at least doubled our size, which means tremendous cultural adjustment for both sides'.

To quote from an earlier chapter, a new organisation means a new dynamic, one that poses a new set of challenges and that demands a new set of responses. So the Executive Committee should work together to scan the environment, building up a picture of the common battlefield that the new allies will have to fight on. As part of this scan, it may be helpful to benchmark a few other acquisitions and to visit those companies to find out what they did to manage integration.

From whatever source, the information that's collected should then be fed into the development of a shared strategic response that provides a context for the workforce to refer to. This response can then be used to foster the idea that 'the enemy is outside' and to ensure that there is a consistent external point of focus to draw people away from navel-gazing.

Executive Leadership

> Management must define the 'commonalities' that can be understood by everyone.
>
> *Patrick J Rich, Retired Chairman, Royal Packaging Van Leer*

Armed with the internally focused data from the Cultural Audit and the externally focused data from the External Scan, the Executive Committee can begin to describe the shape of the future. At this point, they should be able to look rationally at the values and practices that they bring to the new entity and so begin to write their future, *common* history. They'll be able to keep the values and practices that work, and that are applicable to the new market conditions that they face, and lose those that aren't applicable.

This is the moment when the Executive Committee formally establishes itself in the role of sponsor to the integration process. This role is distinct from all of the other roles that it may have, and it's a role that should be kicked off in a formal structured way through a special meeting: the **Executive Meeting**.

The Executive Committee under the Microscope

The Executive Committee is a symbol of the merger: as the first group from the new partners to work together, it is something of a laboratory experiment. Everyone from the employees to the press to financial analysts will watch it closely and will look at it as an indicator of health.

(continued)

In an ideal world, the formal Executive Meeting we describe here would be the first time the Executive Committee had come together in its new incarnation. In reality, this is rarely the case – it may already have met several times to fix a hundred other things. Regardless of this, the Committee members are rarely a 'team' at the point when they gather for this meeting; and until they're a cohesive team, they won't be able to run the new company.

Although they've been appointed, no one will be sure who will hold what role, so there's a very unstable political situation to be managed. Committee members will be watching each other carefully and cautiously. 'Is the line between my role and yours clear? Or are you trying to take over my turf?' With this kind of delicate situation, external facilitation of the Executive Meeting, with a team-building focus, is well advised!

The make-up of the Executive Committee often changes in the early months of integration, with some political appointments being ousted, for example. Equally, the team may not yet have all its members when it comes together for the Executive Meeting.

A word of caution for the CEO: you can expect a tough time! If the group is multicultural, different members will have different expectations of what a good CEO is and does. The CEO will have to adjust to these different expectations.

Because of its unique focus, this meeting should be seen as entirely separate from the regular 'business as usual' meetings that the Executive Committee will have. Together with the follow-up activities that may lead on from it, the meeting should produce certain key outcomes that will form the foundation for success.

- A clearly defined **external focus**. One of the 'golden rules' of Culture Bridging is this: 'If you want to bridge successfully, look to the outside – find the external challenge and focus on it'.

  The Executive Committee should use the knowledge that it has gained from the External Scan to define a strategic focus based on a common threat, something that will make or break the new partnership.

  If the workforce feels that there's a challenge to be risen to, people's motivation to find effective ways of working with their new partners will increase accordingly. It's one of the Executive Committee's key responsibilities to ensure that this mindset is fostered throughout the new organisation.

Once they've determined the external focus, all subsequent decisions about how things will work should be framed and explained for employees by referring to it.

- A statement of the **management style, values and principles** that should be adopted to ensure that the new venture is a winner in the environment that it faces.

Over time, each party will have experienced struggles in its quest for success. At times like these, it will have made fundamental choices about what it believes in; choices that, together, made up the company's culture.

However, as we said earlier, integration is a rebirth and a new period of struggle, bringing with it situations neither company has ever faced before. To move towards success, the new entity has to forge a new way of working by making those fundamental choices about beliefs again. Only this time, they must do it together.

This particular step cuts to the very core of culture. It needs to be handled with the utmost sensitivity. Some people may feel that their personal style and values are being called into question. They may even feel a loss of identity. So it's important that this exercise is framed with respect to the Cultural Audit, and that it looks to the future and asks questions that relate to 'us', to avoid any sense of things being 'judgemental'.

Again, each party is only likely to be able to move on from its *personal* beliefs to a new set of *shared* beliefs, if both parties recognise some common external factor that threatens survival. This approach avoids confrontation, as it's not one partner's model against the other. It accepts that each is unique and focuses the partners on something that is new for all of them, the environment in which they now coexist.

The statement of style, values and principles that emerges from this exercise should describe both the profile of the people who will ideally lead and manage the business, and the type of company that it hopes to be. This statement should feed into the Communications process and be publicised throughout the organisation.

- A decision on the **time frame** for integration. Ideally, this will include both a goal for integration as a whole and some milestones along the way. For example, when they took over Paribas, BNP immediately made a public statement about the proposed time-frame for integration: six days for the Executive Committee level, six weeks for the next layer of management and six months for the organisation in totality.

    While they may provoke scepticism in some quarters, such announcements can be a major source of reassurance for the workforce at large.

- A statement of the **priorities for action**. These should be determined by reviewing the business case and issues raised by the Cultural Audit and will determine the specific projects that will be handled by task forces.

You'll invariably find that the Executive Committee members believe that they can achieve all of the objectives of the Executive Meeting in just a few hours: team building, role definition, establishment of values, etc. But the reality is that it may take them *many* meetings to reach a full agreement on these topics, and they should be prepared for this. Experience tells us that it simply can't be done in one meeting.

    Consequently, the Committee should decide on a specific series of meetings that will focus on managing and monitoring the integration. Otherwise, it is likely to be drawn into running business as usual. Time and resources will not be allocated to implement and monitor the integration process, and Culture Bridging will be submerged.

    Given the nature of its objectives, the Executive Meeting should be held *after* the results of a Cultural Audit are available. If timing makes this impossible, the Executive Committee should be prepared to adapt the work that it completes at the meeting, or in any follow-up sessions, to reflect the findings of the audit once they *do* have the results.

The Integration Team

In all but the simplest scenarios, it will be impossible for the Executive Committee to carry out all of the tasks necessary for successful integration. Responsibility will inevitably need to be cascaded down the new entity, which means delegation.

    The first level of delegation by the Executive Committee should be to appoint a separate **Integration Team**, which will be responsible for the day-to-day management of the integration process. The Executive Committee should provide a clear mandate to the Integration Team, detailing:

- the *context* of the change, including a statement of the key challenges

- the *objectives* and *time-frame* for integration: what has to be achieved, by when; setting the priorities that the Integration Team should focus on to be successful
- the *values and principles* that should guide leaders' behaviour as they manage the integration process, both internally and when facing the outside world
- the *role* that the Executive Committee will play in sponsoring the integration process: what they are ready to do to help the Integration Team, without treading on their toes
- the process for *reporting, measurement and control* as integration progresses:
  - how often will the Executive Committee and Integration Team sit down together for feedback and planning?
  - what are the critical success factors that will be measured? For example, these could relate to people's knowledge of the project, their opinion, the number of people leaving and the extent to which people really participate.

Selecting the Members of the Integration Team

As with all teams and committees formed during the integration process, members should be selected according to clearly defined criteria. In the case of the Integration Team, this means bearing the following points in mind.

- The team should be made up in such a way that it cannot be attacked from a political viewpoint.
- It should include only those who want to 'play the game', i.e. people who view things positively.
- It should be easily brought together: it should be neither too big (we suggest a maximum of eight people) nor too geographically spread.
- Its members should be experienced and willing to take risks.
- It must reflect both the structure and the cultures of all of the partners.

From a cultural standpoint, for example, if you have one partner whose preference around Legitimacy is *intellectual ability* merging with one whose preference is *in-group*, make sure that the Integration Team includes individuals who are legitimate for both. This may mean making sure that you include people with clear records of academic excellence, as well as those whose team members recognise as 'one of us'.

This implies that the Integration Team is best selected *after* the results of a Cultural Audit are available. If timing makes this impossible, the Executive Committee should be prepared to adapt the make-up of the Integration Team down the road when they *do* have the results.

Getting the Integration Team Off the Ground

In essence, it's the Integration Team that will run the whole integration project. It's no surprise then that it must be got up and running both quickly and efficiently.

To build a solid foundation, the Integration Team's initial meeting should focus on getting them to *be* 'a team', and an exemplary one at that, since its visibility in the new organisation will be high.

A team-building session allows the new colleagues to begin building relationships with one another, whilst planning for action using a traditional project management approach. In our experience, this involves working on four 'team pillars' (Figure 4).

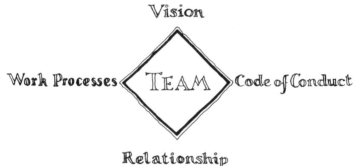

Figure 4

This first meeting should be used:

- to share and take ownership of the mandate handed down by the Executive Committee
- to share the objectives of the integration plan
- to agree on the priorities for action in order to integrate the partner organisations
- to decide, in light of the business case and priorities for action, on a series of integration projects that will be managed by individual task forces
- to agree on the work processes that will enable the team to work together effectively

- to agree on a 'code of conduct': behaviours that will be considered acceptable and unacceptable (let's not forget that the Integration Team is often operating on pretty hot political ground)
- to establish positive interpersonal relationships and a 'winning spirit'.

It is crucial to allocate the necessary time to cover all of these objectives to the required depth. In general, a two-day session will be the minimum time-frame for doing this. Although the Integration Team leader *can* facilitate, an external facilitator may be better positioned to handle the process, given the potential political sensitivity and the fact that team members are unlikely to be familiar with one another.

Once it is successfully established, the Integration Team should initiate action on three fronts to propel the process towards success. These three fronts represent the three 'streams' of issues that are typically thrown up by the Cultural Audit:

- **monitor and solve problems**
- **communicate and measure**
- **develop competencies**.

Let's move on to take a look at what's involved in each of these areas.

(2) Monitor and Solve Problems (Figure 5)

In Praise of the Mixed Task Force

> Mixed teams are a key to success where integration is concerned: it was the sharing of practices at the team level that made integration possible.
>
> *Human resources director, service organisation*

Figure 5

Among the Integration Team's first tasks is the appointment of a series of **task forces** to deal with all of the business issues that integration demands: the alignment of systems, budgets and reporting procedures, the merging of teams to manage clients properly, the merging of R&D departments, the review and restructuring of the product catalogue, etc.

The specific focus of the task forces will be dictated by the priorities decided by the Executive Committee. Each of these priorities will evolve into a project for which a task force should be set up. Some Executive Committees may be ready to launch fifty, but for others five will be a big thing!

In addition to the more obvious areas noted above, two others warrant specific attention. These two areas – purchasing and information systems – have a major impact on the optimisation of business results and also help to smooth interfaces in all work processes. At first glance, a decision to implement a new information system, or to centralise purchasing may seem to be merely a 'technical' decision. However, the political ramifications of these choices can be enormous and often spark resistance to change.

From a Culture Bridging perspective, these task forces are as important as the mandate from the Executive Committee. They are the first opportunity for the new partners to work together and for the cultural influence to be expressed. From marketing to purchasing to production, they are likely to be looking at how things that were done differently, perhaps in quite different ways, can now be done in a single, unified fashion. Corporate cultures being what they are, the natural tendency, if the process is left unmanaged, will be to see who will impose whose system on the other parties! Individuals are likely to go back to their friends and refer to what's happening in the task forces as an indicator of how things will be in the new world. Phrases such as 'So that's how they're going to treat us' or 'I knew they'd put up resistance' may ring around the corridors.

It makes sense then to view these task forces as something of a laboratory experiment. To ensure positive outcomes, it's important to ensure that the Integration Team appoints teams that are mixed, including representatives from all parties, and also that the process is controlled. It may indeed be the case that one partner's system is better suited to the new environment than the others, but the adoption of that system as a solution for the new entity is only likely to be politically acceptable if it has been decided on through exploration by a mixed group.

The Impact of Culture on Task Force Effectiveness

Just as is the case at the macrolevel of the organisation, the cultural profile of the partners will need to be accounted for to enable task forces to put together solutions acceptable to everyone concerned.

For example, a group with a preference for *systems and procedures* around Effectiveness will see a task force very differently to a group with a preference for *action* or *networks*. Different views will be held on how they should work and even who should be a part of them.

We know of a case where a bank with a general preference for *action* merged with a strongly hierarchical organisation with a preference for *systems and procedures*. The new entity began forming mixed teams without completing any kind of Cultural Audit. People from the *systems and procedures* orientated group went along to initial meetings simply to listen to their new partners. Their intent was to get information that could be fed up their hierarchy to enable decisions to be made.

The *action*-orientated group had quite a different agenda. Their intent was to give and get information openly, negotiate a solution that was politically acceptable and develop an action plan that could be implemented with immediate effect. All hell broke loose when they started to interact. Positive intentions immediately went into reverse: the action-orientated partner probed for information, got nothing in response and, after the fourth attempt fell on stony ground, left the room. They felt both suspicious of their new colleagues and cheated by the lack of progress or solution.

Preparing Task Forces to Work Together

This was a clear example of failure to account for corporate cultural differences leading to disaster. But how can task forces be prepared to work together effectively so that this situation is avoided?

- First, by ensuring that the Integration Team fulfils its role and provides task forces with a single, clear mandate to work to.
- Secondly, by determining the partners' profiles through a Cultural Audit. This allows you to predict the kind of gaps that will occur and to plan for navigating them.

There's a lot of value in holding a seminar that brings together nominated task force leaders before any work begins. The overall goal is to share pertinent information about cultural profiles with a view to establishing a mutually acceptable way of working together. Ideally, this session will be facilitated by someone neutral so as to allow those involved to immerse themselves in the experience. The session should be built around four key areas:

- building an understanding of the whole context that has been set for the new organisation by the Executive Committee and of how the task force leaders' part of the jigsaw fits in
- acknowledging and expressing the emotional dimension of the new venture ('How do I feel about my new colleagues?'), leading to an agreed 'code of conduct' for building a trusting environment
- developing an understanding about how the partners' cultures meet (or don't), leading to the definition of a plan for how task forces are going to work together successfully
- defining the task forces' relationship to the Integration Team and Executive Committee.

This type of session, run effectively – and complemented by personal coaching, if leaders require it – will ensure that the necessary pillars are in place to support task force success. It's more likely that task forces will be managed in a consistent way, and that there'll be a shared and common approach to problem solving.

Leaders of the Future

Mixed task forces have one other significant benefit that should not be overlooked: they present a unique opportunity to identify and develop emerging leaders.

Task forces are like 'microcorporations'. They have a mission, measurable goals, a plan to build, implement and monitor, highly diverse people to manage and coach, and results to deliver and evaluate. As a by-product, the people who lead them will develop the very qualities and key skills one expects from a good manager and leader, including the Culture Bridging skills that we'll focus on in Chapter 9.

Human resources departments should pay close attention to how these teams operate in order to pinpoint the talent, the high-potential people with whom the future of the company lies.

(3) Communicate and Measure (Figure 6)

> The messages that are put out must be clear. Everything that's said must be based in fact.
>
> *Patrick J Rich, Retired Chairman, Royal Packaging Van Leer*

Figure 6

Formally or Informally: Just Do It!

The second subprocess that the Integration Team must initiate is that of communication and measurement.

When it comes down to it, the integration process is one big period of change, but that change is rarely so intense as it is at the outset. At this point, uncertainty abounds and everyone wants to know what the future holds. Often, the reality is that there's little to tell them, because it simply isn't known yet.

Even if there *is* information to communicate, there may be issues of confidentiality to be observed, based on the laws of the land. For example, how much can be made public before labour representatives, unions, etc., have been consulted?

Management is often caught between a rock and a hard place, knowing that it must communicate, but powerless to provide the kind of information that people may be demanding. But let's not forget: not communicating *is* communicating! When you're trying to build an environment of trust, saying nothing has precisely the opposite effect, making people feel *dis*trustful of one another.

So how exactly *do* you communicate when you've got nothing to say? It helps to start by remembering that, as with so many elements of integration, there's a human as well as a business side to communication. You may not be able to give people all of the hard facts, but you *can* facilitate 'emotional' interactions, so that people can express their feelings about what they're going through.

Talk about what's going on – tell them that processes are being instigated and let them know when they can expect more information – but, in addition, be clear on those questions to which they won't get a response. It can be much easier for people to accept restrictions when they feel that the lines of communication are open than it is when they feel shut out. So, when you don't have much *content* to share, focus on *process*, in a way that opens up space for questions, even difficult ones, so that people feel listened to and involved.

It doesn't even have to be done formally. Take the example of a divisional head at an insurance company, on hearing that his company was about to be acquired by a huge British group. He had no information to convey and the executive committee was keeping extremely quiet but, naturally, his team wanted information.

Thinking outside the box, he decided to prepare his people for the future by organising a daily cup of tea at 5 pm to discuss where they were and how they were feeling. He didn't hide. He didn't fabricate stories. He chose to gather people around him for an open discussion about how difficult and different it was for everyone to cope with the situation. It was a simple, yet important step in keeping up morale and preparing people for what was to come. It also did more for success than a hundred vaguely worded press releases ever could.

Of course, similar ends can be achieved more formally by allowing people to meet in a structured way through facilitated workshops to talk about what they're experiencing.

> We communicated our strategy to the employees but only in general terms and on a few occasions. Management wanted to be totally sure before anything was communicated to the company – and furthermore we focused on communicating only facts.
>
> Reviewing the process I can see now that we created confusion and insecurity, and unfortunately some key people left the company because of this. We could have reduced much of the mistrust and the rumours by communicating not just what we were sure about but also our thoughts and plans – and what we might need to change later. If we had communicated up front and in a structured way we could have avoided much insecurity and waste of time and energy.
>
> *Senior executive, industrial group*

Honesty Pays?

Informal. Formal. There are choices. What's most important is that communication happens and that, when it does, it's honest. This may be easier said than done. Naturally, people are clamouring to hear good news. No one wants to hear about redundancies, plant closures or savage cost-cutting exercises. Given that some of these may ultimately come to pass, the whole scenario places management under intense pressure.

Consider the example of a manager who decided on the route of honesty when he first heard of his bank's take-over by a new shareholder. He promised himself that he'd tell his people exactly what he knew and understood at all times. In the early stages of the partnership, real information was thin on the ground, but the pressure from his people was unrelenting. Finally, he became so tired of the constant intrusion and his inability to deliver hard facts that he started to give out false news. He'd say that he'd 'met the critical people and everything's OK'. While he disliked the fact that he wasn't telling the truth, this feeling was far outweighed by the sense of relief brought about by the removal of the constant pressure.

The Shifting Nature of Communication Needs

Let's side-step for a moment to think about the different ways in which people can react to the kind of change that's associated with two companies coming together. Resistance is a complex phenomenon and grows out of diverse roots. For some it's born out of nostalgia. For others it comes from giving up familiar working habits. Still others fear that they won't have the competencies needed to 'make' it in the new situation. For another group it's a question of self-esteem and self-image. For many it's just a general fear of the unknown and a concern over 'what's going to happen to me in all this'.

These different sources of resistance can be lessened by open, well-managed and comprehensive internal communications plan. As the Communications task force plans the communications strategy, it should keep in mind that people will have different needs at different phases of the integration process. Figure 7 shows the overall picture.

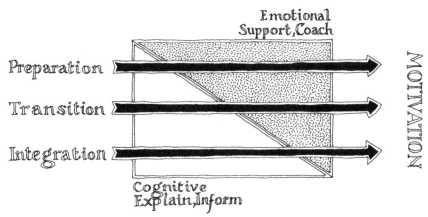

Figure 7

At the outset of an integration process, most of the workforce are likely to experience a greater or lesser degree of resistance to what's about to happen; after all, it represents change, and few of us really like that. Familiar working habits are under threat. There's a sense of professional risk: people are unsure about whether they'll have what it takes to succeed in the new world. As a result, their self-esteem takes a knock and, almost before any change has actually occurred, nostalgia for the good old days has set in. It all adds up to fear of the unknown and an emotional frame of mind.

During the *preparation* phase, therefore, people's needs around communication are largely emotional. Messages need to appeal to their hearts and emphasise support and sharing. As the integration process moves into the *transition* phase, and roles and responsibilities are clarified, and a more equal balance can be struck between the emotional and the cognitive. More messages can now be sent that appeal to the head, messages that explain and inform. By the time things move into the integration phase, although some support is still needed, the emphasis can be firmly on the cognitive domain, explaining results, how things are going, what still needs to be done, etc.

> Intensive personal contacts can often help to open the armour of other cultures. In close talks, where you share your own sorrows and fears in an open way, people develop the trust that is needed to overcome differences.
>
> *Hans Albrecht, Executive Vice-President, Hella*

The Communication Strategy: The Players and Goals

When it comes to putting together a communications strategy that will respond to the shifting needs of the workforce, the featured players are:

- the CEO, to supply the overall vision
- the Communications Director, as the sponsor of the initiative
- management, as a key conduit of information to the workforce
- the press, which gives you feedback on how the outside world views your progress, or lack of it
- the market, which either congratulates you or slaps your wrists!

The goals of an effective communication strategy to address the emotional and the cognitive needs in the right measures should be:

- to provide **knowledge**, by presenting information and informing people about what's going on and where things are going
- to ensure **understanding**, by explaining how things relate to specific teams and individuals and allowing for open discussion
- to gain **commitment** to the change, by involving people in implementation task forces and coaching others for new competencies and ways of doing things
- to encourage **sharing** through co-operation and exchange of ideas and information
- to encourage **action** through reward, recognition and celebration.

The Communications Task Force

To ensure that the complex and critical area of communications is managed effectively, involving the right players and achieving its goals, with no stone left unturned, the Integration Team should form a **Communications Task Force**.

Just as we've recommended for all the teams and task forces born out of the integration process, the Communications Task Force should take a project management approach to the significant task under its remit. Ideally, the project manager should be drawn from the Communications function of one of the partners' businesses. Other team members should be drawn from each of the partners, but should ideally have specific expertise in the area of focus. Key to their success is team members' understanding that the new situation they find themselves in will change the goals and practices associated with their role.

Although they will still be responsible for producing traditional communication tools, this function will be enriched; the team is now likely to find itself providing internal consulting and advice to ensure that managers down the line have the necessary skills and tools to communicate about the new entity and to 'make it happen'.

For example, if, in the early stages, confidentiality laws cause a period of silence in terms of hard facts, the team will need to help managers to deal with the pressure caused by the inevitable press speculation around what's going to happen. This speculation is far more likely to be negative than positive. They'll need to anticipate the effects of potentially damaging articles and be prepared to help managers to respond and cope with the fallout.

As a first step in fulfilling their role, the task force should be launched with a kick-off **seminar**. The goal here is to agree the objectives for the communications strategy and draw up a specific plan. As part of the process, task force members should develop a common understanding of:

- the context for the communication strategy
- the cultures that are to be integrated
- the process that will be used
- the changes that will be involved
- the resistance they will come up against.

The Medium for the Message

Once clear on the specifics of the communication strategy, the task force will need to turn its attention to the *means* of communication. Should existing tools be used? Should new ones be created?

We don't propose to weigh up the pros and cons of individual methods here. Indeed, a mix-and-match approach that chooses from a variety of media often works best, as it increases the chance of reaching and appealing to a greater audience, an audience with a wide range of cultural preferences. It's also fair to say that, whatever mix you choose, there should be elements that involve getting people together face to face, working, playing and having fun together. 'Hard' media alone – video conferencing, paper communication, intranet – just won't do it.

Some of the following methods have been used to good effect.

- **Corporate press**. As well as providing information through traditional intercompany newsletters and magazines, new publications, unique to the integration process, should be considered here. There may even be value in encouraging some healthy irreverence! One such publication surfaced after an acquisition (called a 'merger') in the petroleum industry. Suddenly a magazine appeared that presented a satirical critique of the new organisation. No one knew who was producing it or where it was being published from, but it was seen as a healthy outlet for people's feelings. It also turned out to be a useful way for the senior team to keep its finger on the pulse of the organisation.
- **Video**. In an ideal world, key leaders would make personal contact with each and every employee to relay the context of the new situation. Where numbers and geography make this impractical, the use of video to deliver key messages can be a useful alternative. One caution: because of its one-way nature, video should never be used in isolation.
- **Champions network**. A Communications Task Force alone can rarely spread the message to one and all in the new entity. It should additionally be able to rely on a team of legitimate individuals, throughout the various layers and departments of the new entity, to act as champions. These people, who naturally should be favourable towards the merger, should be targeted to communicate the details and benefits of the change to others. This champions network, by getting much closer to the coalface, can act as a critical conduit in the feedback process.
- **Intranet forum**. Devoting an intranet site to issues surrounding the integration process can generate healthy, positive interaction amongst employees. It's also a place where management can post responses to frequently asked questions and where, on a more general level, an e-mail-based Q&A process can be established. This list is by no means exhaustive, and may be added to by any number of customised approaches. For example, we liked an idea adopted by

Exxon Mobil, who created a specific web-based 'Integration Package' for its managers. This described the theory behind the integration, and gave managers some simple tools to help them to deal with the key issues that they were likely to face.

> Via the intranet it's easy to get quick feedback on the atmosphere and level of information among employees. You can get a quick response by checking how a certain message has been perceived throughout the company and if people have questions around the merging process. It's not enough to check this during the company's yearly opinion surveys because after a year you can't remember what went wrong and it's too late for management to take actions.
>
> *Communications manager, engineering group*

However it's done, what's important here is to reach people with as much honest and useful information as possible. Keep them in the dark or feed them false information, and suspicion will quickly grow, with problems of a far more subversive nature following close behind.

Measure Progress: Take the People's Pulse!

Whatever the strategy and medium for delivering it, it's important that channels of communication are two-way. It's vital that the Executive Committee and Integration Team let people know what's going on, but it's equally, if not more, vital that they should be aware of the voice of the people.

From a motivational perspective, if opportunities for people to express themselves don't exist, trust in management will decrease, the 'emotional glue' that holds people together in the new entity will set more slowly and the process of integration will dramatically slow down. So it's critical to measure what people are thinking and feeling.

An effective communication strategy will ensure that special tools are put in place to capture this kind of information throughout the integration life cycle, and to do so openly.

One such tool is the **Integration Barometer**. This takes the form of a questionnaire, typically sent to a different sample group on a quarterly basis. The feedback received allows leaders to monitor the progress of integration, by observing:

- people's knowledge of the new entity: its products, client base, number of sites, etc.

- opinion and feeling about the change: whether it is good for business, for their department, for their own job and for the future
- the extent to which integration has impacted on people's day-to-day lives
- the extent to which people feel confident that the Integration Team is managing integration issues effectively.

Even with the best of intentions and most carefully laid plans, however, the news coming back to management will not always be positive. This may discourage management from sharing results or from providing any further information that people may construe as negative. This, however, is a mistake, since saying nothing is a powerful act of communication in and of itself. We worked with a client who ran a quarterly integration barometer. The results of the first two were tough; so tough that they decided not to communicate them back to the workforce. But this went down less well than the bad news might have done!

So, it would seem that it's not a case of no news is good news in these situations. Quite the opposite. We'd suggest that, whatever the news is, it empowers people to cope and make decisions. Although honesty may occasionally be painful, it's likely to be highly valued.

The Impact of Culture on Communications Strategy

In our experience, an effective communication strategy should take into account all three cultural orientations: *conceptual*, *relational* and *pragmatic*. There's really no way to choose one over another when looking at an organisation as a whole, since the partners and even different functions within individual partners often have very different profiles.

For example, a sales force may be *pragmatic* in orientation, deeming performance, action and strategic objectives to be important. The Purchasing function within the same organisation, however, may be *conceptual* in orientation, valuing systems and procedures and organisational structure more highly. A message directed towards one orientation may completely miss the mark for the other.

At the partner level, the scurrilous internal publication described earlier serves as a good example. Whilst accepted by the new shareholder as a valid, even useful, expression of people's opinions, to the acquired company it was heresy. Coming, as they did, from a more controlled culture, with less freedom in communications across the organisation, they were scandalised by its lack of respect for the hierarchy.

The bottom line then is that you must embrace all three styles to deliver an effective communication strategy. You need to appeal to people's minds (*conceptual*), using logic-based tools in an intelligent way; you need to touch people's hearts (*relational*), using tools that tap into emotions and a sense of 'being in this together'; and you need to enable people's muscle (*pragmatic*), by using tools that are focused on action and that help people to sort out their day-to-day life.

Above all, you must deliver the kind of information that will reduce anxiety in the early days and nurture people's performance as time goes on.

My advice? Communicate important messages frequently in different ways and different settings. Don't hesitate to communicate about plans and ideas that might be revised later – people like to feel informed.

Communications manager, engineering group

(4) Developing Competencies (Figure 8)

Build the Environment for Success

The third subprocess that the Integration Team must initiate relates to developing competencies. This area, which typically resides with the human resources functions of the partners, is critical to success.

There are two major issues to address here:

- the **alignment of human resources systems, strategy and culture**, elements that can have a significant impact on employees' willingness and ability to contribute their best to the integration effort
- the **development of the competencies** that managing in the new environment will demand. If leaders have never before been exposed to the degree and nature of emotional change that profound organisational changes bring, it's highly likely that they'll need competencies over and above those that they bring to the party.

As a starting point for addressing these issues, the Integration Team should appoint a **Competencies Task Force**, essentially drawing on the human resources functions of the partner organisations, to focus on increasing alignment and developing new competencies. From the

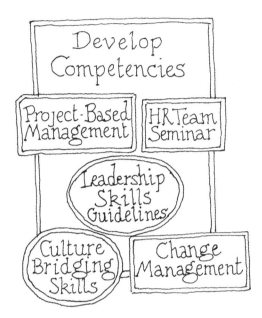

Figure 8

starting point of a team launch seminar, this group should drive initiatives that both bring strategies and processes into line and enable and motivate leaders to manage the integration of partner organisations. The team should use the integration period as an opportunity to redefine some of the traditional activities of the human resources department: to move forward, change and adapt.

Alignment

Early in the process of two organisations coming together, everyone will put appraisal and career development under the microscope. Employees are guaranteed to be asking themselves – and others – a multitude of questions around the way that their performance will be measured and rewarded:

- What will be the criteria for moving up this organisation?
- Do the old rules still apply?
- What sort of performance will be recognised?

Remuneration policy is a particularly sensitive area in this regard, and one which can throw up precious information about the corporate cultures that are merging and the extent to which these are consistent with the strategy for the new entity. Remuneration policies are a good barometer here. For example, during periods of integration, teamwork becomes very important, so people will be naturally sensitive to companies that leverage team bonuses as a way of effecting change.

As an example of the differences that exist in remuneration approaches, and as evidence of why they must be brought into line, consider the example of two organisations merging in the private banking sector. Both operations had regional directors in South America. Although the two people in question had similar basic salaries, one was paid a bonus which, in US dollars, was equal to the entire salary that his counterpart received in French Francs! The 'enormous discrepancy' was immediately presented as one of the major challenges for the merging organisation. Yet, on examination, it emerged that the difference really lay in the remuneration *systems*. When the *overall* packages were correctly analysed, they were much closer together than a cursory glance at salary and bonus would suggest.

It may be a simple moral, but don't just consider salary! If employees consider salary alone, which may be their immediate temptation, the grapevine may quickly become clogged with messages to the effect that 'we're going to get an enormous pay rise' or 'we're going to have our salaries cut', depending on which side of the fence you sit!

Another example of procedures that need to be aligned lies in the area of recruitment. In the language of the Culture Bridging Fundamentals diagnostic, this area will be strongly influenced by each partner's preferences around Legitimacy. We know instances of organisations, with a bias towards intellectual ability and performance, who argue that rank of entry associated with a candidate's SAT or GMAT scores counts, even at 51 years of age! This approach may not sit easily with companies that have a bias towards intellectual ability and in-groups, where the 'club' (for example, being a 'normalien' in France, or having attended Oxbridge in the UK) is critical.

> The solution was to harmonise all working conditions and bonus systems. The management negotiated new agreements that tied in to the desired behaviour in the new company. They were a mix between the two cultures and were perceived very positively by all the employees.
>
> *Human resources manager, services group*

Developing Competencies

Many managers find that they are not adequately equipped for the new and unique situation into which an integration process thrusts them.

The human resources team must develop and implement a plan to help management to acquire the new skills necessary for them to be effective in this type of situation; specifically, to offer them the possibility to display the leadership *style* that the Executive Committee deems appropriate for the success of the new venture.

These skills – Culture Bridging skills as we call them – are the third tool in your integration armoury, and we'll be focusing on them specifically in Chapter 9. Once mastered, they help managers to cope with the uncertainty that is characteristic of integration situations and enable them to manage their culturally diverse teams at such an unpredictable time.

Building a Common Language Through Training

A series of training events is a wonderful way to build consistency in practices and to focus people on results-based behaviour. Many companies start by bringing their world-wide leaders together in business-focused workshops to debate issues, share viewpoints about how to reach objectives and define common ways of working towards them. This often includes strengthening project-management skills. We see this as a particularly high-value activity, primarily because project management calls into question hierarchical and even functional organisations and, as such, is a lever for cultural change in and of itself.

If these training events are successful, they lead to the alignment of differing project-management techniques, and an increased capacity to lead projects and project teams effectively and, ultimately, they increase the overall effectiveness of the new venture.

(5) Celebrate! (Figure 9)

If people have met targets in the US, they celebrate and enjoy the success. And it seems that everyone allows everyone else to be successful without ever being envious. For them the glass is always half full.

Hans Albrecht, Executive Vice-President, Hella

Figure 9

It's so often the case in life that bad news spreads like wildfire, while good news goes uncommunicated. Integration processes are no different. The pain is common knowledge, the pleasure often unnoticed or overlooked. There can be bits and pieces of an organisation that are glowing examples of success, yet no one realises it.

The message here is that, throughout the phases of integration, the positives should be communicated and formally shared. If the integration process has been built on Culture Bridging, an enormous amount of energy will have gone into selecting task forces that will produce all of short-, medium- and long-term results. So when they do produce results, make sure that people know about them. Talk the walk! This is particularly important when it comes to any quick wins. If a new purchasing strategy will allow savings of 20% on annual spending, then shout it from the rooftops! Quick wins give evidence of the benefits of organisations having come together and provide the motivation to keep moving forwards. They're of little use in this regard if they're kept close to the chest of those who are most closely associated with them.

Another aspect of celebration, never to be underestimated, is the importance of simply gathering people together to get to know one another and start building the common history that's so vital to the development of a 'new' corporate culture. A friend of ours who worked in a purchasing role at IBM told us that his first focus when merging new teams of people was to get them drinking together, well before there was any talk of technical integration. The team spirit kick-started by this approach promoted understanding and went a long way to ensuring that technical integration went smoothly.

We can't emphasise this enough though: don't think of celebration as a single, point-in-time step! It should happen throughout the process and allow people to exchange at an emotional level.

The Importance of Building a 'Common History'

So there you have it: a practical approach to managing integration built on the principles of Culture Bridging.

It's unwise to be too prescriptive about the specific action steps that might be taken. Each integration process, and the cultures that it brings together, is too individual for that. But if you plan and implement actions that support the broad steps we've described, we firmly believe that you'll be well on your way to success.

One thought to leave you with. Corporate culture is born out of each partner's responses to the situations that it has faced historically. For a 'new' culture to emerge, the new partners must start building their own shared history. That will happen all the more quickly if people get together to work and celebrate at every opportunity. So, whatever actions you plan as part of your own integration process, ensure that there are as many events as possible that get the different partners face-to-face in the same room.

A contact of ours in the insurance industry once said to us:

> When you hear your company has been acquired, suddenly you have no past. And of course, you don't yet have any future. You're in limbo.

Limbo is a dangerous place to be. The absence of a positive view of the future can encourage people to reinvent their history as a 'past time paradise', whatever the reality may have been! So, the future starts now. Do all you can to help people view it positively.

Proceed in Haste, Repent at Leisure

At this point, it's pertinent to consider the issue of **timing**. Is it too early to think about Culture Bridging when the first discussions around the deal take place? And when does it become too late to introduce for it to have any kind of positive effect on the new entity?

A rather simplistic answer to this question is that it's never too early and it's never too late!

It's never too early because, as we know, bridging cultures requires significant effort, at a time when significant effort must also be expended in many other areas and results are being sought quickly. Integration is a supplementary burden on both managers and employees. Time spent on cultural integration is time *not* spent on servicing customers, developing new products and so on. Yet without cultural integration, those efforts may well founder. So it makes sense to start early so that the company can give its full attention, with full effectiveness, to the market at the earliest opportunity. In addition, moving quickly in a pragmatic and well-organised way will produce the necessary short-term wins that will strengthen people's commitment to their new environment.

It's also the case that mergers tent to 'dramatise' the emotional dimension of a company. Any manager who has experienced an integration process knows the extent to which 'nursing' becomes their major daily activity. So it's necessary to minimise negative emotion by implementing a plan early and monitoring it carefully.

A cautionary note: don't confuse speed with haste. Move too quickly, with insufficient thought, and you'll have plenty of time to reflect on your failure. New partners often take the 'rapid integration' advice too literally, adopting hurried integration plans and trying to resolve problems as they arise, without first obtaining real understanding and buy-in. They're then surprised by people's reactions to the change and the level of resistance that they encounter. If these deals don't get completely derailed, integration ends up being slow and costly.

So, it's never too early. We'd also say that it's rarely too late. In the early part of this book, we considered the encouraging concept that corporate culture is malleable. So, with the exception of the rare disaster scenario, where problems have simply been allowed to go too far and have become too gargantuan, the chances are that it's possible to focus on the cultural dimension and jolt the new entity from a perpetual state of transition into a streamlined, efficient, happy ship.

Some Food for Thought ...

- Manage an integration process as a project. Appoint a project team, the Integration Team, and ensure that it has an executive mandate and support, and that it can access the resources it needs: people, time, authority and budget.

- Identify a few opinion leaders from each company who can play the role of internal champions and influencers to help to shift and reassure others.
- Ensure that the resolution of business issues is at the core of the integration process. Ensure that teams are rapidly set up to work on these issues and to recommend solutions to the Integration Team, so that it can get final approval for change from the Executive Committee.
- Use internal communications to maintain energy and momentum and to share the good news around the organisation. Don't forget to talk the walk!
- The multicultural teams that will necessarily be involved in the integration process will need to develop new competencies. Ensure that a Human Resources Task Force takes this in hand.

CHAPTER 9

Building Your Personal Armoury: Culture Bridging Competencies

> The ability to manage cultural diversity is one of the issues we check
> very carefully with our managers – they should be aware that they'll
> need to be able to do this as part of their day to day job. If they
> can't handle that, they should take a different career path.
>
> *Tryggve Sthen, CEO, Volvo Global Trucks*

So, the Cultural Audit has armed you with an understanding of the similarities and differences in your own culture and that of your prospective partner. You've used that knowledge to build a project-based architecture for managing the integration process between your businesses.

Two valuable tools successfully applied. You probably feel that you're now ready to conquer the cultural divide. But are you? Or is there still something you need to check for in your personal armoury? Leading executives such as Tryggve Stehn would suggest that there is.

As a manager in a newly integrated organisation, you need to demonstrate attitudes and behaviours that will enable you to lead others, develop a strong sense of belonging in a diverse and often international group, and generate commitment to getting results together. The 'traditional' management competencies that would have secured survival in the past may not fully equip you to manage these conditions – conditions that are ever more common in today's dynamic global business village. All of this means that you need to ensure that you're armed with the unique set of competencies that we call Culture Bridging competencies.

Culture Bridging competencies are the attitudes, skills and behaviours that enable leaders to work more and more effectively across cultural borders. They're about the willingness and ability to get things done with people who may be very different to yourself. While the diagnostic model and integration process that we've been looking at in Chapters 7 and 8 provide you with a clear roadmap to help to navigate the cultural divide, these Culture Bridging competencies are the glue that holds it all together.

Culture Bridging Competencies: A Tool Kit

Culture Bridging competencies, we hear you say: aren't these just the attitudes, skills and behaviours that *any* good manager in a modern organisation should be able to call on at the drop of a hat? Yes – and no. You'll see some skills here that should be very familiar to you as an accomplished manager. Active listening, for example. You do that, right? In fact, your people are always saying you're a really good listener. The question is, can you call on that skill when you're out of your comfort zone? When you're exasperated because the person opposite you insists on more small talk, and you want to get down to business? When he or she happily leads a meeting that you feel has little or no structure?

The truth of the matter is, most of us can apply good managerial skills when the road is smooth, but when it gets a little bumpy, that's a different matter. All the evidence tells us that managers aren't quite as good at doing this as they think they are. Right at the beginning of this book we talked about the support from consultants that leaders look for where integration is concerned. One of the requests we hear most often is 'help us to give our managers the skills to manage cultural diversity under any circumstances'. Face it. Culture Bridging skills are a competency for the new millennium!

So let's take a look at how Culture Bridging 'masters' demonstrate their abilities. As we do so, we should point out that our emphasis here is firmly on *what* the skills are and *why* they're important, and less on the specifics of *how* to apply them. We'll save that for Volume 2!

> You make mistakes when you put in a leader who underdelivers. The first 6–9 months is critical. Whether it's your guy or their guy, the person must be totally on board and have all the skills to get the job done.
> *Senior manager, strategy consulting group*

Curiosity and Openness

At the foundation of successful Culture Bridging is an attitude: one of taking pleasure in learning, and of exploring the new and different, rather than being threatened by it. People who are driven by this attitude want to understand how best to implement priorities and reach strategic goals while getting everyone's buy-in. They are naturally open and observant, always looking to understand the environment and the way that things are done, without making judgements. They encourage creativity and innovation.

'Exploring the new and different' in this context doesn't only relate to business practices. It can mean the willingness to try new foods, to get used to new types of clothing, to tolerate new smells and sounds, and so on. Some people almost feel that they are under attack when having to deal with these kinds of differences. Others – those who are driven by a strong sense of curiosity and openness – experience them as an adventure and an opportunity to learn, if not as an outright pleasure.

Why is this 'state of mind' so critical to successful Culture Bridging? Simply because intercultural adjustment depends on leaders being non-judgemental and receptive to the ideas and ways of other cultures, rather than being constrained by their own company's values, ideas, products and ways of doing things.

Anyone who has a role to play in bridging cultures needs to cultivate this state of mind. For some of you, it may come naturally, even when faced with adversity or with something unfamiliar or even disagreeable. Others among you may have to work at it! But it's the key that unlocks the door to success in integrating cultures. Without it, lip service may be paid, but true integration will never happen.

Curiosity and Openness: Self-assessment

Are you curious and open-minded when confronted with new and different situations or opinions?

Look at the following list of statements. If you agree with most of them, curiosity and openness probably come naturally to you. If you *disagree* with most of them, you should think about how you can develop a more positive attitude in this area.

- My reaction in a very different environment is one of curiosity: I'm willing to try new foods, listen to new types of music, test out new behaviours.

(*continued*)

- I'm interested in finding out about different practices in other companies and seeing how they might enhance our own way of doing things.
- I enjoy spending time with managers who have different backgrounds or who see things differently from me.
- In new business situations, I enjoy making a concerted effort to improve my understanding of the other's management cultures.
- When I am in a new environment I actively try to develop relationships with new people rather than staying among those who are most like me.

Self-awareness

Inextricably linked to curiosity and openness is self-awareness. In a cultural context, self-awareness is all about understanding your own cultural 'baggage'. It's about knowing your own personal limits for cultural adaptation. What will you be able to absorb easily? What will be more challenging for you? What are your hot buttons – the issues that may affect your ability to maintain self-control?

Culture Bridging masters cultivate self-awareness. For one thing, it allows them to put their impulsive reactions into perspective by recognising that their own view of what's 'normal' is culturally driven. For another, equally important, thing, it allows them to set limits on how far they are willing or able to 'bend' around their own values and beliefs. This kind of clarity means reduced stress, both for the 'masters' themselves and for others, speedier decision making and, in the long run, a greater level of trust. Knowing your own limits is also a way of *protecting* your own set of values and beliefs by ensuring that they are not absorbed into another way of doing things.

If you're going to build cultural bridges, it helps if you help others to help you. So, Culture Bridging masters think about how they can make the implicit *explicit*, by articulating their own cultural values and beliefs. They're willing to acknowledge that these may not be appropriate for everyone. Similarly, they monitor their own 'negative' feelings, resisting the temptation to feel threatened by other people's core values or approaches to life. Quite the opposite: they respect them and accept them, even though they may not agree with them.

Self-awareness: Self-assessment

How aware are you of your own cultural 'baggage'? How clear are you about your own limits around values and beliefs?

Look at the following list of statements. If you agree with most of them, you probably have a good idea of 'where you're coming from' and what your priorities are. If you *disagree* with most of them, you should think about how you can develop your awareness of your own cultural values.

- I am able to articulate the basic cultural values that are essential to me.
- I can accept certain values held by other people as legitimate, even if they are not the same as mine.
- I feel comfortable saying 'no' rather than engaging in behaviours that do not fit my values.
- I am aware of my own negative reactions if someone goes beyond my cultural 'limits'.
- I know how to react constructively when my basic values, attitudes and behaviours feel threatened.

Risk-taking and Ability to Deal with Uncertainty

It's not unusual to experience the odd impasse as you go about bridging cultures. You're invariably getting to know new people. Sometimes you'll even be working with former competitors. The new ways of doing things won't always be immediately comfortable.

Culture Bridging masters are able to step outside their comfort zone and take chances, even when the outcomes are uncertain. This ability generally goes hand in hand with openness and curiosity. But while openness and curiosity are basically states of mind, risk taking and dealing with uncertainty involve action.

Culture Bridging masters are able to take that action. They make decisions, allocate resources and set priorities without the raft of supporting data that they would ideally like to have. They know that operating in a new environment means that reliable data may be difficult to come by, and that even if they do come by them, the unfamiliarity of the situation means that there's a greater risk of misinterpretation. Consequently, Culture Bridging masters recognise the need to act on intuition if they're to respond to the dynamic new environment that they find themselves in.

Risk-taking and Ability to Deal with Uncertainty: Self-assessment
How able are you to stick your neck out without the backing of hard data? How comfortable are you in taking risks, especially when you have to justify things on the basis of intuition alone? How well do you deal with uncertainty?

Look at the following list of statements. If you agree with most of them, you're probably not phased by uncertainty and may even find risk taking exciting. If you *disagree* with most of them, you should think about how you can develop a more positive attitude in this area.

- I am often one of the first to 'chance it' among my colleagues.
- I feel confident in my own intuition about people and what's going on.
- I consider that risks I have taken have given me valuable experience and good opportunities to learn.
- I prefer doing new and unconventional activities to familiar or repetitive ones.
- I feel confident that I can convince others on the basis of my convictions and intuitions.

Active Listening

When you're confronted with a situation that's 'culturally different', you'll inevitably see and hear things that trigger an impulsive negative reaction in you. When this happens, your immediate response may be to justify your own way of doing things. Not only can this put you into a debilitating 'attack–defence' spiral, it can also prevent you from learning about what's really going on.

When you have a position or opinion that you want to defend, it's all too easy to miss what the other person is *really* saying. Culture Bridging masters are aware of this risk and fight the urge to defend. They strengthen their understanding of what is really going on by listening actively, making a concerted effort to focus on the other person rather than on themselves. Their goal is to build trust by creating an atmosphere where people feel at ease, at the same time as they gather *all* the information that they'll need to pursue the business objectives in a constructive way.

How do they do this? They check whether they have *truly* understood what's being said or done, rather than jumping to conclusions. If they *don't* understand, they take the time to seek greater clarity. They try not to become blinded by what's explicit – the tip of the iceberg – and do all they can to uncover what's not – the implicit drivers that are hidden below the surface. As well as asking questions, this means using their observation skills so that they increase their sensitivity to non-verbal clues. They continue to clarify until they understand what's driving the other person's position or point of view.

When they *do* understand, they say or do something that *demonstrates* that they do.

Throughout this process, it's critical to keep an open mind, to understand, accept and adopt non-verbal behaviours that may be different from your own. For example, a European Human Resources Manager in China, through listening and observation, realises that credibility is an issue for her because she's both European and a woman. Although she doesn't spontaneously feel comfortable with this, she demonstrates her understanding by putting every diploma she has ever earned on her office wall, because she has noted that the Chinese respect academic credentials. As icing on the cake, she adds a couple of photographs taken with important people whom her Chinese colleagues will recognise.

Active Listening: Self-assessment

How well do you apply active listening in tough situations? How good are you at setting aside your own 'agenda' and getting into other people's shoes to understand them better?

Look at the following list of statements. If you agree with most of them, your active listening skills are probably quite strong. If you *disagree* with most of them, you should seek out opportunities to develop your skills.

- I check my understanding of what another person is saying by asking things like 'If I have understood you correctly ... Is that right?'
- I am willing to listen to another person's position – even when it is very different from what I might expect – and then think about how to respond most constructively.
- In new or unclear situations, I ask many open-ended questions for clarification (questions that cannot be answered by 'yes' or 'no').
- I am aware of the impact of my non-verbal communication and can control it to send out the signals I want.
- I believe that the better I understand other people's positions, attitudes and behaviours, the better armed I am to adopt appropriate managerial behaviours and make the right decisions.

Empathic Assertiveness

For even the most seasoned campaigners, there's a significant emotional aspect to a new corporate configuration. This means that 'human' skills need to be in focus as everyone goes about the business of getting the job done and delivering results. Perhaps the key skill that Culture Bridging masters use to maintain this balance is *empathic assertiveness* – the skill of demonstrating care and understanding while still pursuing the business objectives that have been set. A bit of good, old-fashioned understanding is woven in with clarity about what you're after!

Specifically, empathic assertiveness is about responding appropriately to people's emotional make-up to get them to buy into a new way of doing things or a new set of goals.

Culture Bridging masters use this skill after a good dose of active listening to make sure that people *feel* understood and to show that they themselves *have* understood! But it goes beyond that. Listening actively and demonstrating empathy are one thing, but it's equally important for Culture Bridging masters to assert their needs, requirements and expectations, in a simple, straightforward way. If they don't, they run the risk of throwing the baby out with the bath water.

For many people, the idea of insisting on doing something differently causes feelings of uncertainty, unease and even guilt. But while it's important to be culturally sensitive, it's also important not to lose track of who you are or where you want to go. That's the core of this competency: demonstrating that you plan to advance in the way that's most appropriate to the new organisation, while at the same time demonstrating respect for other ways of doing similar things.

Take the example of the new European General Manager of a Chinese acquisition with six years' experience in China, who knows that it takes time to transfer knowledge to Chinese staff. Not only time: it also takes clear objectives, process skills and competence in empathic assertiveness. So, this GM is not afraid of the frustration that may be caused to his expatriate team members when he decides to spend the first hour of a meeting ensuring that *everybody* understands the agenda. This is empathic assertiveness, and it's indispensable.

In a nutshell, it's about thinking and acting in ways that benefit *all* stakeholders. You could say it's about applying 'emotional intelligence' to relationships across cultural differences.

Empathic Assertiveness: Self-assessment

How well are you able to balance the need to meet objectives with the need to respond to people's cultural and emotional make-up?

Look at the following list of statements. If you agree with most of them, empathy probably comes naturally to you. If you *disagree* with most of them, you should think about how you can develop your skill in this area.

- I have the courage not to say 'yes' when what I really mean is 'no'.
- I am clear about my own objectives and can therefore state them simply and with conviction.
- I am able to communicate my objectives in an exciting and charismatic way, including to people very different from myself.
- In my company, when I am convinced of where we need to go, I feel confident about getting others to move in the same direction, even if they are used to doing things very differently.
- I focus on trying to find satisfactory responses to important objections that I may get.

Constructive Influencing and Mediation

With matrix management structures ever more prevalent in organisations, managers generally have no line authority over their project team colleagues. To add to this, their teams may well be remote and international. As a result, they need well-developed influencing skills to encourage colleagues to work together.

Constructive influencing and mediation are applications of the skills of active listening and empathic assertiveness, with the specific objective of conflict resolution. They are important in all managerial situations. During integration and in cross-cultural situations, they are absolutely critical, since managers may well find themselves having to win over people who share neither the same values, priorities nor goals.

Culture Bridging masters excel in these areas. Through constructive influencing, they find win–win solutions to difficulties and conflicts, something that's important both for building trust across differences and for ensuring that any agreement that's reached will be adhered to by each side.

With mediation, they adopt a neutral position to facilitate understanding between different parties, be they teams, functions and line, headquarters and field operations or new partners in an integration process. However, it's important to note that, important as it is, competence alone doesn't always equal successful mediation. 'Position' also plays a part: it's easier to mediate when you're not directly concerned or involved in the issues at hand.

Culture Bridging masters are able to use constructive influencing and mediating to demonstrate their conviction in a charismatic way, and so are able to win over their colleagues without having line management responsibility over them.

Constructive Influencing and Mediation: Self-assessment

How well are you able to influence and mediate when the going gets tough and you don't even 'speak the same language'?

Look at the following list of statements. If you agree with most of them, and if you also agreed with most of the statements in the active listening and empathic assertiveness self-assessments, your influencing and mediation skills are probably quite strong. If you *disagree* with most of them, or if you disagreed with most of the active listening or empathic assertiveness statements, you should think about how you can develop your skills in these areas.

- I try to understand the drivers underlying the other person's position in order to find the most convincing ways of responding to them.
- I look for win–win solutions in situations of conflict.
- I approach conflict resolution as an opportunity for building trust.
- My personal charisma and convictions win people over so that they co-operate with me.
- When appropriate, I am able to remain a neutral facilitator to help parties in my company to resolve their differences.

Focus on Process

Team-working meetings, a negotiation, a project review, the ongoing relationship between headquarters and outlying operational units, the integration of a new acquisition: whatever the interaction, it takes place on two levels. At the explicit, 'above the line' level is the *content* of the interaction. This can be heard, recorded on tape, logged in the form of minutes and debated. 'Below the line' lies another level, the implicit level of *process*.

Whereas *content* concerns the 'what', *process* concerns the 'how'. How is the meeting conducted? How is authority demonstrated? How is the agenda developed and managed? Closely related to 'how' is the question of 'who'. Who is managing the interaction?

Different managers place different emphasis on *content* and *process* as they go about planning an important interaction. Some will pay more attention to the former, while others will pay more attention to the latter, a difference that may well be rooted in national cultures. Educational systems around the globe vary widely in the emphasis they place on process, and often shape the perspectives of the managers of the future as they do so.

But whatever their predisposition, Culture Bridging masters recognise that whenever they have to work through a period of change or across cultural boundaries, it can be just as important and in some cases, *more* important, to manage the *process* side of things as it is the *content* side of things. Take negotiation as an example. Culture Bridging masters realise that the party that sets the agenda and moves things in the direction that suits it, controls the process, and is then in a stronger position than the party that focuses uniquely on content.

Culture Bridging masters know the power of the choices they make around process, so they consciously use it to gain commitment, monitor fears and build trust. For example, as they implement the communications portion of their integration plan, they will focus their energies first and foremost on deciding who should communicate and how, in what kind of forum, with what kind of agenda and with what kind of facilitation. The substance of what they want to say will then flow out of this focus on process.

Focus on Process: Self-assessment

How in tune are you with the *process* side of interactions? How much time do you spend ensuring that you manage this aspect of interactions? How sensitive are you to the immense impact of a well thought through and well-managed process?

Look at the following list of statements. If you agree with most of them, your process management skills are probably quite strong. If you *disagree* with most of them, you should think about how you can develop your skills in this area.

(*continued*)

- When I attend an important meeting or a negotiation, I am aware that the process that is followed has a major impact on how I feel about the event afterwards.
- I spend a significant amount of time before important events thinking about how I can get the flow of the event to feed into my objectives.
- When planning an important meeting, I give serious thought to questions such as 'What should be done first?', 'Who should facilitate?', 'What seating configuration should be used?' and 'How should time be balanced between free discussion and formal presentations?'
- When preparing an important discussion or negotiation, I place as much importance on how I can manage the agenda as on preparing the subject matter.
- I believe that *how* we say and do things carry meanings that are as important as *what* we say and do.

Language and 'Language Management' Skills

Obvious as it may seem, we'd be doing you a disservice if we didn't stress the importance of language skills to successful Culture Bridging. With English being used more and more globally, it's all too easy to overlook how much more easily and productively you can work internationally if you speak *several* languages.

When new colleagues are asked to work in a language over which they have little command, they're placed at a distinct disadvantage. They may only be able to express themselves at the most general of levels, which can lead to costly mistakes and misunderstandings. Leaders who will be working not only across borders, but also across languages, should develop their command of the languages concerned as far as they can, or surround themselves with others who possess those language skills. The goal here is to facilitate communications with people in their own language, maximising the chances both for understanding and for being understood.

When we use the term 'language skills' with respect to Culture Bridging, we're not talking exclusively about the ability to master *fluency* in different languages. We also mean the willingness to take risks with language. Culture Bridging masters listen to the 'music' behind words that they don't fully understand to help them grasp the overall meaning. They 'go for it', making the effort to express themselves in a language, even if they're not fluent in it. Although these efforts may be far from perfect in terms of grammar or vocabulary, they invariably strike a positive chord with new colleagues, indicating a strong desire to meet them halfway in the new venture.

Culture Bridging masters are sensitive to other people's language difficulties. They make sure that everyone around the table gets a chance to speak. Moreover, they make sure that each person is listened to, and clarify anything that they haven't understood. These managers have taken the time to set basic language ground rules with their teams and then ensure that they are respected.

Language and 'Language Management' Skills: Self-assessment
Knowledge of more than one language. Willingness to take linguistic risks. Sensitivity to language management. How do your skills stack up in these three areas?

Look at the following list of statements. If you agree with most of them, and if you agreed with most of the active listening and empathic assertiveness statements, your language and language management skills are probably quite strong. If you *disagree* with most of them, or if you disagreed with most of the active listening or empathic assertiveness statements, you should think about how you can develop your skills in this areas.

- I can use more than one language in a business context.
- When I travel I enjoy trying to communicate in an unknown language, even if I can only say a few words.
- I don't necessarily feel left out when people around me speak their native language, even if I don't understand what they are saying.
- I go out of my way to check that non-native speakers understand what is going on in my meetings and get the chance to participate.
- When speaking with a multilingual group I make a conscious effort to avoid speaking rapidly, mumbling or using idiomatic expressions, difficult words or expressions with strong cultural references such as sports analogies.

Building Trust

Everything we have seen in this Culture Bridging skills chapter adds up to one thing: Culture Bridging masters are old hands at building environments where people trust one another. They understand how important it is to maintain an attitude of mutual trust and faith in cross-cultural environments if meaningful, productive relationships are to be formed, be they between individuals or within teams.

They know how to facilitate interactions between people from very different backgrounds – social, cultural or ethnic, wherever the diversity may lie. What's more, they are also able to help the teams that they work with to develop respect for diversity.

It's worth remembering that trust is the sum total of all the other attitudes and skills in this chapter. If you are able to display these attitudes and skills consistently, you'll be well on your way to building an environment where people work together effectively and confidently, no matter how unfamiliar the territory may be; and you'll be well on your way to being a Culture Bridging master.

Building Trust: Self-assessment

How well do you contribute to an environment of trust in new and unfamiliar situations?

Look at the following list of statements. If you agree with most of them, you are probably able to build trusting relationships relatively easily. If you *disagree* with most of them, you should seek out opportunities to develop your skill in this area.

- Basically, I believe that others will not let me down.
- I'm prepared to take the risk of trusting new people who become involved in my business dealings.
- My colleagues consider me to be a trusting person.
- My colleagues consider me as a trustworthy person.
- I care about forming meaningful relationships in my professional environment.

Putting it all Together

At this point, we'd like you to consider two types of cross-cultural manager – we call them **Red Loop** managers and **Blue Loop** managers.

In independent research into the effectiveness of expatriate managers in the mid-1980s, Indrei Ratiu found that these two types of manager approached the basic, experiential learning cycle in quite different ways. They would ask themselves different types of question as they experienced new things and would develop different types of answer as well.

This meant that they had very different approaches to the *next* new situation they faced. Ratiu concluded that 'Blue Loop' managers are the more effective, based on two criteria: they achieve business objectives and are considered effective by the people in their local and headquarters organisation.

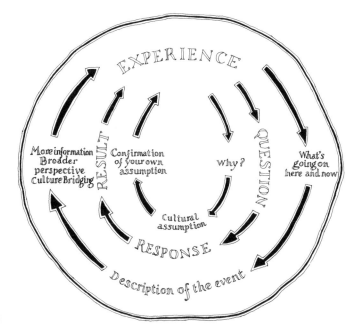

Figure 1

The illustration in Figure 1 summarises these two management processes.

Whenever an important situation arises, Red Loop managers (the inner loop in Figure 1) 'decode' it in light of the cultural assumptions and theories that they've used in the past. Invariably, they find that this new experience confirms these assumptions and theories, so they move on to the next event with their convictions strengthened and their blinkers on.

Red Loop managers rarely take risks. They see process as relatively unimportant. They don't worry too much about building trust or using empathic assertiveness. They tend to do things in the way that they always have, and expect others to fall into line. They can be difficult to work with during an integration process!

Faced with a new and unfamiliar situation, Red Loop managers report experiencing relatively low levels of stress and seem to feel quite happy with the way they are able to manage in this new context. Their colleagues, however, see it rather differently. They give these intransigent types low marks for their Culture Bridging skills.

Blue Loop managers (the outer loop in Figure 1) operate quite differently. They view things far more openly. They won't focus exclusively on the past for answers when a situation arises; they're far more likely to ask 'What's going on here and now?' as they try to figure out how to deal with things. Unlike Red Loop managers, they therefore move forwards with more information and a broader perspective.

When faced with a new and unfamiliar situation, Blue Loop managers generally report feeling a fair amount of stress. They also question whether they're 'doing things right'. Although they may be finding it a little painful, both we and their colleagues would say that yes, they *are* doing it right.

These are the managers who are applying the Culture Bridging skills we've been looking at in this chapter, and are judged to be effective in so doing by their colleagues. They are the role models for any aspiring Culture Bridging masters, because they are the ones with both the willingness and ability to generate commitment and buy-in for new ways of doing things.

> One of the keys to success is an investment in training and competency development. The Accor Academy is a melting pot that really contributes to the development of a common culture.
> *Evelyne Chabrot, Human Resources Director Hotels, Accor Group*

Some Food for Thought...

- Competencies are relevant when they are adapted to the situation at hand. Because 'traditional' leadership competencies have not been developed for successful leadership of cultural integration, they are not broad enough to provide a manager with all of the skills needed to deal with cultural diversity.
- Culture Bridging skills require an open, curious, 'ready-for-change' mind-set, as well as a willingness to put oneself and one's way of doing things under the microscope.
- It takes time, energy and commitment to master Culture Bridging competencies: the attitudes, skills and behaviours that enable leaders to work more effectively across cultural borders. But, together

with a diagnostic and integration process built on Culture Bridging, they are a key ingredient in the recipe for 'making it happen'.

- It may be easier for an individual to manage across cultures in a 'Red Loop' manner without worrying too much about Culture Bridging competencies. However, this short-sighted option will not deliver results over time and runs the risk of demotivating good people, disappointing new clients and confusing the development of new work processes.
- Linking Culture Bridging Skills to an increasingly shared vision of the new organisation is a powerful way to reinforce both the importance of these skills and the robustness of the vision. Then, as with all competency development, they need to be embedded in all of the human resources systems and processes.

CHAPTER 10

Seeing the Light

The Culprit Unmasked

It was, one might say, time for the tough to get going. On a late winter afternoon, Ingo found himself staring failure in the face. There was a very real prospect that the deal between JPMT and InterComm was going to result in an organisation that was less than the sum of its parts, a minor player left out in the cold, looking in at the select group of mega-businesses to which it had aspired to belong. But the prospect of failure was something that Ingo found both unfamiliar, deeply unpalatable and like a red rag to a bull. He was going to sort it and sort it good.

At least he felt that he now had a better understanding of what 'it' was. When he set out on his series of walkabouts some weeks ago, with Jenny Anderson's words about 'merging two different tribes' ringing in his ears, he knew that he was on a quest to understand the impact of corporate culture. Yet he really had little idea of what he was going to find.

So, he'd talked to a lot of people; gathered a lot of information; faced the ire of several less-than-happy-shipmates; and quickly established just how spot on Jenny's observations were. Ingo was amazed by how frequently 'culture' was mentioned by the people he spoke to:

They just didn't seem to get our culture.

It was a total clash of cultures.

It was all about **them**. I didn't see one iota of respect for **our** culture.

A picture had begun to emerge, one which became clearer and sharper by the day. It seemed that InterComm's approach to its very existence was significantly removed from JPMT's. The way the new partners went about things, whom they trusted and respected and how they communicated the future were a million miles apart, and nothing had been done to bridge the divide. Quite the opposite: the perception among the workforce was that JPMT had used its position as acquirer to impose its 'way' on InterComm in all aspects of the business. As InterComm people began to sense this, their readiness to co-operate dwindled by the hour.

By the time he'd completed his walkabouts, Ingo was in no doubt that the lack of appreciation for each other's culture was the key culprit in the case of JPMT and InterComm's rocky marriage, and that the key to putting the deal back on track lay in bridging the gaping cultural divide. All he needed to do now was to figure out what to do about it…

Putting a Language to the Challenge

Although he'd already put together a 'fix-it' integration team, and although he already had enough facts, comments and opinions to write an epic to rival *War and Peace*, Ingo still didn't quite feel ready to move.

He couldn't help feeling a little concerned that all of their analysis had been done from the inside: JPMT InterComm contemplating its navel. While he didn't doubt the importance or validity of the data, he felt that they needed some external input, an expert eye with no territory to protect to take an unbiased view of their situation and provide a foundation of critical data that they could act on with confidence.

Ingo had heard from colleagues in other businesses about 'cultural audits'. Coming from the school of thought that 'smart people should be able to work together', he'd always been a little cynical of their value. But with his new-found sense of open-mindedness, he began to think that a cultural audit may be just the tool to help them to decide what they needed to do to get the juggernaut rolling. At this stage, there was nothing to be lost and much to be gained.

So, Ingo called in an outside agency to conduct the audit. The resulting 'cultural profiles' showed that JPMT was generally a 'formal' organisation, with an orderly approach to everything. In the language of the analysis, they were generally more **conceptual** in nature, particularly when it came to the way things were done and to communicating about the future. They liked evidence and used the past as a predictor of the future. When it came to who to trust and bestow power upon, this conceptual orientation was combined with a more **pragmatic** side: they valued people with strong track records, who delivered results.

InterComm, by contrast, were far more 'emotional' and people orientated. Theirs was a culture of informality. In the language of the analysis they were generally **relational** in orientation. They trusted their people and let them get on with it, unencumbered by onerous systems and procedures. They gave them space to take risks on fresh approaches and bore the consequences together, be they positive or negative. They were like a family and, as such, the values that had helped them to be so successful historically were of great importance to them. Perhaps because of this, when it came to communicating the future, the cultural audit showed a more **pragmatic** side: InterComm liked to make sure that all of their people had a clear picture of the company's objectives and of the part they would play as individuals in reaching them.

It wasn't hard to see why the new partners had clashed on so many fronts. As he and Jerry Meulen, InterComm's CEO, listened to the findings, Ingo could hear many of the comments that had been fired at him over the last few weeks slotting into place. Some of the realisations he'd already had were confirmed. Others were enriched. But perhaps most usefully, the analysis put a language to an area that was not always easy to define, and that made the picture crystal clear for the first time.

For example, when it came to **Legitimacy**, JPMT trusted and bestowed power on people with degrees and stellar performance, InterComm on bright, yet often unproven people who 'fitted the mould'. So when JPMT parachuted in its personnel, the result was a workplace where people neither trusted nor respected one another.

In terms of **Effectiveness**, JPMT had a procedure for everything, whereas InterComm saw procedures as restricting their creativity. So when JPMT imposed its working practices on the new organisation, the result was a workplace where it was impossible to get agreement on anything or to come up with workable solutions to problems.

When it came to the **Future**, JPMT felt most confident if they had a strong, yet flexible organisational structure in place, while InterComm looked to clear objectives and the protection of their values. So when JPMT created an informational black hole after the acquisition of InterComm, the result was insecurity and a lack of direction.

Had they possessed this wisdom in advance of bringing their two businesses together, things may have panned out quite differently. The differences would still have been there, but the language that they were now able to use would have made the issues less personal and easier to confront. It would have given them the power to build strategies to manage them, like the adults that they were!

Back to the Foundations

In its current state, JPMT InterComm was like a poorly constructed building, a building without foundations. It had been born out of a vision – a great one at that – but they'd rushed into construction, focusing their attentions above ground on what the world would see, forgetting about what needed to be done *below* ground to keep the building strong and upright. No surprise then that it had begun to sway at the first signs of inclement weather. What they needed to do now was to go back and underpin the building.

So they did just that. The team meetings, walkabouts and cultural audit had all given JPMT InterComm's leaders a much clearer understanding of what it would take to lead the business to success. Ingo now set about putting more structure to things. A business school alumnus to the last, he relished the opportunity to apply his finely honed project-management techniques to such a critical situation.

His first step was to combine formally the loose collection of executives who had been 'managing' the integration to date into a more formal Executive Committee, under the combined leadership of himself and Jerry Meulen. Ingo made sure that the Committee balanced both JPMT and InterComm people and that, more importantly, it reflected the different cultural preferences that the audit had highlighted. That meant **not** choosing people just because of their rank or perceived position in the hierarchy of the new organisation. Again, being able to use the data from the cultural audit to explain their choices ensured that no one's nose was put out of joint when they were not chosen.

Armed with new knowledge from the cultural audit, and under the watchful eye of their chosen external consultants, the Executive Committee got together to shape the future. One of the few advantages of having suffered so much pain in the recent past was that they were now able to negotiate agreement on goals, values, time frames, etc., with remarkable ease, and to prepare a clear mandate that could be communicated throughout the organisation.

One 'nugget' that emerged from the Executive Meeting came from Jerry Meulen. He offered the insight that, as they'd been trying to integrate, two businesses that had succeeded historically because of their unwavering focus on the customer and market, had become consumed by internal wrangling. They'd taken their respective eyes off the ball and the effects were all too clear to see. Jerry's suggestion was to couch everything moving forward in the light of an external challenge, one that was bearing down on them fast. This external focus would provide the context for everything they did forthwith and, since it affected their very survival, it would focus people on success.

So it was that all subsequent communication about the merger was related to the need to maintain JPMT InterComm's place in a market that was contracting under economic pressure and subject to increasing consolidation, meaning bigger competition and a smaller cake.

Spreading the Load

Although ultimately accountable for the success of the merger, the Executive Committee knew that it would be unable to manage the day-to-day details of the integration process, whilst still maintaining the high-level strategic viewpoint that was so critical to future success.

The short-term 'fix-it' integration team previously set up by Ingo had already shown that it could work well together and produce results. As such, it was the perfect candidate for assuming responsibility for the day-to-day running of the integration process. Consequently, the Executive Committee formalised this arrangement, giving the existing team a longer term perspective and a wider remit as it did so.

As part of the handover, the Executive Committee applied the wisdom of the cultural profile to the make-up of the Integration Team. They noticed that, in its current incarnation, the team was not a true reflection of the different preferences of the partners, so Ingo set about making one or two changes. Armed with solid data and a clear external focus as a rationale, there was nothing but co-operation from those individuals affected. Besides, there was so much to be done to bring about the rebirth of JPMT InterComm that it was easy to find new and valuable supporting roles for those who were leaving the team.

If there was one thing that the cultural audit had highlighted, it was the need to balance actions that appealed to the head with those that appealed to the heart. At this particular point, the Executive Committee realised that it was becoming a little too 'conceptual' and overly focused on process. The human dimension of JPMT InterComm was in sore need of attention and now was the time to give it.

It was fair to say that the Executive Committee, and now the Integration Team, were some way ahead of the rest of the business attitudinally. Although there had been communiqués assuring people that steps were underway to improve things around the business, it was only at the upper management levels that people really knew what was going on. Further down the organisation, there were still daily struggles, misunderstandings and temper tantrums, all as a result of the culture clash.

So the Executive Committee decided to allocate some budget for people just to get away from the business and enjoy themselves. The 'Awaydays' that were planned as a result were initially greeted with frowns and raised eyebrows. JPMT people feared that this would be one more occasion when they would be made to feel like the black sheep in Inter-Comm's family. InterComm people had nightmare visions of team-building activities that would no doubt be managed with JPMT's usual rigorous sense of process. But the event organisers were on the case and carefully constructed an event that would appeal to both company's styles. The result was that JPMT and InterComm laughed together for once.

A Time for Celebration

Simple as it was, this idea of 'celebration' was a new one for Ingo. Always a voracious reader, Ingo had complemented his walkabout through JPMT

InterComm by researching business texts and journals, looking for inspiration and cutting-edge practical thought on what could be done to help mergers to go smoothly. One of the key pearls of wisdom he'd picked up, and that always brought a smile of amusement to his face, was: 'If you want something to grow, pour champagne on it'.

The last few months had been hell for all of them. Now Ingo wanted to bring back some of the pleasure and pride that he believed everyone had once felt when they walked through the doors of JPMT or InterComm. He made sure that the mandate to the Integration Team included celebration as a key component. At the simplest level, he encouraged everyone to shout when they had successes, through newsletters, when they talked to the outside world and perhaps most of all when they talked to each other. At a more formal level, he encouraged them to create opportunities to get together, be it for work or play, as often as possible as they went about building a culture that they all owned and were proud of.

TICs and Task Forces

As employees went about getting to know one another better on the 'Awaydays', the Integration Team began the job of 'retrofitting' the foundations of JPMT InterComm.

Even though most of the business functions were some way down the road to integration, many were experiencing difficulties and some seemed to have reached an impasse, unable to find a way through their differences. Few of them were taking a truly structured approach to merging systems and processes, with many falling prey to the 'too many cooks' syndrome.

So the Integration Team appointed a series of mixed task forces to oversee the integration of all JPMT InterComm's key processes. Where a process had already been successfully, if painfully, integrated, the task force was primarily focused on monitoring and improving, and on spreading the benefit of their wisdom to other teams.

One innovation here, which participants and observers would later credit more than anything else for the resurgence of JPMT InterComm, was the creation of the role of Team Integration Coach (TIC). These individuals were charged with providing guidance and support to task forces and to a small number of specified individuals each. TICs didn't come from any particular rung on the management ladder. They were selected for their unique combination of qualities – empathy, communication and conflict resolution skills, a passion for the business – and an ability to let it all hang out!

Holly Arthur was a prime example. Part of the team that had succeeded in integrating the partner's financial systems, Holly was made TIC to the task force looking at the client relationship process, a team that was truly struggling to find an approach that worked for everyone. JPMT's conceptual Account Management Process was totally at odds with Inter-Comm's relational 'we work as a team and bring people in when we need them' approach. The task force's inability to negotiate one acceptable approach had had a high cost: clients were directly touched by the friction between old and new team members, and their confidence was undermined by seeing people that they needed to trust bickering in front of them. Relationships were damaged and, in the worst cases, lost.

Holly, who had demonstrated her ability to manage extremely challenging situations to successful outcomes in her work with the financial systems task force, began to attend client relationship team meetings. She sat on the sidelines at first, engaging team members in one-on-one coaching conversations after the meeting closed. Gradually, as she earned the trust of team members, she became more involved in meeting proceedings and, as time went on, was often to be found on the phone with a task force member dispensing valuable advice and insight that had been gained the hard way.

In general, the TICs helped task forces to take an objective viewpoint, negotiate differences, apply solid project management discipline to their work and often to learn to have fun again. Over the months, they also became one of the most valuable conduits of information between the Executive Committee and the ground.

Tooling Up

One of the key factors recognised by the Steering Committee as it considered how to move from the present to the future was that the environment they found themselves in was new and different for every employee, and that most, if not all of them, lacked the knowledge and skills needed to deal with it. At the grass roots level, for example, many had a limited understanding of change, how it might affect them or how they could develop a personal strategy to deal with it. At an executive level, team leaders lacked the skills to manage difficult situations. Although they were all personable people and had the capacity to get on well, they lacked the ability to coach one another, something that would be essential to their success on this difficult journey.

Training was the logical answer. Training had always formed a part of the JPMT way. In its traditional forms, it fitted perfectly with the company's conceptual approach to doing things, putting things in neat little boxes and following structured processes. You could always tell the JPMT delegates at any training session: they'd be the enthusiastic ones with their hands in the air waiting to answer every question. The

InterComm guys would be at the back of the room with their arms folded, asking what time the seminar would end on Friday afternoon. Training in the lock step sense was an anathema to them.

So the Integration Team was faced with a dilemma. They were all agreed that they needed to help people to develop their competencies. They just didn't know how to achieve it in a way that fitted everyone's cultural preferences. To this end, they put together a Development Team, made up of 'culturally selected' members of the partner's Human Resources functions, and tasked it with creating a programme to equip everyone in the business with the knowledge and skills they needed to fulfil their part in achieving successful integration.

The team was highly motivated, working hard, fast and long into the night to build a programme that would deliver results to the business quickly. They were acutely aware that, if they didn't fulfil their brief, the workforce could well lack the capacity to dig the new organisation out of its hole. They went into the workplace and talked to their target audience – everyone from board directors to the most junior artists – to get their perspective on what they needed and how they would like to see it delivered.

Within a few short weeks, with external help, the Development Team had devised and timetabled a curriculum of training modules that included approaches and activities that would appeal to the entire range of learning styles. The new initiative was launched with a solid communication strategy, comprising a series of voluntary informal workshops that everyone was invited to attend.

Indications from early pilot sessions with mixed groups were extremely positive. Better still, delegates from these sessions were going back to their workplace and praising the experience they'd been through. To respect individual ability and choice, the Development Team had made all of the training elective, yet quickly found that good press was leading to a level of demand that they were almost unable to meet. Particularly successful was a short half-day workshop on personal strategies for managing change. Delegates clearly valued its focus on them and their feelings, as well as the fact that it equipped them to deal more effectively with the choppy waters that they were sailing through.

From a personal perspective, Ingo was highly impressed with the way that the Development Team worked. They were a model of the very end that they were trying to achieve, bringing two disparate cultures together to work in harmony. They succeeded in applying a tight project management process to what they were doing, while maintaining enough of a sense of informality for everyone to be happy. Their entire approach to implementing their strategy seemed to respect cultural differences: elective training, using carefully mixed methodologies. One more cause for celebration!

Opening the Channels of Communication

At the same time as they were passing the mandate to the Development Team, the Integration Team turned its attention to another area that had been highlighted by the cultural audit: the way in which the sensitive issue of communication was being handled in the new organisation.

JPMT had always been a place where information was given out on a 'need to know' basis. More by luck than judgement, this approach had never caused any problems, perhaps because the company was always on an upward path, with everyone sharing in its success. It was so much easier to tolerate being kept in the dark when your stock options were growing in value by the day! So it had come as something of a surprise to Ingo to learn that even JPMT people were unhappy about the level of communication around where things were heading and what each of their roles would be. Add to that the very vocal reaction of InterComm people, for whom the informational void and lack of direction was a dark abyss the likes of which they'd never experienced before, and you had a very clear case for change.

Responding to the mandate from the Executive Committee, the Integration Team therefore set up a team to devise and implement a communications strategy that would leave employees with the clear vision of the future that they'd lacked until now. The Executive Committee had already set the trend by recognising the immediate need to talk to the troops. To this end, Ingo and Jerry, working as a double act, ran a series of meetings to acknowledge the difficulties that JPMT InterComm found itself in, and to express their desire to work with everyone to put things right. They followed this up with a series of lunchtime Q&A sessions – lunch thrown in! – to which everyone was invited and encouraged to express their opinions and feelings about what they were going through. As a side-benefit, the sessions encouraged cross-functional mixing, something that the new organisation had been less than good at as it doubled in size.

The Communications Team's strategy built on this new platform of openness and honesty. One of their early initiatives – a brave one, in that it opened them up to interrogation before any hard information was really available – was to open an 'Integration Hotline'. From 9 to 5 each and every day, a member of the team would man a phone line that employees could call anonymously with questions or concerns about the merger. More than anything, the team wanted to signal to everyone in the business that they intended to communicate transparently going forward.

The take-up was dramatic, and not just by those who'd worked in the more information-orientated InterComm environment. The early days were tough. With task forces and committees still working out the specifics of what would happen and where things would go, there was often precious little information to give to callers. But armed with skills that had been honed through training provided by the Development Team, they were able to manage the emotional side of the interaction. So, even if they didn't have precise answers to their questions, at least people felt that they were being listened to, and for many of them, that was a first in the new world of JPMT InterComm.

With the Hotline running in the background, the Communications Team set about devising a strategy for the regular communication of developments, in a way that would appeal to everyone's tastes. They considered multiple options. Video updates from the Executive Committee were cast aside; at this stage in the game, a personal commitment and physical presence from key players was vital to people's trust and buy-in. Ingo and Jerry took little persuasion to fall into line with this, and agreed to continue their walkabouts, presentations and lunchtime Q&A sessions for as long as they could without compromising the business.

The 'soft' side of the communications strategy was enhanced by involving the budding network of TICs. Once a week, they were briefed by the Communications Team on the pertinent issues of the day, so that they could act as integration 'champions' whilst coaching and supporting task forces around the business.

To complement the personal touch, the team decided to draw on the creative orientation of their business for the 'hard' side of their strategy. A monthly newsletter focused on the integration process was launched with the prime objective of drawing people towards a dedicated section of JPMT InterComm's intranet site. As well as being updated daily with pertinent news items and comments – good, bad and downright ugly – from people around the business, the site featured an e-mail discussion forum through which people could exchange ideas. For those who didn't want to talk to the Hotline, a Q&A process was set up that promised anyone posing a question a response within 48 hours. If a specific response couldn't be given, people would be told why and would be given a date by which they *could* expect a response.

As the icing on the cake, once the series of lunchtime Q&A sessions came to a close, Ingo or Jerry would be available on-line at a specified time each week to talk to anyone who wished to pick their brains.

In the early days of the communication strategy's implementation, the various media used were still predominantly crammed with gripes and grumbles. But comments on the level of two-way communication itself were never less than glowing. It also seemed that the mix of media meant that there was something for everyone, from the conceptual, through the pragmatic to the relational. Finally, employees had a voice and, what's more, the voice was being heard. As the weeks went by, the

Communications Team began to realise that a corner really had been turned, when what started as a series of places where people could let off steam evolved into a forum where people exchanged ideas.

Epilogue

The new approach didn't eliminate problems. If you were counting, you might even have noticed that it brought more to the surface. But that in itself was part of the value of the Bridging Process that JPMT InterComm had adopted. Instead of being hidden from view, being muttered about unfavourably by all and sundry, issues were now on the table, warts and all, which undoubtedly spelled progress. It meant that problems and conflicts could be analysed and solved, in the common knowledge that, if they weren't, the company that you'd given so much to may be left lagging behind, as bigger and more efficient media conglomerates forged ahead.

Results didn't come easily. Small steps didn't necessarily become giant leaps. Yet there was a definite sense that things were moving forwards. Gradually, some of the irritations that were preventing people seeing to the real problems beyond were removed. Once that happened, they began to find solutions to those bigger problems. The communications strategy meant that people knew about any wins quickly, and the new emphasis on celebration meant that people enjoyed their successes. Throughout the business, a new spirit was gradually emerging, one that said 'we're in this together and we're in it to win'.

Ingo could almost smell the change in the air as he walked round the building. As he observed mixed teams laughing together at round tables, it suddenly began to look possible. They really were going to be able to merge these tribes.

Back in his office, Ingo caught a wry smile reflected in the window. He suddenly felt that he was riding another winner.

CHAPTER 11

The Culture Bridging Code

*What I'd like to stress is the necessity to adopt some guiding principles in
any acquisition. We must avoid focusing solely on the use of specific tools,
but need to apply these tools through a set of guiding principles.*
Philippe Dabas, Human Resources Director, Henkel-Ecolab

As we move further into the twenty-first century and look at what lies
ahead, it's hard to see any let-up in the trend towards alliances, mergers,
acquisitions, joint ventures or any other permutation in the burgeoning
array of partnerships designed to respond to an increasingly dynamic
business environment. Even if it hasn't happened to you already, as an
ambitious business professional, it's highly likely that you'll find yourself involved in, maybe even leading, one of these adventures.

Yet if we look at it today, all the evidence would suggest that your
chances of achieving genuinely successful integration will be slim, no matter how 'obvious' the synergies, no matter how 'perfect' the fit of the
partners. If there's one thing that we hope we've put across through the
pages of this book, it's our absolute belief that it doesn't have to be this
way! If you stick your head in the sand and deny that there's a problem,
you're probably heading for trouble. But if you decide to acknowledge
the myriad of studies showing the importance of the cultural factor in
a successful integration, and put cultural issues squarely on the table,
you're already on the road to success. Furthermore, if you recognise
that, for the manager in the new millennium, Culture Bridging skills are
a key competency, you've moved into the fast lane.

Having read this far, you've probably begun to form your own opinions about what really counts when it comes to 'merging the tribes'. We
hope that we've given you some of the ingredients that can be blended
to achieve successful integration in your own unique situation. Now, as
we come to the close of this book, we'd like to share with you, by way
of summary, the guiding principles that we believe underpin successful cultural integration – our *Culture Bridging Code.*

The Culture Bridging Code

- Put the cultural dimension on the agenda.
- Agree on the real enemy.
- Embrace and bend with the differences.
- Build a map of the merging cultures.
- Plan, plan, plan.
- Implement quickly.
- Communicate openly and honestly.
- Make promises realistic and stick to them!
- Walk the talk ... and talk the walk.

Put the Cultural Dimension on the Agenda

My advice is to put culture management at the top of the list of priorities for action by senior management.

General manager, beverage industry

Simple as it may sound, just making sure that the issue of corporate culture is in everyone's minds as they make decisions and take actions is one of the keys to unlocking the door to successful integration.

Be deliberate in your efforts to understand and consciously address cultural issues. Make sure that, under the pressure to deal with *hard* issues, the *soft* issues are not overlooked, that the emotional is not overwhelmed by the rational. After all, a merger is as much an emotional as a rational process and you'll need 'Emotional Intelligence' to bridge the cultures involved.

Advocate the use of tools and activities that nurture a common understanding and open dialogue. In short, put the issue of culture firmly on the agenda, cultivate an environment where it's the backdrop to communication and you set yourself on the right track.

Remember: it's never too early to start wrestling with the issue of culture!

Among the biggest problems of integration are the commitments made in front of the financial analysts. The 'synergies'. These tend to speed up the integration process in such a way that results have to be obtained even before people get real ownership of their new situation, function, task, objectives and so on. The pressure is enormous. And painful. Most of us felt weary at such times. And in the company, we heard things like 'We have lost our people value', not knowing exactly what it meant. We misinterpreted it as a loss of what one would describe as a 'family feeling'. But no, there was a feeling that something human had been damaged.

Terry Morgan, Group Managing Director Operations, BAE Systems

Agree on the Real Enemy

It's a natural human tendency to defend ourselves and what we stand for in the face of an enemy. But in a merger or acquisition situation, your 'enemy', the company with whom you battled for so long to win customers and market share, often becomes your new partner.

Sadly, people don't always make the mental shift from a combative attitude to one of partnership as they join forces. Afraid that their values, beliefs and ways of doing things are under threat, and at the same time believing that those same values, beliefs and ways of doing things are the key to future sustainability, each side adopts an attack/defence mindset. As they become more and more self-absorbed, they allow the *real* enemy, the competition, to take ground from them, ground that they may never be able to win back without a titanic struggle.

It's critical for those involved in a deal to break out of this emotional, judgemental mindset. The reality is that no one side is 'right'; no one side is 'wrong'. The new organisation faces a new reality and the parties involved have to negotiate, with the foundation of Culture Bridging, a new set of responses to the challenges that they will face.

The first step towards this is to recognise that the enemy is not within. The new partners must work together and scan the external environment to find their *common* enemy. The shared, strategic response that this can generate often acts as a trigger that can change both sides' points of view. And that enemy is always 'outside'.

Embrace and Bend with the Differences

There must be a willingness on both sides of the acquisition to accept change.

Ed Shipka, CEO, Pe Ben Oilfield Services

'Integration' is tough enough when there are just two individuals concerned. Put us together and we often struggle to find the common ground that allows us to coexist in harmony. When the equation involves two or more monolithic corporate entities, the challenge is magnified many times over. Corporate cultures are carved from shared history, a history that has often involved pain and a struggle for survival. They're ingrained; they're defended; above all, they're unique. There *will* be differences. Those involved in an integration process shouldn't see this as an obstacle, just as a fact of life, as any other issue that must be managed.

This willingness to accept and to be flexible on both sides is critical. Although it certainly begins with the leadership team – as we know, curiosity and openness are characteristic of Culture Bridging masters – it's an attitude that must be fostered throughout the businesses. Although similarities in cultures may occasionally make this relatively easy, don't *expect* people to immediately change the way *they* do things to meet *your* way of doing business.

Encourage a climate where diversity is accepted as part of life, where individuals and teams see differences as something that can enrich their own world view. Although it may not always be easy, work towards a workplace where everyone's approach, so long as it is for the common good, will be listened to and accepted. Help them to understand that no one's approach is 'best', and that imposing one on another is unlikely to produce the best outcome for *anyone*. Create well-facilitated occasions for people to meet, formally and informally, to exchange ideas, work through their differences and bridge them to arrive at a solution that everyone can buy into.

The bottom line? Foster a mindset that sees an integration process, whatever the extent of the integration, not as something that threatens the status quo with the spectre of the unfamiliar, but that offers opportunities to discover very different ways to run the same business!

Schlumberger's culture is based on diversity, not on a view that there's one way to do things. This goes back a long way – diversity is part of the culture. Being different is part of our culture. This makes acquisitions possible and easier.

Euan Baird, CEO, Schlumberger

Embracing and bending...
Another principle was 'respect for people, respect for cultures'. No one was in a position to impose his or her culture. And we knew that the issue was not to create one 'global' culture but to manage diversity.

Jean Favarel, Head of Social Development, BNP Paribas

Once it's clear that people share a common sense of purpose and direction, the Alcan culture allows for a lot of diversity.

Gérard de Saint Remy, retired CEO of Alcan de France and its major subsidiary, Technal

If you find people willing to sit down and work things out sensibly, things will work. We succeeded in merging the pilot lists of BA and British Caledonian in only 12 weeks. This was due to the willingness of the union side to work with flight management, and the logical, reasonable approach of flight management. Both sides worked trying to find solutions, without raising each other's hackles.

Lord Colin Marshall of Knightsbridge, Chairman of British Airways, on British Airways' acquisition of British Caledonian

We look on cultural differences as an opportunity rather than a problem.

Tryggve Sthen, CEO, Volvo Global Trucks

Build a Map of the Merging Cultures

A model would have been very helpful in giving us support during a chaotic time and in helping us to accelerate organisational effectiveness and performance.

Ed Shipka, CEO, Pe Ben Oilfield Services

Corporate culture isn't the easiest thing in the world to define. There are no hard edges to give it shape, no universally accepted language with which to describe it. It can be particularly difficult to define what it is when you're within it.

In an integration situation – perhaps the time when your own corporate culture comes to the fore – you're under pressure from all sides. It can be almost impossible to see the wood for the trees. But this is precisely the time when you need to understand your own cultural profile and that of your prospective partner. Only if you understand where your similarities and differences lie do you stand any chance of building a plan that will take each side's needs into account, and that will lead to the win–win solution that's one of the foundations of successful integration.

Don't be fooled into thinking that you can apply 'general recipes' for integration to happen. Each situation is unique and that uniqueness needs to be understood if the potential synergies are to be realised. So build a cultural map that will provide both a common understanding of your cultures and a common language with which you can discuss them.

Get outside help. Engage someone with the expertise to examine *objectively* the cultures of each party; someone who can bring the unspoken and taboo into the open; someone who can provide you with comprehensive, comprehensible and *actionable* data that can feed into your integration planning. If you can, commission a Cultural Audit – applying a model such as the Culture Bridging Fundamentals diagnostic – probably the most practical and beneficial vehicle for generating a cultural map.

In the absence of a formal Cultural Audit, be your own cultural cartographer. Think culture at all times. Like a Blue Loop manager, ask 'What's going on here?' Then use your initiative to structure the answers. Share your thoughts with others and encourage them to share their thoughts with you.

> The culture bridging diagnostic raised awareness among our people as to the importance of cultural integration. It helped them better understand why managers coming from a company other than their own would react in such and such a way when working together.
>
> It helped us unify our vocabulary, and we sent out a glossary on our intranet, defining key words like 'challenge' or 'target cost'.
>
> *(continued)*

We then launched training programs in the areas of cost management, quality management and time management, based on the best
practices of each of the partners.

Sector president, European plastics company

Plan, Plan, Plan

Before you begin, you need a battle plan.

Patrick J Rich, Retired Chairman, Royal Packaging Van Leer

An acceptance that culture is an issue, a climate in which diversity is
embraced and solid information on which to act are all part of the
foundation for success when it comes to integration. That foundation
is further strengthened by a fourth element, planning.

The partners in a new organisation need a detailed, well thought
through plan to help to turn their good intentions into reality: a project-
based plan, built on the principles of Culture Bridging, that will provide
a roadmap for addressing the business issues, human resources issues
and communications issues that will need to be managed.

This plan is as important as any strategic plan that the organisation
will ever have to come up with. It should be simple enough for everyone in the new organisation to understand and buy into. As a roadmap,
it should be explicit, including a few clear goals, as well as key milestones
and achievements.

As you build your plan, focus on the three key areas highlighted by
the Culture Bridging Fundamentals diagnostic: Legitimacy, Effectiveness
and Future. If you keep them at the forefront of your analysis and decision making, you'll be addressing the challenges that are the hotbeds of
cultural conflict.

Remember too as you decide on actions, events and communication
to aid integration that you should appeal to each of the head, heart *and*
muscle. For example, to appeal to those whose style is *relational*, plan
events that get people together to share thoughts and feelings. For the
pragmatic, ensure that you devise processes for getting things done that
are free from red tape. For the *conceptual*, make sure that you explain
the reasons for doing what you're doing.

Remember: planning doesn't stop when integration begins. An integration plan cannot be static. Because you won't be able to plan for *all*

the eventualities in advance – sometimes you just don't know what you don't know! – the integration plan should be seen as a dynamic, living, breathing thing.

> Having a good sense of what you want to do with the business is very important. You can't invent as you go.
> *Senior manager, strategy consulting firm*

Implement Quickly

The prospect of a merger or acquisition often causes worry and uncertainty for anyone who's not in the driving seat. The longer the period between the deal 'going public' and tangible indicators of things starting to happen, the more those concerns are likely to grow.

As they grow, speculation – rarely a positive thing – increases by the hour. Facts are thrown into the mix that may not be true but that have a way of becoming self-fulfilling prophecies. Myths emerge and suddenly become reality. Before you know it, the new partnership is on the back foot before it's even left the starting blocks, and rather than beginning its new journey in a spirit of excitement, it begins it in turmoil.

So, implement quickly! Follow tight timelines for planning and get things happening. Squash the rumours with swift action that demonstrates how things are really going to be. Focus on quick wins that are visible to the workforce. If they aren't visible, make them visible!

A cautionary note though. In your haste to make things happen, make sure that you give people enough time to breathe. Moving *too* quickly can have a detrimental effect on motivation that may neutralise the very value that you were aiming to create.

> One of our most important principles was: **go fast**. We really gave a timeframe to the market and we were forced to stick to it. This is the famous 6 days to appoint the Executive group, 6 weeks for the key executives of the businesses, 6 months for the management to be nominated and for the organisation to be settled. 6, 6, 6 – it had a tremendous psychological impact internally as well as externally.
> *Jean Favarel, Head of Social Development, BNP Paribas*

An integration should be fast enough to maintain the momentum, but not so fast as to kill motivation.
Terry Morgan, Group Managing Director Operations, BAE Systems

Communicate Openly and Honestly

One success factor for integration is certainly the openness of the first interactions.
Terry Morgan, Group Managing Director Operations, BAE Systems

My advice to top management is to be very open in the early phase of the merger. We were honest when we revealed that this merger would lead to a reduction in the number of production sites, as well as in the number of employees. We didn't hide the fact. But at the same time, we argued that bigger and more modern production sites would provide better working conditions and climate. The new structure would be of benefit not only to the owners, but also to the employees.
Jens Bigum, CEO Arla Foods, on the merger between Danish-based MD Foods and Swedish-based Arla

Just as dragging your heels over implementation is a recipe for discontent, so is poor communication – either the communication of misinformation or, in the most extreme cases, the lack of any communication at all.

People need information to be both willing and able to perform their role. They need to know what's in store for them, how changes may affect their world and those of the people around them. The longer they're kept in the dark, the lower morale slips. Even though it may be painful, bad news is rarely more damaging than dishonest or partial communication that later turns out to be untrue. This tends to have a much more widespread damaging effect that can be difficult to reverse.

Although there will undoubtedly be times when you don't have *information* to communicate, don't use that as an excuse for not communicating at all. Content isn't the only aspect of communication that sends a message, the very act of communicating does so too. Keep the channels open, even when you have few of the answers that people might ideally be looking for. Gather people together; listen to what they have to say; tell them what you can tell them; and when you *can't* tell them, tell them why and tell them when you *will* be able to tell them. As long as you then keep your promises, you'll go a long way to building the trust and buy-in that you'll need to help integration happen.

> Communication has to be reliable and honest and in the right order. It's important to promise the employees that they will be the first to get the news about their specific working place – and to keep that promise. Don't let them get any important information via the newspapers or the television.
>
> *Kjeld Johannesen, CEO, Danish Crown*

Make Promises Realistic and Stick to Them!

All of us know just how disappointing and demotivating it is when promises are broken. Apart from the simple fact that things we expected to happen *don't* happen, a dangerous new precedent is set: we start to *expect* future promises to be broken. When this happens, trust – a cornerstone of successful integration – breaks down, sometimes irrevocably.

The leaders of a new organisation will be under major scrutiny by their troops. The more cynical of those troops will be watching and waiting for slip-ups, maybe looking for the opportunity to say 'I told you so' to colleagues whose attitude to the new entity may be in the balance.

Don't give them the chance to upset the hornet's nest! When you promise something, make sure that you deliver it, particularly in the early days of the merger when people are likely to be most nervous and cynical. If anything, err on the side of caution when you communicate what will be. If you deliver more, it will only come as a pleasant surprise!

> The success of the merger is dependent on your ability to meet the results you have promised – or better than that: a bit more than you have promised. Being eager to get the top job often makes people
>
> (*continued*)

(the new top manager) promise too much – which leads to disappointment and lack of motivation – and the risk of getting sacked by the owners. For this reason, it's very important to set low economic goals for the first and second year. Promise a bit less than you expect. In this way you gain respect and win over the sceptics.

Kjeld Johannesen, CEO, Danish Crown

Walk the Talk ... and Talk the Walk

They really weren't interested in facilitating individual points of difference in the business culture – they talked a lot about 'diversity' but the reality was very different.

Commercial vice-president, beverage industry

There's another angle to keeping the promises that you make, and that's making sure that your words match your deeds. Just as with promises broken, there's little more demotivating than seeing managers espouse openness, active listening, empathy, etc., and then watching them keep people in the dark, fail to respond to concerns or behave in a way that's 'unfeeling'.

In short, the members of the Executive Committee and the Integration Team must also be Culture Bridging masters. They must walk the talk. Although it may take effort at a time when there's so much else to do, leaders must consistently check their own behaviour to ensure that there's synchronicity between what they say and what they do. Lip service just won't cut it. They'll tumble you in an instant.

In the process, don't forget the other side of the coin: talk the walk as well! Communicate and broadcast the steps that you're taking to manage the integration process, take diversity into account and move forward together with your new partners. These are not things to be kept secret: quick wins and real commitment are wonderful levers for change, so use them fully.

The company we acquired had individuals representing them who were very positive and open to the whole idea. They saw opportunities rather than problems and that was a good starting point.

Tryggve Sthen, CEO, Volvo Global Trucks

Conclusion

Our motivation for writing this book came from the profound conviction that culture matters; and that if it's factored in to the planning and implementation of mergers, acquisitions or any other type of strategic alliance, the organisation that results can make a far more powerful contribution to the global economy.

Our motivation also came from the observation that this relationship is all too often overlooked. We hope that, by reading this book, we've at the very least heightened your sensitivity to the issue of corporate culture in integration situations. If we've succeeded in doing that, we hope that we've *also* given you some serious food for thought about how the issues raised when corporate cultures come together can be managed, through the tools and techniques of Culture Bridging.

There's no precise formula for Culture Bridging, no recipe that we can give you that will guarantee success. But we know that with the right attitude and the three tools we've worked through in this book – the Culture Bridging Fundamentals diagnostic, an integration process built on Culture Bridging and the Culture Bridging competencies – woven together in a way that fits your own unique circumstances, you'll make a whole lot more progress than the frightening array of managers who stick their heads in the sand at the mention of the word culture.

Treat it right and integration can be a real thrill ride, with ups and downs, but with an overall effect that leaves you feeling that you've really conquered something.

It can be scary; but go on! Take your blinkers off, get your head down and prepare to tackle the two-headed monster. Who knows, you may find yourself quoted in that book about 'The World's Most Successful Merging of the Tribes' that's just waiting to be written.

Leaders Talk About Their Experience

The following set of interviews captures what senior leaders have to say about their experience of mergers, acquisitions and alliances. Each one tells his or her story in terms of their specific experience. Some are more technical, others are more impressionistic. Some come from large multi-nationals, others from medium-sized companies. But all of them insist that the management of cultural issues is critical to success when you bring two or more companies together. All of them highlight the kinds of difficulties that they faced in the integration process and each of them gives his or her own recommendations, based on personal experience, about how to engage successfully in a similar adventure.

Interview with Gérard de Saint Remy

Retired CEO, Alcan de France and its major subsidiary, Technal

What acquisition situations did you face when you were CEO of Alcan de France and of its major subsidiary, Technal?

There were two. The first was the acquisition by Alcan, a large, inter-national Canadian group, of Technal, a small- and medium-sized com-pany in southern France. The second was the development of Technal as a mini-multinational within the Alcan group through acquisitions outside of France.

Can you tell us something about the Alcan acquisition of Technal?

The cultural differences and values of the two organisations lay at opposite sides of the spectrum. The Alcan culture is a technological, production culture, with strong requirements for financial results. The business is closely monitored and planned. What counts is performance against objectives. It is a culture of engineers and financial controllers, closely monitoring performance such as production per person per hour, etc. The Alcan 'Blue Book' of procedures forces rigor and provides a sense of 'justice' since decisions are made on the basis of objective facts.

Furthermore, Alcan's culture had developed in an international context. Canada is not a culturally monolithic culture, and Alcan's culture isn't either. Upper echelons of management are open to people from different cultures and this was the case in how they approached Technal, demonstrating a tolerance of difference – so long as everyone agrees to pursue the same objectives and work in the same direction. Once it's clear that people share a common sense of purpose and direction, the Alcan culture allows for a lot of diversity.

Technal on the other hand was a family-owned company, with all that implies in terms of lack of transparency and subjective decision-making. Its enormous strength lay in its commercial culture. Technal has always been highly reactive, non-strategic, and totally client-focused. It's a culture of design, marketing, creativity, and paid little attention to figures except for annual turn-over. For Technal at that time, results and turn-over were basically considered to be the same thing.

To some extent, I'd even say that the client-focused aspect was extreme. When Alcan took over Technal, the client was king to the extent that the company never said 'no', even if it meant getting into a non-profitable situation. Marketing and sales teams lived under constant stress of satisfying the client.

These were the two cultures that needed to be bridged.

What were the critical success factors for Culture Bridging between Technal and Alcan?

Shared purpose, direction, principles and objectives. The first thing I decided was to bridge the gap between Technal and Alcan by drawing up a Technal Charter. Alcan had prepared one, with underlying principles and values. I believed this was important, but there was also a Machiavellian side to this. If we could draw up a Technal Charter, compatible with the Alcan one, then we'd have our shared mission and objectives. I would be able to demonstrate the compatibility between the two organisations and turn to Alcan to plead for tolerance as Technal evolved. This is what I did, orienting the Technal charter around the concept of 'wealth creation' (people were not saying 'value creation' at the time) for clients, employees and shareholder. In other words, I decided to build on *the* basic block in the Alcan culture that would make differences easiest to accept. Demonstrating a shared sense of purpose within Alcan was my ticket to diversity. This was a paradoxical move often used in change management: you affirm one position in order to obtain its converse. In this case, I wanted Technal to demonstrate similarity in order to obtain more lee-way for its differences.

Share and cascade objectives. The next step was to ensure each person knew the objectives and understood how s/he contributed to meeting these and we achieved this through a cascading process via the management line.

Tighten up procedures. As is the case with many family-owned companies, particularly sales and marketing ones, Technal did not have many systems and procedures. We built on the Alcan 'Blue Book', which got us out of the family-style subjective management practices into something that felt more 'fair' and 'just', including with respect to remuneration.

Deliver results. An essential critical success factor is that Technal quickly generated increasingly good results, thanks to improving financial controls and implementing a performance management system. This was fortunate because we had to fight against a far bigger system and I was afraid that the Technal culture would be swallowed whole by the industrial culture of Alcan. But our performance really helped us and these excellent financial results came very rapidly. In addition to helping us build our credibility, as a result of our profit contribution the Alcan people didn't care – perhaps not even realise – how different Technal really was.

What about Technal's acquisitions?

Technal's internationalisation was built on the same concept of shared values, clients, service and transparency as existed within Alcan, and that Technal had developed as a result of its integration into the Alcan group. However, here, I ran into differences in national culture here, around the issue of values. To give just a few, rapid examples:

'Transparency'.

- In France, the notion of 'transparency' evoked anecdotal curiosity, and sometimes even an unhealthy insistence that everyone know everything. 'Transparency' here did not inspire confidence.

- In the UK, transparency was an essential feature of the organisation. People needed to know what was important for them to do their job, but that was it.
- In Spain and Portugal, this notion created surprise and people wondered 'why are they telling us this?'

Conflict resolution.

- In North America, people discuss, they express issues openly and explicitly. This is part of what I call Anglo-Saxon professionalism.
- In Latin countries we are more emotional about things. People confuse 'task' and 'person' and so it is more difficult to discuss openly.

What Culture Bridging strategies did you adopt here?

Performance management system. It was difficult to implement but was one of the levers for bridging cultural differences. Depending on the country, we had to communicate, communicate, communicate, explaining every step of the process, and how it would work. Finally, we got the point where people who had not had their annual performance appraisal were requesting it, because they had understood it was a moment for them to express their views and to reduce conflict. Nonetheless, in countries like Spain and Portugal it was very difficult to implement and took about two years to get it going.

International transfers. This involved transferring people for significant assignments (two years, for example) between the international subsidiaries of Technal. Alcan had never sent Canadian trainees to us to acquire the Technal marketing competence. We found that this policy of mobility created strong personal links as well.

Multidisciplinary, multinational task forces. We set up task forces for product development, marketing, information systems, in order to get people working together on a subject of interest, and with the obligation to deliver results.

Training. I sent high potential managers to Canada for training courses. People appreciated this and it created a sense of complicity between the international participants on the course. This is the cement that topples cultural differences: you set common objectives and you strengthen the networks.

Common information system. We encouraged subsidiaries to propose information system resources to one another. The strongest lever for integrating the UK subsidiary turned out to be when they adopted and implemented an information system that had been developed in one of the French subsidiaries. And then we moved it into the other French subsidiaries as well.

Bottom-up. An information system is a strong lever for integration, but the other important point here is that we were ready to adopt systems developed within the group, not only at the centre. This information system was developed within the group and then adopted at HQ and in the largest subsidiary. This kind of 'bottom-up' movement is important for generating buy-in to an integration process.

Interview with Ivar Hafsett

Strategic Advisor, Hydro Light Metals

What were your biggest surprises when acquiring companies?

For one thing, acquisitions are all different. Two acquisitions are never similar because there are different components in each culture. For example, if you buy a privately-owned company or a subsidiary of a large multinational, you immediately notice differences in the decision making processes and in existing managerial competencies. Local management really acts differently depending on previous ownership. After a few acquisitions you understand there is a pattern in post-acquisition processes and then it's possible to prepare oneself. In any case, what will matter most is attitude: our attitude with respect to those we acquire and their attitude with respect to us.

What is the impact of these differences in management style on an acquisition or merger?

The biggest issue is that a very successful local management, with a 'hands-off' private owner, may not find a 'good home' in a multinational company. The local manager may be used to a certain type of decision making process that makes it difficult for him or her to work in a new and global organisation. By the same token, former management may feel like a lid is being taken off if a new, less autocratic and less centralised owner gives local management freedom.

The Nordic culture is not very hierarchical and this is felt to be an advantage by local 'doers'. But there is a drawback. We do not have a managerial culture, and so are not the best placed to follow up on a performance plan. When ABB was formed in the mid eighties, it was perceived to be a good match between the Swedes who defined policy and the Swiss who were the doers. It might not have worked well had the roles been reversed.

What have been the major difficulties you have faced?

The biggest difficulties are on the people front, when people cannot communicate and have bad feelings. 50% of acquisitions fail because of that.

Of course communication is time consuming and sometimes people's concerns are not the most important issue around. However, *communication is critical* for the success of the acquisition.

The human resource factor is the main factor for success and it needs a lot of attention.

What Culture Bridging strategies did you employ?

First of all, I would never attempt to make an acquisition if the acquisition is not perceived as a good thing for the target company.

Then, our corporate philosophy is to try as far as possible to retain the management of the acquired company and give them a 'better home' in order to increase motivation. We believe that this contributes to our reputation and that the reputation of the acquirer towards the management of the acquired firm is important. We try to make our way of doing concrete things and to demonstrate concretely what we bring in terms of tools, market knowledge, operational concepts, financing, etc.

In the worst case, if all else fails and if there is real incompatibility, the management needs to be replaced. This is a case-by-case issue. And if power was never shared in the organisation or if the employees feel they have lost their 'legitimate managers', the challenge is greater. That's why we believe that the legitimacy of the project is so important – it is the only justification for getting rid of existing management.

What advice would you give a colleague about to acquire a company?

It is an advantage for multinational companies not to be mono-cultural. If they are neutral, they will more easily be able to take up valuable elements of newly acquired companies from other cultures. For example, our headquarters are in a neutral place (Switzerland) and top management is recruited from many nationalities, preventing our culture from becoming 'too Nordic'.

We believe it is important to integrate national cultures, to try and understand them and not try to change too much. We should let the Italians stay Italian, but we have to try to understand them and take this learning into account in our dialogue with them.

Corporate culture also has to be taken into account. So Hydro Aluminium goes beyond language and national differences and acknowledges that ways of doing things and managing business are different within companies, even from the same country or in the same business.

You have to be perceived as a 'good owner'. In other words, if you don't think that you can offer a 'better home' for the company you acquire, then cancel the deal. As a corollary, we believe it's important to give local management a kind of ownership of their business – to take the lid off so they can create their own performance. Nobody wants to be 'talked to', so we offer them a 'menu' (tools, etc.) and let local managers choose their meal. However, if we give power and independence to local management, we also expect accountability.

In some industries, it's possible to let the acquisition stand alone. But when you acquire a company that is in the same business, you have to integrate it and make it part of your organisation. In those situations, work at removing obstacles and don't wait too long to do this. People need to accept that you are the new owner.

And finally, select your management team carefully. When working in the same industry, you have the opportunity to know who the managers of your competitors are. So you know them when you sit across from them at the negotiation table. You can 'test people' and make your selection at that time.

Relationships between the new owner and the subsidiary are particularly critical during the post-acquisition integration process.

Interview with Håkan Hallen

Executive Vice-President Human Resources, Volvo Global Trucks

What were your biggest surprises when you first interacted with the companies you acquired?

I was coming from the outside and had only been two years with Volvo. I expected the Volvo people (acquirer) to expect a lot from the deal and for Mack and Renault VI (acquired) people to be more resistant, not wanting to be involved. But in fact, the reverse happened! The Renault VI/ Mack people were very receptive and cooperative. They wanted to understand what Volvo was all about. And the Volvo people were less willing to change, whereas they need to change!

What were the main differences you noted in the ways of working?

I noted two major differences:

- Expectations of managers and management style, both with respect to people's own managers and with respect to feelings about what they should do themselves. The different partners had different views and practices here.
- Different senses of urgency. The closer the culture is to the customers the faster it goes. State-owned companies have a different sense of urgency – for example, they allow more time for meetings. Differences in decision-making styles, which create frustration in multicultural meetings. For example:
  - The Americans are always ready to speak up whenever the top guy is in the room and even if they do not know the subject.
  - The French also speak up. They need to talk about things and explore different options. They have no problem with decisions if they have had a chance to discuss.
  - The Swedes don't speak up as much and get frustrated to see the Americans talking about things they do not necessarily understand and they get frustrated with the French whom they feel never stop discussing.
  - These differences between the Latins and the Anglo-Saxons, which have a lot to do with how we use time, are a source of a lot of frustration.

How did you bridge in the area of selecting managers, identifying success criteria and recruitment guidelines?

We generally had no difficulty selecting people for the level just below the CEO and there was no competition except in one or two cases. The decision criteria were a mix of need for diversity and respect for the different companies. We did face culturally different approaches.

- The French were very quick to identify candidates. Often they already had a person in mind before and they defined the job profile around the candidate.
- The Swedes were more open to considering a variety of candidates. They were not so strongly linked to the persons they knew.

- In the USA, the President went and talked to the people before advertising the jobs.

Our staffing policy placed our strategic target at 25% non-local managers in the top teams of each company/country. We strongly believe that multicultural teams are essential for global success.

What got people on board?

All three parties want to contribute to success, although their behaviours are different.

- In Mack (USA), what counts is the possibility of being at the table and influencing products and decisions. They want to feel personally part of the success.
- In Sweden, they also want to be at the table to influence decisions, but then they want to be left alone to implement them. Daily contact/control is by definition negative control.
- In Renault VI (France), they want to be able to talk and be seen by their bosses. They excel in technical issues, even with complicated things.

At one level, we discovered a willingness to change. Our aim was to hear people say: 'I will do whatever I can to change and commit to changing my way of doing things. I am ready to engage with your guys to change things together'. And we did. But it's not a linear process. For example, once people agreed to something new together, like having a new and common Performance Management System, they also started arguing for their own existing system.

How did you go about facilitating integration?

To begin with, we quickly noticed that the word 'integration' was badly received by people. So we stopped talking about 'integration' and began talking about 'shaping' our new culture and group.

We first defined a list of behaviours that would lead us towards profitability and efficiency. Our behaviours are broad enough to be accepted by the different cultures.

The Group Executive Team then signed off on four main work streams that would help shape our new culture. We selected a network of cultural champions to implement the various activities. These included:

- *Leadership*: a global and very focused leadership program. We insist on 2 roles for the manager – his/her role as a coach and his/her responsibility for shaping the new culture

- *Policy Progress Alignment*: implementing a common performance management system
- *Team building*: a 34-question internet tool to help teams improve their teamwork skills
- *Internal communication*: we have communicated a lot in our corporate magazines, and published a special edition on cultural aspects. We also use our e-magazine, organise feedback sessions on the results of our cultural audit, etc.

What advice would you give to a CEO who has to integrate a new acquisition?

If you want to avoid major problems, my four recommendations are:

- Take these cultural issues seriously.
- Sit down, define and shape common processes together.
- Identify the similarities and differences between the corporate cultures, but be sure you have a clear idea of what you want to do with that information to move things forward.
- You need to integrate cultural findings to how you then manage your priority business issues.

Interview with Torben Laustsen

Head of Group Identity and Communications, Nordea

What is the 'acquisition history' of Nordea?

Nordea is the result of two recent mergers and one acquisition. The first merger took place in 1997 between Merita (FI) and Nordbanken (SE), resulting in the formation of 'MeritaNordbanken'. The second one took place in April 2000 when MeritaNordbanken merged with Unidanmark (DK). In December 2000 they acquired the Norwegian bank K-Bank. Nordea is a pan-Nordic financial corporation integrating banking and insurance.

How did you approach the second merger between MeritaNordbanken and Unidanmark?

We began by developing a shared vision. In a merger process companies often start by spending a lot of time designing the new organisation, then clarifying the synergies between the companies and only as a last step formulating a corporate statement for the new merged company. In this case we did it the other way round. We began with the values and corporate statement, then moved on to synergies and as a third step designed the organisation.

In other words, even before the official announcement of the merger, top managers spent a lot of time testing and discussing values and vision: What were our common values and where did we differ in opinion? What were our common Nordic culture and values? How did we view our common Nordic future? In this way we formulated our corporate statement, which enabled us to point out the synergies in our combined businesses. Without this common frame of reference we might have ended up with ideas about possible synergies that would prove to be unrealistic when people actually began to work together in daily operations. Furthermore, this proactive approach ensured a relatively high degree of commitment and buy-in among the top managers that were to be ambassadors of the new reality after the merger.

We were able to use 70% to 80% of our former corporate statements as a basis and then we added the new elements which were further stretching our new common corporate statement. This included a strong brand focusing on Nordic innovation and partnership with our customers. Our corporate statement provides the direction for everything we do in our business. This is the foundation of our value-based leadership. On this basis we have launched a process we call 'From words to action'. This involves each of the 40,000 employees in a discussion of how the Nordea values can be an asset in the daily operations of their local units benefiting their work, customer service and thereby ultimately our shareholders.

How important was the name change?

Our new name became a driving force in the integration process. We all left our former names behind and this very visual and noticeable change creates momentum without which reengineering business processes would be difficult.

We looked for a name that mirrored our corporate statement and the region in which we are doing business. We wanted a name that could be used in all our markets without cultural barriers and misunderstandings and that would signal the future – something we could grow into. Nordea is a combination of 'Nordic' and 'Ideas': we share Nordic ideas and exchange Nordic ideas to create value for our customers and thereby for our shareholders.

What differences did you identify?

Although we are all Nordic, significant differences exist between us. Both the Danish and the Swedish decision cultures are very consensus-driven. You are expected to involve all stakeholders who will be affected by a decision in how that decision will be implemented so they can feel part of the decision process. Swedes continue to discuss the matter until they have found a solution that everybody feels good about and can support, while Danes might reach a decision faster and respect that a decision has been taken and then implement it, which may sometimes lead to changes later in the process. The Finnish decision-making culture is more hierarchical – management often makes decisions without involving so many people. The Norwegian decision-making culture seems to be most like the Danish one.

On an overall level though, we feel that we, as Nordic 'brothers and sisters', are similar enough to be able to communicate well while different enough to inspire one another.

Decision making. I experienced the difference between the Finnish and the Danish way of making decisions in my own organisation when I found out that my Finnish middle managers were already implementing a decision we had *talked* about, but in my mind not yet taken. 'But you said that you preferred this decision and you are the boss', said my Finnish counterpart. 'Yes, but it is your responsibility to provide me with the necessary information regarding local conditions so we can avoid making the wrong decision. I don't intend to overrule your professional expertise', I answered him.

Language. When Merita and Nordbanken merged, Swedish was chosen as the corporate language because many Finns understand and speak Swedish. But some Finns may have perceived this as a defeat. When Nordea was created after the next merger, we chose English as our corporate language because it would give all four nationalities the same conditions and is more international.

So our challenge is to see to it that the fact that we all have to speak in a foreign language does not result in communication becoming the lowest common denominator.

The lack of language skills can slow down the change process because some people can't manage to contribute their opinions in English. For some, it even nourishes antagonism because they perceive their lack of language skills as a barrier and feel left out of the process. We try to highlight the challenge by saying: 'Beware that you do not go from being a "master" of what you can say, to becoming a "slave" because of what you *fail* to say'.

On a positive note it should be said that the translation from local languages into English and vice versa has increased our awareness as to the importance of nuances. This has probably made our communication in local languages more precise and accurate than before.

Still, language problems may reinforce cultural differences and do increase the challenges for many employees, leaders and project managers. They suddenly need to have good group dynamic skills in order to understand and feel how people with different cultural backgrounds may react in certain situations and enhance mutual understanding. It becomes a common challenge to develop such social and inter-cultural bridging skills which become as important as the professional ones.

While not everyone may be equally good at developing such inter-cultural skills, for those who do, this truly widens their horizons and lifts their overall level of competence.

What advice can you give to others engaged in a cultural integration process?

There are four things I'd like to leave people with:

- Be aware that it is very important to allocate enough time in the first phase to investigate the cultural differences and test existing opinions and values. Do this together with your new partners so that you can formulate, together, the values and vision for the new company.
- Find a new name. This can be the key to shaping the new corporate culture. Don't choose a name that simply combines past cultures. Create a name that embodies your unique contribution to the market and reflects something that you can grow into.
- Engage in open and honest communication with all stakeholders. Prepare them for new decisions and get them onboard as rapidly as possible.
- Good interactive skills are perhaps the most important leadership skill in the merged company. Choose new leaders accordingly and ensure that they have a good platform for being ambassadors of the new reality.

Interview with Fred Reid

President and COO, Delta Airlines

Can you tell us how the SkyTeam Alliance started out?

SkyTeam now has six sides. Before it had two. There was an early recognition that the two need to co-exist. We started out with a number. We started there: this alliance must produce X and here are the 7 things we need to do to achieve it. Having done all that, there was a broad awareness that our good intentions could become subject to derailment through cultural miscues.

What cultural miscues did you come up against?

None of us came into the deal with a cultural template. The Europeans are by definition more international than Americans. I was the executive responsible for building the alliance and by fate had spent 31 of 50 years outside of the USA.

There were a lot of common features between the two companies and they were more prevalent than the differences. There was an enormous desire to succeed and not to fall into cultural pitfalls. We each were fully aware that the other guy had something we didn't. The French wanted to learn about hub management, IT, etc. And we wanted to get more global and savvy about other markets.

Delta was willing to dive in earlier. Americans generally seem to feel that 60% of the information is enough to start applying it and adjust as we go. But the French wanted to test and analyse more. There's no right and wrong to that.

We underestimated the way people come to conclusions. The problems we face are the same. The hard thing is that people can come to the same conclusions through different logical structures. If you argue over these, you lose.

For example, our business involves trading inventory and we have completely different philosophies on inventory management. So when Air France said 'Give us 100 seats, and we'll give you 100, whether we use them or not', we said, 'No let's have it be more fluid'. Well, neither side would move. Then I said 'We'll do it your way for 1 year for 80% of the flights and for the rest we'll do it my way. At the end of the year, if you are disadvantaged, I'll write you a check'.

As it turned out, we were making money with their system, but we thought we could get more with our system. In any case, you need to test your assumptions. It's about trying something one way, even if it isn't your way, and adjusting if it doesn't work. Compromise is the answer.

What are the key qualities of a leader that will make an integration work?

Two words: patience and tolerance. Without losing the rigor of the end game, which is all about profit, synergy, productivity, sense of urgency and creating something good. Having been on the ground floor of building the Star Alliance, I've had a lot of time to play in this sandbox.

Another quality is open-mindedness.

The last notion is willingness, not making assumptions too early.

What advice can you give other leaders on making an alliance work?

Ask yourself the one important question: am I better off with you or without you? That's the only question. And don't carve up the pie. The small guy will get *much* more than the big guy in a relative sense, so don't look at the size of the pie. The only thing that counts: am I better off with you or without you?

Expand the hub. You need a tightly linked alliance team as a hub. But don't have the intersection occur only at the alliance team. You need to bring the spokes into the room too: maintenance with maintenance, finance with finance, etc. We asked people on both sides of our alliance to make up a plan and work it out and learn from one another. You need to spread the interaction across a wide base and get the functional experts together. It's important to have governing board meetings at least two times per year. That's the meeting of the heads of state.

Interview with Mr Sheng

Chairman, The Romon Group

The Romon Group manufactures clothes for domestic and export markets in China. The textile sector generally provides China with its first or second most important source of international currencies. The Romon Group owns its own brand (Romon) that is sold through its own distribution network of more than 1,500 outlets in China.

The Romon Group was founded in 1984 by Mr Sheng's father, who started his first business at 18, with no formal business education.

Mr Sheng is currently 31 years old and took on the Chairman position two years ago, raising turnover by 25% to US$1 billion.

This text is a compilation of many long discussions with Mr Sheng on the issues surrounding doing business internationally.

What have you found difficult in working internationally?

I have tried to learn from others which companies succeed in Europe and what they have done in order to succeed. They are always ready to give me answers, which makes me think they must know something that I do not know. However, their answers are always vague. For example, one French executive explained to me that textile companies in Europe survive because they 'optimise their organisation'. But this does not mean very much to me, here in China.

Americans have offered to make deals with us. They are very concrete and they have all sorts of technical processes. But can I use all of this in China? Which are the tools that will be most relevant here?

The Japanese understand us best. They know we are not able to integrate all new things all at once. The most important thing for us when dealing with the Japanese is that we can see very concretely *who*, in their company, is going to be in charge of working with us, and so who we will be able to turn to in our dealings.

So you find that people from different countries approach work with you in different ways?

Yes. My staff reports to me that the French always keep explaining to us why we should not do one thing or another. We are not so interested in 'why', and not so interested in what we should 'not do'. What we want to know is what we 'should' do, and 'how'. We already know that things are managed differently in China!

For example, we want to know direct outcomes. We want to be able to see what we'll get if we work together. And then we want to know, concretely, what should we do first? And how, in practical, concrete terms, will this help us reach our target. The French managers we have talked to begin with emphasising why we should do one thing or another and then talk about the decisions and actions that will be implemented. None of this is very concrete.

With the Japanese, again it's different. They don't get into the big picture, but give only a brief reminder of objectives. Then they immediately get into what we will do first and, most important, *who* will be in charge on their side. Then that specific person immediately presents what s/he will start with and who s/he wishes to work with on our side in terms of profile and experience. This makes things much easier.

Are there any other things that are important for you when you work with people from other countries?

Yes. I believe it is essential that my people are all involved, at their own level, in decisions and actions. I have had problems with some projects when one European partner has consistently escalated problems to me, complaining that things are not being done efficiently by my people. This is a problem for me.

With other partners, it has been easier. They understand that they have to deal with their counterparts in my organisation first. I don't want people to deny there is a problem. They have to address it. But to address it with the appropriate people. This way they save face for people working on the ground and involve the people who have the real power to change things in solving the issue.

Interview with Edward Shipka

CEO, Pe Ben Oilfield Services

Pe Ben Oilfield Services Ltd (Pe Ben) is a public Canadian company engaged in the provision of oilfield support services, stockpiling and stringing of oil and gas transmission pipe and the transportation of bulk petroleum products. The mission of the company includes positioning Pe Ben to meet the challenges of an industry in transition through innovation, expansion of our service base, mergers and acquisitions, strategic alliances and partnering relationships, so that these are obviously critical to the organisation.

What first struck you when you started to interact with the people from the company that you acquired? What were the main differences in the way people work?

Value differences. They weren't used to operating in an environment that encouraged independent thinking and problem solving. Employees came from a parochial style of management where roles and responsibilities were clearly defined and boundaries were not to be crossed. Employees were not motivated and looked to others to make decisions.

Basically, what they were after, and what made for success in that company, was keeping key management happy. They did not have multi-layers of management. Their communications process was top–down and they sought to protect investments through directive management.

Motivation was through paychecks rather than through leveraging an interest in helping the company to succeed. Our values are based on building and enhancing organisational success through our employees. Their value system did not encourage independent thinking and did not provide employees with a sense of the bigger picture.

What difficulties did you encounter that were directly linked to these differences? How did it impact your relationship? How did you overcome the difficulties?

Due to the issues noted above, we let go of 90% of the managers within three years. The social integration of the companies has been a slow process. However, most of the employees from the acquired company are happier. Results have improved and employees are encouraged to be independent thinkers and decision makers. There was a drastic change in policies and procedures once the acquisition was complete.

What advice do you have for others who acquire a company?

Thoroughly research the opportunity. Spend time interviewing key players. Find out what their approach to business is. However, this is very tough, as the company who is trying to sell often does not want you to know what their existing contracts are, what problems they are facing. Owners are putting their best foot forward, and you always can't see their socks.

Acquisitions are time sensitive and are usually focused on the financial and legal issues. Decisions are made on economics and a set of limited criteria, such as a company's reputation. This makes it difficult to know what you're getting into.

In any case, don't expect that employees will immediately change the way they do things to meet your way of doing business.

The most unexpected thing I had to deal with were the issues I didn't know about. For example, the acquired company had stopped making repairs on their equipment and consequently we were faced with huge, unexpected equipment costs. This led to the toughest thing I had to deal with, which was adjusting to the fact that we had acquired a low yield company. This is why I say the first thing to do is to know what you're getting into as fully as possible.

What do you feel is the true role of a leader in an alliance situations?

The role of the leader is to provide direction as to expectations, organisation resources and to successfully address economic and quality of life issues. The leader must also set out what the company expectations are. S/he must have a good understanding of people.

Critical success factors for acquisitions

People and communication make the difference. There must be a willingness on both sides of the acquisition to accept change. If you can analyse the cultural features of the two organisations, this will help you diagnose, immediately after the acquisition, what the gaps and overlaps between the two companies are. You will know more about how to frame the challenges that face social integration and how to develop a strategy for addressing these issues. Finally, this kind of data can give you support during a chaotic time and help accelerate organisational effectiveness and performance.

Index

Acquiring a company, personal
    experiences 205–207, 209–210,
    211–212, 214, 222
Action cultures 46, 73, 76, 83
Alignment of human resources
    strategy 155, 156–157
Alliances 4–6
Assertiveness, empathic 170–171
Authority 56
Automobile industry 4, 14, 38, 64, 86,
    101
Awareness of cultural issues in
    leaders 17

Beverage industry 31, 50, 59, 61, 99,
    100, 194, 203
Blue Loop managers 176–178
Bright side 48–49
Building trust 175–176
Business issues 115, 133

Celebrations, importance of
    158–159, 185–186
Champions network 152
Chemical industry 50, 59, 60
Common history, importance of
    building 160
Communication
    needs 148–149
    issues 115, 134
    style, example of culture 13
Communication and measurement
    142, 146–147
Communications strategy 151–153
    goals 150

impact of culture 154–155
    players in 150
Communications Task Force
    150–151, 152
Competencies Task Force
    155–156
Competencies, development of
    142, 155, 158
Conceptual style 47, 49, 128,
    129, 130
Conflict resolution. 208
Consolidation phase 130
Consulting companies 58, 100
Corporate culture 10–12, 38
    forming 11–12
    see also Culture
Corporate press 152
Corporate style 47–49
Credibility 56
Critical success factors 140,
    206, 223
Cultural Audit 41, 107–108, 126,
    133, 163, 198
    benefits 109–112
    conducting 112–115
    report 115–120
    three 'streams' of issues
    142
Cultural autonomy 27–28
Cultural awareness, senior
    management and 18–19
'Cultural blindness' 16–17
Cultural clues 41
Cultural differences 13, 16–17
Cultural flashpoints 43

Cultural harmony 30
Cultural integration 86–87, 217
Cultural respect 128
Cultural snapshot 43
Cultural understanding 37–38
Culture
  'clash' 13–15, 38–39, 62
  definition of 6–8
  educational systems and 19
  effect on task force effectiveness
    144
  explicit aspects 40
  formation of 8–10
  implicit aspects 40
  sensitivity to 40–41
  see also Action cultures, Corporate
    cultures, Heritage cultures,
    In-group cultures, Multinational
    cultures, Network cultures,
    Systems and procedures
    cultures
Culture Bridging 30–31, 32, 33, 37,
  62–63, 134–135, 163–164
  strategies 208, 210
Culture Bridging Code 194
Culture Bridging Competencies
  164–176
Culture Bridging Fundamentals
  model 42–43, 48
Culture-driven preferences 45

Dark side 48–49
Decision making 216
Detractors 43
Due diligence process 41, 109, 114,
  121, 126–127

Educational systems, culture and
  19
Effectiveness 43, 44
  mixed task forces 82
  national cultural differences
    84–85

Effectiveness challenge 72–73
  different preferences 79–80
Effectiveness preferences 73–74
Effectiveness triangle 74
Empathic Assertiveness 170–171
Enablers 43
Entertainment industry 60
Entrepreneurs 59–60
Executive Committee 17, 108, 110,
  114–115, 121, 133, 134, 136–137,
  203
Executive Leadership 136–139
Executive Meeting 136–138
External focus 137
External Scan 135

Family-owned companies 78–79
Focus groups 114
Future dimension to integration 43,
  44–45, 46–47

Globalisation 4–5, 11, 29, 96, 101, 102,
  104, 197, 209
  see also Multinational cultures
Group survival 9–10
Groups, response to threats 9

Heritage culture 46, 94, 99–102,
  105
  vs strategic objectives 104
Hierarchy of Needs 9
Honesty, need for 148
Human resources 145, 199
  issues 115, 134
  role in developing competencies
    158
  systems 111–112
  alignment of 155, 156–157

In-group cultures 45, 47, 57, 61,
  62–63, 64, 65, 140
Influencing skills 171–172
Insurance industry 147

Integration
degree of 24–26, 28–30, 134
facilitating 213–214
four phases of 125–130
time frame 138–139
total 26–27
Integration Barometer 153–154
Integration phase 129–130
Integration plan 110
Integration process 110–111
Integration team 35, 70, 86, 90, 111,
114–115, 129, 139–142, 143, 144,
146, 150, 185, 186, 189, 203
selecting members for 140
Intellectual ability 45, 57, 58, 63, 65,
140
Intellectuals 58–59
Internationalisation,
see Globalisation
Interviews for cultural audit 113
Intranet forum 152–153
Invisible response to threat 9

Japanese–European partnership 64,
86

Language skills 174–175, 216–217
'Language Management' skills
174–175
Launch meeting for cultural audit
113
Leaders, approach cultural issues
17–18
Leaders, future 145
Leadership team, see Executive
Committee
Legitimacy 43, 44, 45, 48, 65–66, 140
challenge 56
preferences 57
triangle 57
Local operations 5

Management style 138

Manufacturing industry 63
Media, range available for
communication 151–152
Mediation skills 171–172
Mentors 10, 78
Mergers 214
Mergers, failure of 6
effect of cultural issues 16
Merging partners with different
style 49
Microcorporations 145
Mixed task force, see Task forces
Multinational cultures, integration
13, 14, 29, 37, 38,
50, 58, 59, 61, 63, 65–66, 75, 104,
105, 127, 207–208, 212, 218,
219–221

Naming of new company 215–216
National Cultural Differences 84–85
Network cultures 46, 73, 77–78, 83,
87

Operational integration vs cultural
integration 23–24
Organisational preferences 43
Organisational structure 46, 94,
95–97
vs heritage culture 102–103
Organisational style 43

People like us 60–61
Performance evaluation, different
approaches 83–84
Performance-driven cultures 57,
59–60, 62–63, 64
Petroleum industry 13, 152
Planning, role in mergers 6
Pragmatic style 47–48, 49, 128, 129,
130
Preferences, culture-driven 45
Preparation phase for integration
125–128

Priorities for action 139
Problem solving 142–145
Progress measurement 153–154
Publishing industry 65

Questionnaires 113, 115–116

Red Loop managers 176–178
Relational style 47, 49, 128, 129, 130
Remuneration policy 156–157
Resource optimisation vs market optimisation 5

Seminar, kick off 151
Semiology 119–120
Service industries 65–66
Start-ups 78
State-owned companies 58–59
Strategic objectives cultures 46, 94, 98–99, 104–105
Styles 47–49
Superficial homogenisation 16
Survival 9–10
Synergy 6

Systems and procedures cultures 46, 73, 74–75, 83
  vs action culture 81–82
  vs network culture 80–81

Task forces 82, 142–145, 150–151, 155–156
Telecommunications industry 13, 53, 74
Time frame for integration 138–139
Timing 160–161
Training events 158
Transition phase 128–129
Transparency 207–208

Understanding of cultural issues in leaders 17, 85–86
Understanding, three key themes 43–44

Video 152
Visible responses to threats 9

Willingness to address cultural issues 17–18